£5

£5

STARTING WITH GRACE

STARTING WITH GRACE

A Pictorial Celebration of Cricket 1864–1986

BOB WILLIS AND PATRICK MURPHY

STANLEY PAUL
In association with the BBC Hulton Picture Library

Stanley Paul & Co. Ltd

An imprint of Century Hutchinson Ltd
62-65 Chandos Place, London WC2N 4NW

Century Hutchinson Australia (Pty) Ltd
PO Box 496, 16-22 Church Street, Hawthorn, Melbourne,
Victoria 3122

Century Hutchinson New Zealand Limited
32–34 View Road, PO Box 40–086, Glenfield, Auckland 10

Century Hutchinson South Africa (Pty) Ltd
PO Box 337, Bergvlei 2012, South Africa

First published 1986

© Bob Willis and Patrick Murphy 1986

Set in Linotron Palatino by
Input Typesetting Ltd, London SW19 8DR

Printed and bound in Great Britain by
Anchor Brendon Ltd, Tiptree, Essex

British Library Cataloguing in Publication Data

Willis, Bob
    Starting with Grace : a pictorial celebration
    of cricket, 1864–1986.
    1. Cricket—History
    I. Title   II. Murphy, Patrick, *1947–*
    796.35'8'09   GV913

ISBN 0 09 166100 5

Applications for further use of
copyright photographs from the
BBC Hulton Picture Library must be made to:
BBC Hulton Picture Library
35 Marylebone High Street
London W1M 4AA

Contents

ACKNOWLEDGEMENTS

To the Hulton Picture Library for introducing us to so many great cricketers who had been lost through the mists of time. In particular Bob Bright and Peter Elliott were at all times supportive and constructive and kept the coffee flowing at the Hulton.

Our thanks to three of the best cricket photographers of our generation – Patrick Eagar, Adrian Murrell and Graham Morris. Just when they thought they had finished their part in the book, we would return with further requests – and could we have them yesterday?

Robert Brooke has provided a statistical appendix in his customary comprehensive style. We agonised over statistics: on the one hand the book is meant to be a generalised treatment of cricket, yet some readers will want to check out some points of fact. Hopefully Robert Brooke's imaginative use of statistics will act as a happy compromise.

Finally Roger Walker, our long-suffering designer. He knows a good deal more about cricket than a year ago – we hope the experience has not been too chastening for him. We admired his expertise whatever he thought about our inadequacies.

Bob Willis
Patrick Murphy

Introduction

BY BOB WILLIS

This book is the result of a chance visit to the BBC Hulton Picture Library in London. I happened to be chatting about cricket in general to Bob Bright and Peter Elliott and they mentioned that the Hulton had a generous amount of pictures in their vaults. They asked if I fancied having a browse and as I had always been interested in cricket photographs, it was no hardship. To my delight, I stumbled upon a treasure trove, a veritable Pandora's Box. The pictures encompassed a whole century of cricket – from the young, slim, W. G. Grace to Geoffrey Boycott with hair! Some of the players featured were legends, others forgotten through the mists of time, but as I flicked through the files, I was very conscious of a sense of history.

It occurred to me that such a vast stock of photographs could be condensed into an attractive book, reflecting the changing face of the game. I called in an old friend, Patrick Murphy, a collaborator with me on three previous books, and he too was beside himself with fascinated curiosity. We sat there for day after day, sipping the occasional BBC canteen coffee and sifting the high-class wheat from the occasional chaff. In the process I learned more about the game's history and the society in which a particular player flourished. The short hair of the immediate postwar years reflected the National Service disciplines, and it was interesting to see how many spectators wore hats during the period between the two World Wars. So many players bowled in their caps in the early days of the century, and they all seemed to smoke! Almost every off-field picture of Jack Hobbs or Walter Hammond saw them with a cigarette between their fingers – and Hammond was supposed to be a great athlete! Today smoking has decreased among people in their twenties and thirties, and only a small percentage of first-class cricketers puff the dreaded weed. One thing has not changed, though: the dedication of the autograph hunter. Throughout the decades of the twentieth century we came across pictures of youngsters swarming around the big names of the day. I have often wondered what they did with all those indecipherable scrawls, but the passion for autographs shows no sign of ever abating.

Golf seems to have retained its fascination for the top cricketer: we unearthed golfing pictures from W. G. Grace onwards, and, speaking as someone who has just taken up the game, I have to admire the businesslike swing of Sir Donald Bradman. Some of the fielders trapped by the Hulton camera looked blissfully unconcerned about the contest between bat and ball, particularly in some matches before the First World War. As someone who never threatened to be my team's best fielder, I have to say that I would not have been happy to see gully standing with his arms folded as I delivered the ball – but in those days, fielding standards seemed less exacting. Yet batting and bowling techniques remain timeless, and it was fascinating to analyse Ray Lindwall's bowling action or look at Bradman destroying the unfortunate Essex bowlers on his last tour of England.

We have tried to select pictures that reflected unusual insights into the great names of cricket. The shelves are full of cricket books that feature action from bygone games, but we wanted to highlight those moments when the immortals were pictured off-duty, as it were. It was surprising to see Hammond smiling over a cup of tea with the inevitable cigarette in hand, fascinating to find Jack Hobbs posing for a sculptor, and we loved the picture of Denis Compton dancing with Anna Neagle. Homage has been paid to the cricket orthodoxies as well – hence action shots of the featured great players. We have selected a gallery of famous players who spanned more than 120 years and we make no claim to have provided an exhaustive list of significant, influential cricketers. All we have done is sketch the contemporary canvas of the game, while focusing on a certain player who was outstanding at that time.

Where necessary we have supplemented the selection from the Hulton Picture Library with photos from other sources. For example, it would have been wrong to feature Victor Trumper without that wonderful shot of him jumping out to drive from the G. W. Beldam Collection. The selected cricketers of the past twenty years have been covered by some of the game's best photographers of this age – and to that end we thank Angela Patmore for her tireless research. Our thanks to Roddy Bloomfield, our energetic publisher, who was always ready with fresh ideas and who helped conceive the shape of the book from a selection of marvellous photographs.

My favourite picture? It has to be the one of Keith Miller getting out of a taxi with something other than cricket on his mind. I must pull his leg about those socks when I next see him – they hardly go with the smart suit, do they?

I hope this book can give a flavour of cricket over the last century or so. It is not meant to constitute a history of cricket but Patrick Murphy has endeavoured to point out the important signposts as the game developed. The pictures are the product of long hours of discussion, agonizing sifting of options, and finally some ruthless decisions. We can only hope that our final selections hint at the enjoyment we have had from plundering the archives of the Hulton Picture Library.

Preface

BY PATRICK MURPHY

We chose the year 1864 as our starting point because it marks the time when modern cricket really started. In 1864 overarm bowling was finally legalized – the last major change in bowling styles after the sanction of roundarm in 1828. The year 1864 also saw the debut of one W. G. Grace in important cricket: a few days before his sixteenth birthday, he scored 170 and 56 not out for the South Wales Club against the Gentlemen of Sussex and Brighton. Even in those days of highly competitive, financially conscious cricket, it was clear that an influential figure had emerged. Over the next four decades, he became the most important player in history. One final landmark came in 1864: the publication of John Wisden's *Cricketers' Almanack* for the first time. It cost one shilling, ran to 116 pages and padded out the cricket information with diverse items like a list of the battles in the Wars of the Roses and a brief account of the trial of Charles I. As cricket spread its wings, such historical data was dropped and *Wisden* became simply the cricketer's bible.

In researching this book, I have been struck by recurring trends. Of course the game has changed drastically over the past century but human nature remains idiosyncratic. Consider Lord Harris, that indomitable England captain of the Victorian Age and influential martinet at Lord's until his death in 1932. Ostensibly the embodiment of cricket's capacity to refine behaviour, Lord Harris bowled grubbers along the ground to stem the flow of runs a century before Trevor Chappell did it to a cacophony of disapproval from traditionalists. Lord Harris also specialized in chattering at batsmen while in the field – a pioneer of 'sledging' as popularized by Tony Greig in the Packer era. Consider the role and power of the cricket press, a thorny topic today. It is generally claimed that the modern press are far too keen on fanning the flames of controversy. If so, contemporary journalists could have taken their cue from one Mr C. F. Pardon way back in 1882. He covered the Australian tour to England that year and in the sports journal *Bell's Life* in London, he divested himself of the following trenchant observations: that the standard of umpiring was poor, that A. N. Hornby should not have captained England, and that W. G. Grace was guilty of sharp practice when running out S. P. Jones after he strayed out of his ground following a quick single. More than enough there to keep the pot of controversy stirring; W. G. Grace would have been a godsend to the news hounds of a century later.

Those who criticize the various bodies at Lord's for alleged tardiness in decision-making should know it was ever thus. In 1872 the MCC first discussed a knockout cup; it came to pass ninety-one years later, courtesy of a razor blades company! It took twenty years before a method of deciding the county champions could be sanctioned by Lord's in 1890. In the interim, the winners were selected by the various cricket magazines and newspapers. And to think that the modern player often feels the press are too powerful!

Cricket has always attracted the 'laudator temporis acti', the zealot who comes to the painful conclusion that the game has gone to the dogs. Consider the following profundity: 'Cricket, to maintain its hold on the national character, must be eager, quick and full of action. Today it is the reverse.' The words are those of A. G. Steel, England all-rounder and captain against Australia in the 1880s. He was talking in 1900, at the height of the Golden Age, by common consent the period when cricket reached its peak of attraction, variety and positive intent. The nostalgic Mr Steel would have loved discoursing at length today, if a microphone happened to be anywhere in the vicinity. Every succeeding era has seen former players willingly don the curmudgeonly cloak.

The overall standard of behaviour on the field has sadly deteriorated in the past decade, but there have always been iconoclasts at hand, willing to test out the guidelines. Warwick Armstrong, that successful Australian captain of the early 1920s, could have been a soul-mate of Ian Chappell; he disliked cricket administrators just as much, and he allowed Gregory and MacDonald to bowl as short as they wished. Armstrong was the only cricketer to upset Jack Hobbs when he accused that model sportsman of gamesmanship. He would have loved the macho posturing and umpire-baiting of the Packer era. Talking of Packer, the dispute in 1977 that rocked world cricket had been foreshadowed in the 1930s, when the Australian Broadcasting Commission had to fight off several commercial stations for the exclusive rights to radio commentary of the Ashes battles.

'Plus ça change, plus c'est la même chose' could almost be the sub-title of this book. In celebrating a great game and its illustrious figures, it is worthwhile to keep in mind not merely its social context but man's enduring capacity to dissemble, to argue and to flirt with philanthropy while consummating his love affair with materialism.

'Back and across'. Grace's technique remained correct throughout middle age

W. G. Grace

William Gilbert Grace was an uncomplicated country doctor with a high-pitched, squeaky voice, a dominating mother and a keen eye for the main financial chance. He was also the most important figure in the history of cricket. There have been better bowlers, more prolific batsmen, superior captains and better sportsmen – but W. G. Grace revolutionized the game. When he entered first-class cricket in 1865 it was still a shady pastime, with the pursuit of quick money by the players the overriding motive. Cricket was still provincial. The first tour by an English side to Australia had just taken place, but only through the late cancellation of a lecture tour by Charles Dickens. Something else was needed – and quickly – to appease the abrasive Australians, so why not a cricket tour? More than forty years later, when W. G. Grace played his last first-class game, cricket was the national sport. The Royal Family asked after his health and he gloried in the fame and adulation. After Gladstone, he was the best-known Englishman and was quick to remind any sceptics of that. 'They've come to see me bat, not you umpire. Play on!' he once said, after being given out – and he stayed at the crease. The word 'superstar' had not been coined in those days, but Grace was undoubtedly the first of that genre. Legend has it that the sign outside county cricket grounds would state: 'Admission threepence; if W. G. Grace plays, admission sixpence.'

Like all influential characters, W. G. Grace was in the right place at the right time. As the game grew in popularity, he was ideally placed to influence its tactics. From the days of the 1850s, when the Factory Act created the Saturday half-day, there was time for cricket to seep into the public consciousness. The growth of

Grace became, in 1895, the first to score 1000 runs in May

railways meant that cricket could now be played all over England and the introduction of piece-work in midland and northern textile industries at last gave many the freedom to play. Southern dominance was gradually eroded and Leeds, Manchester, Sheffield and Nottingham became major cricket centres, while in the mining areas, cricket meant social emancipation and the chance of respectability. The values of Victorian

England – jingoistic, enterprising, materialistic – were mirrored in the growth of cricket. The appalling poverty in the cities spurred many players on to the pursuit of rich pickings. Tours abroad were organized and the best players fell over themselves to make money. The 'star' system was created to boost gates and the top performers ensured they were rewarded handsomely. None more so than W. G. Grace. It was estimated that he made more than a million pounds from the game in his career – including three separate testimonials that raised £9000 in 1895. It cost Lord Sheffield a little matter of £3000 to persuade Grace to captain his touring side to Australia in 1891/2: his wife was also on the trip and a locum for the Grace practice in Bristol had to be financed. As early as 1873 he received £1500 plus generous expenses for an Australian tour, even though he was officially an amateur and should not have been paid. A century later, traditionalists who railed at the alleged cupidity of Kerry Packer's disciples might have recalled the financial opportunism of the good Dr Grace.

Yet Grace's influence on the game was so profound that no one can surely begrudge him his material comforts. He dominated thirty of the forty seasons he spent in first-class cricket. The supremacy was not just statistical, or the realization that he was far and away the best all-round player in the world; he altered the game's terms of reference, transcended the social divisions and placed cricket on the map as a national spectacle. He revolutionized the art of batting by playing the right shots to the appropriate ball in a way that no other batsman had achieved with any degree of consistency. He played back and forward where

W. G. Grace taking a gentle net. Not everyone behind the net is giving the great man the rapt attention he always felt was his due

necessary against fast bowling and adapted supremely well to any bowling variety over a period of forty years. As C. B. Fry wrote, 'He turned the old one-stringed instrument into a many-chorded lyre. The theory of modern batting is, in all essentials, the result of W. G.'s thinking and working on the game!' As a result of his batting supremacy, new methods of bowling were necessary – variations in flight and speed – and more imaginative

placing was introduced to try to curb Grace's uncanny ability to find the gaps in the field. Grace blocked the shooters on treacherous wickets of his youth, he mastered the lob and spin bowlers in late years and routed the fast bowlers with illegal actions in the 1880s. Such was his mastery of the fast men that critics began to complain about a surfeit of slow bowling. Captains had turned to that method of attack in despair, yet Lilly-white's *Cricketers' Companion* of 1880 complained about 'This dreary and monotonous prevalence of slow bowling.

No less than five of the leading six counties have found it necessary to begin their attack with two slow bowlers.' All because of one man's towering ascendancy. As one county bowler ruefully observed, 'I put the ball where I likes and 'e puts it where 'e likes.'

In the halcyon years of Grace (from 1865 to 1890), the bowlers were dominant, with the exception of the massive bearded figure who had been taught the virtues of a straight bat by his indomitable mother, Martha. The pitches were invariably dangerous – hardly surprising when the main method of preparation involved putting sheep out to graze. There was no groundsman at Lord's till 1864, the year Sussex refused to play there because of the hazardous conditions. One day at Lord's in 1868, W. G. Grace blocked the first four deliveries of the match, after they had all shot along the ground at high speed. The crowd rose to him and cheered him to the echo. In 1870, Lord's claimed a victim. George Summers, a young Nottinghamshire batsman was struck on the head by the first ball he received and he died three days later. It is surprising that more batsmen were not killed on those wickets. W. G. Grace was the only man to look at ease. As James Shaw, the Nottinghamshire bowler remarked, 'Oh yes, he blocks the shooters, but he blocks 'em to the boundary.' Not until the 1890s could a batsman look forward to a pleasant day at the crease on a pitch of true bounce.

Grace was the living embodiment of the game as it developed in the Victorian period. He was there in the first crucial decade – the 1860s – when overarm bowling was finally allowed, when

The Harrow XI of 1869

matches between county sides became accepted practice, and the first tour to Australia took place. In 1868 we had the first tour to England from Australia. A team of Aboriginals played 47 matches until mid-October, giving displays of spear and boomerang throwing after each game. They rejoiced in such nicknames as King Cole, Red Cap and Dick-a-Dick and although the cricket was only semi-serious, the game was spreading around the world. Events in the 1870s confirmed the growth in popularity: county cricket regulated its qualification rules, the wonderful feats of W. G. Grace brought the game to a wider audience, and England and Australia began to play Test cricket. The first historic game at Melbourne in 1877 was described as 'Victoria and New South Wales or Australia versus England' – simply a chal-

Frederick Robert Spofforth. Known as 'The Demon', he was the first great Australian fast bowler. He eventually settled in England, became a pillar of the business community and left £164,000 on his death
The Australian tour party of 1878. Back row (left to right): J. McC. Blackham, T. P. Horan, G. H. Bailey, J. Conway (manager), A. C. Bannerman, C. Bannerman, W. L. Murdoch. Seated: F. R. Spofforth, F. E. Allan, D. W. Gregory (captain), W. E. Midwinter, T. W. Garrett, H. F. Boyle

lenge match with no plans to make it a regular part of the cricket calendar. The English players would have scoffed at such a suggestion; they felt the Australians were far inferior to their battle-hardened professionalism. A rude awakening lay in store: victory for Australia by 45 runs. Although a hastily arranged return game was won by England by a four wicket margin, it was clear that Australia cricket was developing rapidly. They hastily organized a tour to England in 1878 and proceeded to dent a few complacent egos. They were not accorded an international match and had to be satisfied with a game against a strong MCC team. In a single day, the Australians won by nine wickets – bowling out the MCC for 33 and 19. The news was greeted with incredulity all over England; perhaps the Antipodean upstarts had some talent after all. There had to be some merit in bowlers who had dismissed W. G. Grace for just 4 and 0. Spofforth (six for 4 and five for 16) and Boyle (three for 14 and five for 3) modestly accepted they were not without ability.

Spofforth's skill was underlined within the next twelve months, when England again toured Australia. The team was called 'The Gentlemen of England with Ulyett and Emmett', an acknowledgement of the need to play the two best professionals of the day. No matter: Spofforth took thirteen wickets in the game and another win for the Australians. By now tours to both countries were becoming a regular feature, yet there

seemed no real desire to capitalize on the obvious talent of the Australians. They arrived in England in the spring of 1880 with no plans to take on England again. They had no fixture list and at one stage they were reduced to advertising for opponents. Games at Oldham, Keighley and against Eighteen of Dublin were hardly the stuff of representative cricket. Finally, in early September the Surrey secretary, C. W. Alcock persuaded Lord Harris to raise an England side. The match was played at the Oval and England, chasing 57, scraped home by five wickets. Even the insular cricket hierarchy in England admitted to admiration of the Australians' tenacity. The idea of international matches had finally taken root, even though the term 'Test Match' was not coined until 1884 – by the *Melbourne Herald*. By that stage, Australia had not only achieved self-respect, it had won 'the Ashes'. The name was invented after the thrilling match at the Oval in 1882, when Australia beat England by 7 runs in a game of unbearable tension. England needed just 85 to win but Spofforth again bowled sublimely and the last four wickets fell for just 7 runs. A few days later the *Sporting Times* published its famous obituary notice of English cricket with the footnote: 'NB. The body will be cremated and the Ashes taken to Australia!' Later that year, when the Honourable Ivo Bligh took another England team out to Australia, he was said to be going out to recover the Ashes. The famous Ashes urn thus became the symbol of the gripping contests between the two countries.

By the end of the nineteenth century, they had played nineteen Test series and a galaxy of great players had made their mark on cricket history. Australia's great bowlers included Spofforth, Turner, Trumble and Ferris while George Giffen, their splendid all-rounder, was dubbed the 'W. G. of Australia'. Their excellent wicket-keeper J. McC. Blackham toured England eight times and their best batsman W. L. Murdoch was captain in seven series. On England's side were batsmen of the calibre of Shrewsbury, Abel, MacLaren and Stoddart. Among the bowlers, Peel, Lohmann and Richardson were notable performers. Within a few short years, Test cricket had been firmly established and the Victorian pioneering spirit led to official English tours to South Africa, India and the West Indies.

If the missionary zeal of the Victorian age was apparent in cricket's worldwide development, a hard-nosed desire to make money was also never far away. The last two decades of the nineteenth

Arthur Shrewsbury, the foremost English professional batsman of the Victorian era. He died tragically in 1903: labouring under the mistaken belief that he had an incurable disease, Shrewsbury shot himself.

century were full of attempts by the professionals to throw off their shackles and improve their financial lot. They resented the way the Australian tourists were termed 'amateurs', even though they made exorbitant demands about gate money whenever they toured England. In 1880, seven Nottinghamshire players demanded £20 each to play against the tourists. A year later five Nottinghamshire players went on strike for most of the season and there was talk of a union. In 1888, nine professionals asked for £20 each before they would turn out for the Players against Australia and in 1896 the sum of £20 was again invoked by five players who had been picked for a Test Match. The demands were fuelled partly by the financial opportunism of the Australians, partly by the acumen of English amateurs like W. G. Grace and partly by insecurity. The relationship between county committees and professionals was often semi-feudal. Players could only request a raise; they did not get lunch on match days, that was the amateur's privilege. All too often the professional would have a few drinks at the bar, with the inevitable consequences. Many famous professional cricketers of

the Victorian age squandered their money on drink and drifted into alcoholism and an early grave.

Thanks to enlightened captains such as Yorkshire's Lord Hawke, the English professional slowly developed self-respect. Hawke dedicated himself to improving the social standing of his professionals and in the process did more than any other nineteenth-century cricketer for the men who were the backbone of the game. Hawke had to make painful decisions: he dismissed the England slow bowler Ted Peate at the height of his powers and in 1897 he did the same to Bobby Peel, Peate's successor in the England side. The genial Peel had arrived at the ground in the morning in a state of some intoxication. He proceeded to bowl at the sightscreen and urinated on the outfield. Despite Peel's high talent and deserved popularity, he never played again for Yorkshire. Lord Hawke demanded high standards of behaviour from his professionals, but in return he supported them financially and morally. By the turn of the century, the average professional was earning around £275 a summer, while the unskilled labourer was picking up about £100 a year. More and more professionals were becoming pillars of rectitude in their villages – walking down to the local pub in best tweeds, enjoying the attention of their admiring friends. Slowly the autocratic attitude of county committees towards the professionals was being eroded as men of influence agreed with Lord Hawke that players sound be paid well for skilled labour.

As cricket developed apace, there was no lack of attendant turmoil. Chronic financial squabbles were just one manifestation of the game's enduring knack of evoking strong passions. In 1862, Edgar Willsher was no-balled for throwing in the England versus Surrey match; he threw the ball down on the pitch and stalked from the field, followed by his fellow-professionals, leaving just two bewildered amateurs to carry on the bowling. Three years later, five Yorkshire professionals refused to play against Surrey because they were convinced that the umpire who no-balled their teammate Willsher had been acting on instructions from the Surrey club. The following decade, the MCC ruled that 'no gentleman ought to make a profit by his services in the cricket field' – a statement that much have been greeted by cynical smiles by the likes of W. G. Grace. No wonder many newspapers in that period campaigned to depose the MCC 'and its

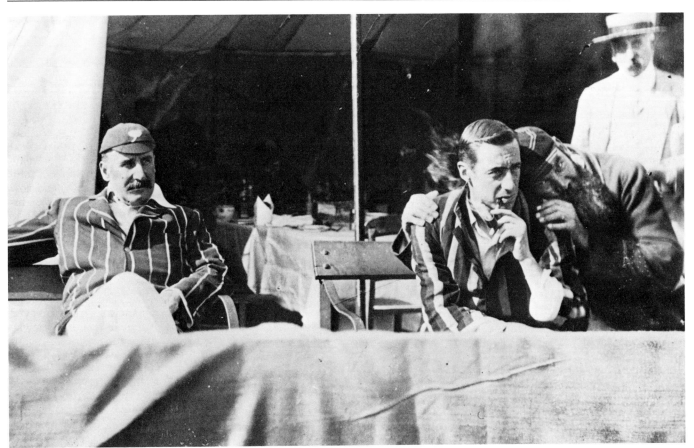

The Hastings Festival in 1901 – Grace reveals the puckish side of his nature. The broad shoulder belongs to J. R. Mason, the highly talented all-rounder who graced the Kent and England sides at the turn of the century. To the right of Mason sits Lord Hawke, brilliantly successful captain of Yorkshire and firm supporter of the professional cricketer

deplorably lethargic and out-of-date committee', a century before a similar call from Mr Michael Parkinson after the D'Oliveira affair. Crowd disturbances were not rare. In 1879 the pitch was invaded three times at Sydney, after the Australian hero W. L. Murdoch had been given out. Lord Harris, the English captain, was struck and surrounded by a hostile crowd and his team-mate A. N. Hornby was brave enough to chase some of the protesters away. Some illustrious players were not immune from social peccadilloes. Ted Pooley, England's wicket-keeper missed the historic first Test in 1877 because he was still languishing in a New Zealand jail after a betting coup that ended in brawls. Twenty years later, the England captain A. E. Stoddart had to defend his players against charges of heavy drinking after England lost a series 4/1 in Australia. A century later, as we bemoan the less palatable side of Dennis Lillee, the self-

The London County ground, Crystal Palace. W. L. Murdoch is on Grace's left

W. G. Grace indulging in one of his favourite
winter pastimes – hunting. The year is 1900, when
the Grand Old Man was aged 52

The good doctor played golf even when his
spreading girth impaired his vision of the ball!

indulgent streak in Ian Botham and the
boorish character of many cricket
followers, a certain historical perspective
might be in order. When it came to
bending and occasionally ignoring the
laws of cricket, W. G. Grace made Lillee
seem a paragon. The good doctor was
also less than obsessional about physical
fitness, as a letter from Arthur Shrewsbury to his team-mate Alfred Shaw
confirms: 'Grace would drink enough to
swim a ship.' Yet no one indulged in
censorious public moralizing about Grace:
the press contented itself with a solemn
recital of his great deeds instead of
considering the heinous possibility that
the colossus of cricket might actually be a
cheat.

Any character defects of W. G. Grace do
not matter when his influence on cricket is
assessed. He was not of the university or
public school classes yet he was idolized
by the MCC members and the amateur
clique. He was an amateur with a
hypocritical attitude to making money,
yet the professionals admired and
respected him. He was simply above the
usual criteria we set for normal cricketers
and human beings. The most innovative
cricketer in history was autocratic,
occasionally petty, the pioneer of gamesmanship on the field – but above all he
was unique. He established the guidelines
for the game of cricket that have broadly
lasted to this day. In the process he established a chain of continuity that stretches
over a century. The grizzled veteran who
played his last Test in 1899 saw the debut
of the great Wilfred Rhodes in the same
match. Rhodes played long enough to
bowl at Sir Donald Bradman in 1930 and
Bradman batted against Jim Laker –
another legend who until recently was
still very much a part of the contemporary
English summer. Grace would probably
approve of many aspects of the game
today – especially the money available to
the best players – but one suspects his
greatest satisfaction would be the
enduring appeal of a sport that he played
better than anyone else in his life.

Victor Trumper

Victor Trumper adorned the game during the most illustrious period of its history. His Test career lasted from 1899 to 1912, an epoch generally accepted to be unrivalled in its entertainment value. Trumper's first Test, at Trent Bridge, was the last for W. G. Grace and it was fitting that the Grand Old Man's remarkable career should be closing with dignity as another blossomed. For Trumper was a batting genius. Like Grace, his statistical achievements may seem modest, but mere figures cannot do justice to the charm and gallantry of Victor Trumper's batting.

Before the 1902 season in England, only Grace had dominated the game to the extent that many other marvellous players were merely cast in a supporting role. Trumper did the same in 1902: in a vile, wet summer his ability to play so beautifully and so securely astonished the harshest of critics. He made 2570 runs, with eleven centuries (the rest of the Australian squad only managed thirteen hundreds between them). He won golden opinions from the likes of C. B. Fry, a man with a high opinion of his own batting standards and an exacting judge of other techniques. Fry wrote, 'He is a wonderful player, consistency from first to last and he possesses the ability to successfully play the same game on all sorts of wickets – fast and slow, wet and dry, sticky and dead.' The verdict of *Wisden* was equally enthusiastic: 'He reduced our best bowlers to the level of the village green.' The suffering bowlers were of the highest class – they included Wilfred Rhodes, George Hirst, Bill Lockwood – but they all came alike to the young man of twenty-four on rain-affected wickets that completely overwhelmed team-mates who were simply Test-class batsmen

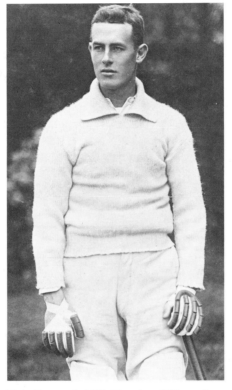

Victor Trumper in 1902. More than 2500 runs in a wet summer

rather than touched by the hand of genius.

This from a man who had been on reduced pay at the start of his first tour to England in 1899. The established players received about £900, while young Trumper had to be content with £200. After all, he was very inexperienced, would probably be out of his depth on English wickets and was only in the squad at the insistence of the wisest contemporary Australian cricketer, M. A. Noble. A century from Trumper in his second

Test, a little matter of 300 not out against Sussex, and Trumper was soon on full pay. The unanimous opinion of all cricketers during that era was that Victor Trumper was priceless. Forty years later, Trumper's great contemporary, Clem Hill, would assert, 'He was streets in front of anyone else.' This from a man who had seen all the great players, from W. G. Grace to Don Bradman. He was at his best when the side needed him most – not for Trumper the remorseless accumulation of runs on smooth, blameless pitches. His duels with Wilfred Rhodes on rain-affected surfaces are the stuff of legend. 'Please, Wilfred, give me some peace,' he implored the implacable Yorkshireman after he had teased him with cunning variations in flight for over after over. Yet Trumper won the battle that particular day: 185 not out at Sydney in 1903, as Australia faced a deficit of 292, with Rhodes licking his lips. He scored a remarkable hundred before lunch in the Old Trafford Test of 1902, when Trumper realized that he had to make quick runs while the wet footholds prevented Bill Lockwood from bowling in the first two hours. At Melbourne in 1904, Wilfred Rhodes took fifteen wickets in the match, on the classic 'sticky dog', where the ball leapt and fizzed, spat and darted: Trumper made 74 in a total of 122. Always he would take the attack to the bowler, especially when the conditions were unfavourable.

When Len Braund bowled leg-theory at him in the 1903 Sydney Test, Trumper leant back and cut him away repeatedly through the off-side – a ploy repeated by Bradman in more exacting circumstances thirty years later in the Bodyline series. Like W. G. Grace, Trumper had the peerless ability to play back and forward with

Trumper dancing out to drive at the Oval in 1899

Below: Oxford v. Cambridge at Lord's in 1909

equal facility; his dazzling footwork, matchless range of strokes and his dashing insistence on using them established him as a supreme attraction in an age awash with cricketing talent, audacity and charm. Even England supporters hoped he would dazzle in every Test Match – as long as Australia contrived to lose.

Trumper's glorious example epitomized a time of cricketing brilliance and hectic activity on the Test Match front. Between his debut in 1899 and 1912, his last year as a Test player, England and Australia played nine series – a salutary corrective to the modern player's lament that there are now far too many Test Matches. Australia won five of the series, including sixteen victories to England's fourteen. The seeds planted by W. G. Grace were blooming into a healthy, vigorous institution. As the game grew in its appeal, sound administration became more vital to ensure it would remain the national summer sport. In 1899, a Board of Control was appointed to administer Tests in England. A selection committee was used for the first time, replacing the practice of allowing the ground authority to pick the Test side. That summer saw the first series of five Tests between England and Australia. The following year the first West Indies team toured England. In 1903 the MCC took over responsibility for England tours overseas: no longer would

the organization be left to cricketers with a flair for making money out of long trips. In 1905, the Australian Board of Control was set up and in the same year Pelham Warner took the first MCC team to South Africa, and played five Tests. South Africa returned to England in 1907, its first tour as a Test-playing country and the first time a Test was played in England without Australia providing the opposition. In 1909 came further proof that the infant of 1877 was now a vigorous, mature 32-year-old: the Imperial Cricket Conference (ICC) was formed. The founder members were England, Australia and South Africa. Test Match cricket was spreading its wings, acquiring status, respectability and vast newspaper coverage. In 1912, the ICC organized an event that purported to be the most impressive celebration of Test cricket so far – the Triangular Tournament, to be played in England between the three founder members of the ICC. It proved a sad, anti-climactic project. The weather was dismal, England outclassed South Africa, and Australia – weakened by the absence of six star players following a disagreement with their Board – were no match for an England side that had beaten the full-strength team by 4/1 in Australia the previous winter. The Triangular Tournament was never revived: too much depended on the vagaries of the English weather and in any event, weightier matters were to distract international cricketers within a couple of years.

That damp, three-Test series of 1912 was to be the last between England and Australia for eight years. The absence of six players of the calibre of Trumper, Armstrong, Hill, Ransford, Carter and Cotter robbed the contests of much of their traditional verve and character, but it was not unusual at that time for top players to be at loggerheads with their Board of Control, or simply unavailable for a Test series. For the 1901/02 England tour to Australia, amateur batsmen of the quality of C. B. Fry, Ranjitsinjhi and F. S. Jackson could not travel for business reasons, while Yorkshire, ever the pragmatic county, refused to allow Wilfred Rhodes and George Hirst to tour. Yorkshire had won the championship in 1901, with the two great players performing valiantly, and their employers decreed that a rest from cricket was preferable to a winter's labour in Australia. The following summer saw Yorkshire retain the championship, with Hirst and Rhodes earning their keep without any signs of fatigue. Two years later, A. C. MacLaren, Fry and Jackson were all unavailable for

April 1912: some of the Australian team arriving at Plymouth

Warwick Armstrong – indomitable all-rounder and archetypal tough Australian

the next Australian tour, but the amateurs did not have the monopoly on financial considerations. The 1907/08 tour to Australia went without four of the best professional cricketers: Tom Hayward, Johnny Tyldesley, Dick Lilley and George Hirst. They objected to the terms offered and decided to stay at home. The English professional cricketer had come a long way since the Nottinghamshire strike in 1881. He was now a highly respected member of the lower middle class, with the England player a model of waistcoated conformity. The amateur was admired for his flair, his altruistic inclination to entertain the spectators – but the skilled professional knew the value of his own talents.

It is a tribute to the quality of the cricketers that the absence from England tours of some of the best players never proved to be disastrous. There always seemed to be a fresh young amateur batsman available, or a class bowler from the ranks of the professionals. The roll call of great English players from the time of Grace's last Test to the Triangular Tournament is peerless. The batsmen included Fry, MacLaren, Ranjitsinjhi, Tyldesley, R. E. Foster, Hayward, Jessop and the young Hobbs and Woolley. Among the all-rounders Jackson, Hirst, Rhodes, and Len Braund, with bowlers of the calibre of Lockwood, Barnes, Blythe, and the creator of 'googly' bowling, B. J. T. Bosanquet. Australia was equally favoured:

The Edgbaston Test of 1909. Here George Hirst bowls to Charlie Macartney: note the legside field to accommodate the pronounced inswing of Hirst

Trumper and Duff were a marvellous opening pair, with batsmen such as Hill, Gregory, Bardsley, Darling and Macartney to come. The class all-rounders included Noble and Armstrong while Trumble, Cotter, and Laver were superb bowlers. Great names, illustrious performances that still stand up to the most exacting scrutiny. Between them they managed to fashion some of the greatest Tests of all time.

The 1902 Ashes series in England remains the most remarkable one in Test history, despite the dreadful weather that ruined two of the Tests. Only the 1981 series can rival it from the modern era, but even the most fervent admirer of Ian Botham and Mike Brearley would have to concede that the cricketers of 1902 were rather special. The England eleven for the Edgbaston Test of that year is widely considered to the greatest ever assembled. The names deserve detailed consideration:

A. C. MacLaren (captain)
C. B. Fry
J. T. Tyldesley
K. S. Ranjitsinjhi
F. S. Jackson
G. L. Jessop
L. C. Braund
A. A. Lilley (wicket-keeper)
G. H. Hirst
W. H. Lockwood
W. Rhodes

MacLaren the imperious, extravagant stroke-maker, Fry the solid technician, Tyldesley the most gifted professional batsman of his day, Jessop the most consistent hitter in the game's history, Ranji a wristy, supple genius. Six of the side performed the 'double' – 1000 runs and 100 wickets in a season – and Hirst remains the only man to take 200 wickets and score 2000 runs in a season. Jackson headed both batting and bowling averages in the 1905 Ashes series, and for good measure won the toss all five times. Lilley kept wicket for England in his calm, unfussy way for a decade, and he was a good enough batsman to score sixteen first-class centuries. The bowling was superb – the classical slow left-arm spin of Rhodes, the leg-breaks of Braud, the deadly fast-medium of Lockwood, the swerve and swing of Hirst, Jackson's

medium pace and the uncomplicated fast bowling of that gloriously uncomplicated cricketer, Jessop. No wonder they bowled Australia out for just 36 at Edgbaston (Trumper made 18, worth a century on such a wicket). It seems incredible that such an awesome side could lose the series to Australia by a margin of 2/1.

They managed it due to a combination of circumstances. The rain saved Australia at Edgbaston, ruined the Lord's Test and gave the Australians time to re-group and come to terms with the damp conditions. After Edgbaston, the England selectors made a series of crass errors and MacLaren's idiosyncratic captaincy reflected the nature of the man. Full credit must be paid to the Australians for battling to the series victory. They were almost as strong as England – Trumper and Duff to open, followed by Hill, Darling and Gregory, with the all-round skills of Noble and Trumble, the competent wicket-keeping of Kelly and the brisk spin of Saunders, a dangerous bowler on the damp wickets of 1902.

Not quite the vintage Australian eleven of 1921, or 1948, but a very fine side nevertheless. The batting of Hill and

Trumper and the bowling of Noble and Trumble brought them deserved victory at Sheffield and the next two Tests proved historic.

Old Trafford 1902 and the Oval 1902 remain in that select group of Test Matches which will never be forgotten. For sustained excitement, towering individual performances and human drama they must eclipse even the two great games in Botham's year of 1981. Although the final day's play at both Leeds and Edgbaston in 1981 was sensational, it must be admitted that some of the cricket was substandard and that some of the players lacked genuine Test class. That does not apply to the 1902 Tests. Right from the start of the Old Trafford game, when Trumper scored his bewitching century before lunch, the quality of cricket was tremendous. The hundred by F. S. Jackson that took more than four hours was a masterful innings on a treacherous pitch – a point underlined when Australia were soon bowled out for 86. England were left to get 124, a tall order against Trumble and Saunders on a rain-affected wicket. The bowlers worked their way through the batting until 8 runs were needed with the last pair together. A shower interrupted the play for a time, increasing the unbearable tension. After a delay of forty-five minutes, the imperturbable Wilfred Rhodes walked out to bat with his partner, the Sussex bowler, Fred Tate. The England selectors, in one of their more memorable aberrations, had dropped Hirst and brought in Tate for Old Trafford. Hirst would show what they had missed at the Oval but this occasion proved too much for poor Tate. He jabbed a nervous 4, but then flailed at a faster one from Saunders and was bowled. Australia won by 3 runs and it became known as 'Tate's Match' for the most poignant reason. He had also dropped Joe Darling on the square leg boundary as he tried to smash a few runs on the difficult pitch. Darling ended up top scorer with 37, 30 more than he should have made. As Tate sat, inconsolable, in the England dressing-room, he vowed that one day his son would restore pride to the family name. A little matter of twenty-four years later, Maurice Tate was in the team that won back the Ashes at the Oval and Fred Tate – who played just the once for England – was alive to see the great day.

Old Trafford was climactically successful for Australia, but the following match at the Oval brought joy to England in the most spectacular fashion. After 'Tate's Match' it was 'Jessop's Match'. England needed 262 to win and when

Jessop came in, they were 48 for five. He scored a hundred in just seventy-five minutes with his usual mixture of clear-eyed aggression. An innings of 104 off just eighty deliveries, within the context of that match and the quality of the bowling, establishes Jessop's performance as one of the greatest of all time. When he was out, Hirst took on the extra responsibility,

S. F. Barnes. One of the greatest bowlers of all time, a proud, prickly man who knew his commercial worth and brooked little interference in his bowling from incompetent amateur captains

determined to rid himself of the disappointment of Old Trafford. With just 15 needed, Hirst was joined by the last man, his fellow-Yorkshireman, Wilfred Rhodes. Legend suggested that they agreed 'we'll get 'em in singles', but both men denied that in later years. They nudged a couple here, a single there and

calmly proceeded to inch towards victory amid scenes of unbearable tension. When Rhodes hit the winning single, the spectators forgot their traditional reserve and stormed the pitch – crowd invasions are not the invention of the tempestuous 1980s! Hirst finished with 58 not out and the point had been made to the selectors in no uncertain fashion.

Despite stoppages of rain, both these great Tests were completed in three days. One can only wonder at the scorn that would be poured on the concept of the 'Timeless Test' by the players of the 1902 series. One cannot imagine the likes of Trumper and Jessop taking kindly to the suggestion that they should occupy the crease without taking the kind of chances that endeared them to so many.

If the 1902 series stands out as the most remarkable in the pre-1914 period, there never seemed to be any lack of incident during those years whenever England and Australia locked horns – with the exception of the Triangular Tournament. In the 1907/08 series, there were echoes of Old Trafford and the Oval, when Australia won the Sydney Test by two wickets after slumping to 124 for six, with 150 still needed. Then England won the next Test by one wicket. They needed 282 to win and at 209 for eight, their cause seemed lost. Syd Barnes and Arthur Fielder put on 39 to win the match, which would have ended in a tie if Gerry Hazlitt had elected to throw the ball calmly from cover to the wicket-keeper. Instead he panicked, shied at the stumps and Fielder scrambled home as the ball whizzed past him.

Cricket, especially England v. Australia cricket, never lost its capacity to surprise during that halcyon period. The mystery googly bowling by Bosanquet that won the 1903/04 series in Australia for Pelham Warner; the remarkable debut of S. F. Barnes on the 1901/02 tour, after being plucked from the obscurity of league cricket by MacLaren to bowl at Trumper and the others; ten years later the brilliant bowling of Barnes and F. R. Foster that turned a 1/0 deficit into a 4/1 thrashing after Barnes had managed to persuade his captain Johnny Douglas to let him open with the new ball. Wilfred Rhodes began this period as a number eleven batsman and ended it as Jack Hobbs's regular opening partner, adding 323 together at Melbourne in 1912. George Gunn, on holiday in Australia for health reasons, was asked to play in the first Test at Sydney in 1907 – and scored a hundred. One assumes his health picked up fairly rapidly.

England captain Johnny Douglas bowls to H. V. Hordern, Melbourne Test, 1911–12

Through all cricketing vicissitudes, one man remained a constant factor: Victor Trumper. From 1899 to 1912, he made forty consecutive appearances against England, in the process charming a generation of cricket lovers and establishing a reputation that has never been besmirched or challenged. It was a pity that he could not bring himself to a compromise with the Board of Control in 1912; it was not in Trumper's generous nature to dig his heels in over a trifling matter. His consistent support for Clem Hill, the captain under fire from the Board, was entirely typical. At the time it did not seem too dreadful to be without Trumper for one summer in England – the popularity of Test cricket over the previous decade had ensured a healthy turnover of Ashes battles. Yet by 1912 Victor Trumper and the civilized world were both beginning to lose vital battles. In 1914 came the Great War, and a year later, Victor Trumper died of Bright's Disease, a kidney ailment. He had never been robust and had been visibly waning for a year. Yet his death shattered the Australian nation, hardly the most sentimental race. Such was his impact on cricket that news of his death was plastered on billboards in England, even though the latest details on the war would seem to have been more important. Trumper symbolized that pre-war age of innocence. He combined wondrous cricketing ability with outstanding personal qualities. He never made anything out of his sports goods business, because he would insist on giving away equipment to those he felt deserved it. He even gave one boy the very bat with which he had scored a Test century. When a testimonial match raised £3000 for Trumper in 1913, the authorities invested the money for him and paid him only the interest from the sum; they knew he would have given away the money to friends down on their luck. This the man who once bought up all the song-sheets that a lad was trying to sell outside a London theatre – Trumper said it was cold and wet and the boy should be at home, instead of shivering on the pavement.

The year 1915 remains a seminal one for cricket, despite the interruption of the war. Within the space of four months, the game lost its two greatest figures: Victor Trumper, the thrilling embodiment of modern cricket, and W. G. Grace, the inspiration of the sport that Trumper later embellished with such distinction. Whatever the post-war years might bring, cricket would never re-capture the careless rapture of a Trumper century before lunch or another Indian summer from the portly bearded figure who never thought he was out.

C. B. Fry & Ranji

Charles Burgess Fry and Kumar Shri Ranjitsinhji were two of the most spectacular talents of the so-called Golden Age of cricket. That period could be said to have lasted from around 1890 to the outbreak of war in 1914. Afterwards cricket was never so glamorous or – depending on your sense of realism – so naive again. The game flourished at every level, reflecting Victorian, imperialist self-confidence that merged into the gaiety of the Edwardian age. It was a time of privilege in England, a period of literary and artistic enlightenment, with the likes of Arthur Conan Doyle, J. M. Barrie, Rupert Brooke, Siegfried Sassoon, A. A. Milne, E. V. Lucas and P. G. Wodehouse in love with both cricket and their art. Conan Doyle, the creator of Sherlock Holmes, wrote verse to commemorate his feat of taking the wicket of W. G. Grace. Conan Doyle's brother-in-law, E. W. Hornung, created the cricketing burglar Raffles – the slow left-arm bowler known as 'The Amateur Cracksman'. P. G. Wodehouse, a fine bowler for Dulwich College at the turn of the century, rarely resisted the chance to insert a cricketing theme into his work: Jeeves, his famous butler, was named after a Warwickshire all-rounder who was later killed in the Great War.

In England it was a time of complacency, of jinogistic pride. Many agreed with Cecil Rhodes that the master race was to be found in the British Isles and that it was beneficial to the world at large to have the Union Jack straddling the globe. When Queen Victoria died in 1901, she left behind a country glorying in its missionary zeal; her son Edward VII decided that the nation would enjoy its privileged position in the civilized world. It did not seem to matter about the class

The supreme technocrat – C. B. Fry in his pomp

divisions that held firm throughout that age, or the high rates of infant mortality, the widespread prostitution, the poverty, and the fact that the average male life lasted just forty-six years. Only 58 per cent of men could vote – a privilege denied to every woman – and factory wages were pathetically small. For all that, there was a deep pride in being British at that time: the old Queen may have gone, but there was still W. G. Grace to idolize. The streaks of grey in his beard were now more pronounced, the girth fit to rival that of the new king – but he symbolized the evolution of cricket and gloried in his status as the Grand Old Man of the game. With W. G. still around, what could possibly be wrong with our national summer sport?

The short answer to that was 'very little'. Cricket was now more or less the finished product, broadly the same game that we play in the 1980s. The splendid Nottinghamshire batsman Arthur Shrewsbury had developed back-foot play, so that batsmen now agreed there were alternatives to the front-foot lunge; swing bowling, perfected by George Hirst, had set stern examinations; and the 'googly' bowling of B. J. T. Bosanquet had brought a new dimension to spin bowling. Bowlers with illegal actions had been banished after a campaign lasting twenty years, and improved grounds-manship had allowed batsmen to flourish without fear of suffering the same fate as poor George Summers in 1870 at Lord's.

Above all, the players were outstanding. Other generations have thrown up greater cricketers in more exacting times – when captaincy was more subtle, fielding vastly superior, pitches more problematical and the overall approach infinitely more professional. Yet between 1890 and 1914 there was a spirit of adventure about the English game, an endearing conviction that batsmen would be dismissed by getting them to play their favourite shot, rather than blocking off the opportunity.

Wilfred Rhodes, that great bowler who flourished throughout this age, main-

The predecessors of Rachael Heyhoe-Flint and Sarah Potter in the grounds of the Bournville Chocolate factory, Birmingham, in 1909

Right: The Bat and Ball Inn at Hambledon in Hampshire in 1908. The most famous cricket inn of all, it is situated close to Broad Halfpenny Down, where the English game was established in the latter part of the 18th century. In the same year of this picture, W. G. Grace unveiled a monument dedicated to the great days of Hambledon cricket

Kumar Shri Ranjitsinjhi, circa 1896, at his batting and charismatic peak

Below: Lunchtime in the Worcestershire v. Australians game at Worcester in 1909. The cathedral (inspiration for generations of cricket photographers) presides majestically over the proceedings while the young autograph hunters keep a respectful distance from their heroes. In the foreground, Syd Gregory (with pads) discusses the burning topics of the day with the Worcestershire captain, H. K. Foster

tained to his dying day that he always had two men out on the boundary when he bowled. He expected to fox them in the flight and he bowled quite deliberately to force the batsmen to hit him in the air. It was commonplace to see a slow left-arm bowler open with a fast bowler at the other end; variety, rather than uniformity was the key to successful bowling attacks. The bulk of the bowling was aimed at or near the off-stump and the length was a good deal fuller than in these days of short-pitched, intimidatory bowling aimed at the body, rather than the stumps. As a result, the off-drive, the most beautiful stroke in the game, flourished throughout the Golden Age: the day of the inswinger to a packed leg-side field was still to come in more pragmatic times. The wickets were excellent – the motor roller had not yet been fully developed and the heavy roller (either horse or hand-drawn) compressed the surface and bound it tightly together. When it rained, we had the 'sticky dog' – the time when a bowler held the ascendancy, although the great batsmen could, and often did, fight a fascinating battle.

The tempo of cricket in those days was brisk. Points for first innings lead had not been invented, so an outright win was vital. Over rates were never a problem with so many slow bowlers available – and among the faster men, a run-up of twenty yards was exceptional. As a result, scoring was very fast, aided by fielding that was generally unathletic and captaincy inclined to fatalism if the game

Wilfred Rhodes, the historic left-arm slow bowler for Yorkshire and England who later proved an obdurate opener. His tally of 4187 first-class wickets on retirement in 1930 is unsurpassed

was running away from the side. The general air of chivalry, of 'May the best team win' would find no support in the breast of a Bradman or a Jardine, but it made for exhilarating cricket.

This comparative naiveté in tactics was a product of the age and the presence of the amateur. He would drift in and out of country house cricket – all striped blazers, champagne, parasols and languid grace – into the sterner world of county and Test cricket, with hardly any alteration in approach or technique. A product of the public school system, he accepted the social divisions that made him change in a separate dressing-room from the professionals but would be horrified if someone had called him a snob. With a place in the family business looming, or a career ahead in law or the army, the amateur invariably had a limited amount of time at his disposal to disport himself on the cricket field. What time he had was to be enjoyed. If possible, a cricket match would not stagnate through bloody-mindedness. An amateur who had

Tom Richardson in 1897, at his peak. C.B. Fry called the great Surrey and England fast bowler 'a cheerful, brown-faced, Italian-looking brigand with an ivory smile'

Eton. Captain H. S. Hatfield leads admirers to the pavilion, 1907

experienced the horrors of Ladysmith or Mafeking while serving his country was unlikely to *play* for his country in too obsessional a manner. His public school training had given him exquisite table manners whenever he played for I Zingari or Eton Ramblers at an elegant country house – but it also gave him a refined batting technique. The front-foot drive was the hallmark of the amateur batsman – the straight knee yards down the wicket, the ball despatched through the off-side with lordly disdain. The style was embodied by the likes of Reggie Spooner (Marlborough College), R. E. Foster (Malvern College), Kenneth Hutchings (Tonbridge School) and Lionel Palairet (Repton School), all of whom played for England. Yet they were just the national symbols of the public school style. It was important to these amateurs to stamp their personalities on what was to them only a game, a self-indulgent diversion from the sterner issues of life.

The amateur cricketer of that period was usually a bold, restless spirit in the manner of the age, with the solid achievements of the Victorian period yielding to a frivolity that epitomized the Edwardian Age. They could afford to be daring, adventurous and creative because that was simply the philosophy of life at that time. Cricket was just one of many pleasures available to the talented man of independent means. Consider just a few of the amateur personalities of that era:

C. Aubrey Smith – Captain of England in two Tests in South Africa, he also acted on stage with Ellen Terry, Mrs Patrick Campbell and Ethel Barrymore. He eventually moved to Hollywood, starring in *The Prisoner of Zenda, Clive of India, Lives of a Bengal Lancer* and many other films that captured his quintessential Englishness. He was knighted for his contribution to Anglo-American relations.

F. S. Jackson – Winston Churchill was his fag at Harrow and after Cambridge, he captained England with style, gallantry and great success. He served in both the Boer War and the Great War, ending up a colonel. Son of Lord Allerton (a member of Lord Salisbury's Cabinet), he became an MP, Governor of Bengal and President of the MCC.

A. E. Stoddart – Captain of England at cricket and rugby. A first-class hockey player, splendid golfer. He moved easily among the upper classes yet when his financial prospects terminally declined, he took the traditional course of the gentleman who feared great social embarrassment. He shot himself.

R. E. Foster – One of seven brothers who played for Worcestershire, he made 287 in his first Test against Australia. He also played soccer for England and remains the only man to have captained his country at soccer and cricket. He won four sporting blues for Oxford and died from diabetes in 1914.

B. J. T. Bosanquet – After Eton and Oxford, he turned his fertile mind to a revolution in cricket – the 'googly', the ball bowled with a leg-break action which goes the other way, because the wrist is dropped. He won two Tests against Australia with the googly and his success led to a clutch of South African spinners who won two Test series against England. Bosanquet loved the social round, lending his languid, humorous personality to Free Foresters, I Zingari and Eton Ramblers cricket and also excelling at billiards, ice-hockey and hammer-throwing. His attitude to life was summed up by 'Spy' in *Vanity Fair* magazine: 'His friends make persistent efforts to see more of him . . . but the short interval between close of play and the beginning of dances gives them little opportunity.' His son Reggie, the famous television newsreader, did his considerable best to follow the family tradition.

In such diverse company, C. B. Fry and K. S. Ranjitsinhji were never outshone, either on the cricket field or in the social whirl. Ranji, as he came to be known for the convenience of headline writers, came to Cambridge with very little money and an air of eastern mystery. While at Cambridge he made speeches in favour of Indian federation – an early indication

Ranji in 1912. A decade and a half and several stone heavier since his glamorous entry into cricket

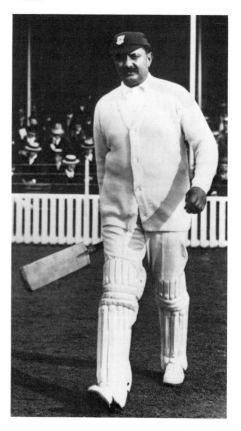

Above: C. B. Fry, aged 49, practising in the nets in 1921, when he considered a return to the Test side

Right : Charles Burgess Fry – handsome of bearing even in his seventies

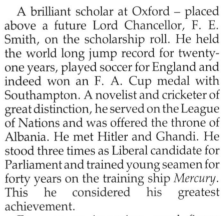

that political ambitions would always run ahead of any cricketing hopes. He later became Jam Saheb of the State of Nawanagar at the age of thirty-four and proceeded to repay many past kindnesses when he had not been quite so wealthy.

In Nawanagar he re-shaped the state's economy and in the Great War served as aide-de-camp to Sir John French. He then served on the League of Nations, where he was joined by his great friend C. B. Fry.

Fry and Ranji were born in the same year (1872), and their cricket careers seemed inextricably linked. They played for Sussex and their prodigious batting exploits illuminated the Golden Age. Somehow Ranji and Fry always seemed to be 150 not out in balmy weather at Hove on a perfect batting wicket. If Ranji was an impressive all-round personality, Fry made him seem an under-achiever. He was the complete, well-rounded man of that generation. His cricketing deeds can wait for a moment, but reflect on these accomplishments:

A brilliant scholar at Oxford – placed above a future Lord Chancellor, F. E. Smith, on the scholarship roll. He held the world long jump record for twenty-one years, played soccer for England and indeed won an F. A. Cup medal with Southampton. A novelist and cricketer of great distinction, he served on the League of Nations and was offered the throne of Albania. He met Hitler and Ghandi. He stood three times as Liberal candidate for Parliament and trained young seamen for forty years on the training ship *Mercury*. This he considered his greatest achievement.

Fry was an imposing, regal figure throughout his life but he encapsulated the supreme self-confidence of the gifted amateur in the Golden Age of cricket. As Neville Cardus put it, 'The cricket field has seen no sight more Grecian than the one presented by C. B. Fry in the pride and handsomeness of his manhood.' He had every justification for such pride. One of the great captains in a period undistinguished by tactical acumen, Fry never once tasted defeat when he led Oxford, the Gentlemen or England. He rationalized the technique of batting to a greater degree than anyone else of this time: that brilliant mind occasionally tired of composing Greek or Latin verse while waiting to bat. He wrote *Batsmanship*, the complete batting textbook, a work that still reads soundly almost a century later. No other amateur of his day thought as much about batting as C. B. Fry; he had an awkward, stiff presence at the crease and set himself to work out a method that suited him. He decided to work the ball to the on-side, using his powerful arms, steely wrists and gift of timing. The wickets were good enough to let him play across the line of attack and he was sound enough to go on to the back foot where necessary. Let the Spooners, MacLarens and Fosters dazzle with their off-side pyrotechnics: Fry was content with his own method. For twenty years and more, it was more than satisfactory – only Grace and Tom Hayward had scored more than Fry's ninety-four centuries when the Great War came.

If Fry was the supreme technocrat, Prince Ranjitsinjhi was a bewitching genius. At Cambridge, he hired English professional fast bowlers to bowl at him in the nets and he fashioned his remarkable technique. Arthur Shrewsbury had pioneered back-foot play with defence in mind, but Ranji opted for attack off the

back-foot. His timing and eyesight were so remarkable that he could flick the ball through the leg-side off the back-foot. He felt that he would lose sight of the ball for a split second if he went forward to drive it, so he would go back, watch the ball on to the bat and despatch it with a turn of the wrists. He invented a new stroke – the leg glance – although he admitted that was purely by chance. He tried to fend off a bouncer and to his surprise, the ball was flicked to the boundary by dint of his instinctive reactions. It became his most productive stroke and gained respectability among cricket sages as he continued to play it, with spectacular results.

So Ranji was the next creative batsman after W. G. Grace. Arthur Shrewsbury may have perfected the art of back-foot play, with the pads as a last line of defence, but that was solely with the aim of keeping the ball out of his stumps, to wait for loose deliveries on good wickets. Ranji's leg-glance and general back-foot technique were consciously aggressive. Throughout his career, he scored at a rate of 55 runs an hour and, when free of asthma and bronchitis, Ranji was a devastating,

thrilling sight. He was the first to score 3000 runs in a season and for good measure did it again the following season (1900). He once scored 47 off twelve balls in ten minutes for the Gentlemen against the Players, the most prestigious fixture of the season outside the Tests. Against the all-conquering Yorkshire attack, he scored two centuries in a day and he made hundreds in his first Test against Australia in both countries.

That hundred at Old Trafford was an effective answer to the MCC's ruling that the Indian prince was ineligible for England in 1896. With the ground authorities still allowed to select the Test side, the Lord's establishment kept Ranji out of the first Test. The Lancashire authorities had no such scruples and scores of 62 and 154 not out justified their selection. Ranji had the knack of charming his detractors with the bat and his own delightful personality.

By the mid-1890s Ranjitsinjhi was an acknowledged sensation. The cricket writers of that period usually described the game's intricacies in great detail and ignored the 'star' syndrome, unless W. G. Grace was involved. This young, graceful Indian prince was different, however: the

Parsee ladies enjoying the game, circa 1900. The first Indian team to tour England was made up entirely of Parsees, in 1886; it was purely an educational trip and the players had to pay their own expenses. Eleven Parsees have played Test cricket, including Nari Contractor, Polly Umrigar, Rusi Surti and Farokh Engineer, who was the last to represent his country in 1975

purple prose washed all over his beguiling performances. He was a pressman's dream, once his name had been shortened to Ranji – the 'lithe, dusky hero', with 'lean but steely muscles under his smooth brown skin'. The *London Daily News* wrote, 'He handles his bat like a walking-stick and dispenses runs like a millionaire disgorges sovereigns.' His majestic batting contained 'an Oriental calm with an occidental quickness, the stillness of a panther with the suddenness of its spring'. Adjectival excess is not the preserve of our hyperbolic age.

The press were not the only ones to acknowledge Ranji's unique attraction. He became cricket's first sex symbol. In those uncomplicated late Victorian days, a dusky figure was a rare sight and whenever Ranji practised at the nets, he was watched by a legion of female admirers with little or no interest in his leg-glance. After his wonderful 175 at Sydney in the 1897/98 series, the hero worship almost reached the proportions of Beatlemania. A cartoon in a Melbourne newspaper showed a mass of ladies confined behind iron railings to prevent them 'getting at Prince Ranji and eloping with him in a mass'. On that tour, tobacconists sold Ranji matches, sandwiches bearing his name were sold in railway bars and barbers started to sell Ranji hair-restorers. Eighty years later, the playwright Ben Travers said that when Ranji walked out to bat in the Tests of that time, 'the crowd burst into song'. Ranji was too sensitive and intelligent to take such adulation seriously. At the height of his cricket powers, he was never deflected from his aim of becoming a statesman. Victorian versatility was not confined to Anglo-Saxon amateurs. He nearly stood as Liberal candidate at Brighton and although nothing came of it, his close friendship with Fry also included a political consensus. Ranji had the politician's eye for the opportunity; his air of opulence at Cambridge was a sham, but he realized he would only be accepted by white Englishmen if they thought he was fabulously wealthy. He also possessed the politician's knack of putting his foot in it: on his only tour to Australia he ignored all the fan worship, criticized Australian crowds for their rowdiness and accused the fast bowler Ernest Jones of throwing. When bush-fire surrounded the ground, he remarked that 'Australia seemed to be the only country happy to set fire to itself to win a Test match'.

Like Fry, Ranji was not slow to express an opinion. In 1902 he was so disgusted by the standard of fielding in the Sussex side that he refused to play in the last few matches of the season. His suggestion of fielding practice before each day's play had been ill-received and although an uneasy truce was cobbled together, Ranji's relations with Sussex were never quite the same again. His trenchant remarks on the poor quality of fielding in the English game are a salutary counter-balance to the brilliance of the batting and bowling in the Golden Age. It seems Ranji was one of the few batsmen prepared to seek improvement in an area that could have limited his supremacy. Yet he was never one to seek advantage for himself at the expense of the game at large.

Ranji hardly played any English first-class cricket after 1904, when he was just thirty-two: wider responsibilities claimed his attention, as they did for so many gifted amateurs of that time. A gentleman of reasonable physique was expected to spend time on the cricket field, while keeping a sophisticated eye on the social opportunities. The Eton *v.* Harrow match at Lord's was the high spot of the social and sporting season, as the privileged mingled with their own class, secure in the conviction that their world would never be thrown off course by anything as common as a world war. The *Sunday Times* captured the flavour of those hedonistic times in its report of the 1898 Eton *v.* Harrow match:

Lord's is the rendezvous, the 'bien entendu' of the majority of those fortunate individuals who can follow the brilliant cortege of a London season, while, moreover, to be found at the Bois of the saint who subsisted on locusts who, so to speak, have Pullman seats in the express train of life, of those who travel through the world so rapidly that they have no time for sorrowful emotions, or in fact, for any other than pleasant ones.

One assumes the writer's tongue was not firmly in his cheek: satire of high society belonged to a later, more astringent age.

The public's appetite for cricket was not confined to the world of John Galsworthy's Forsytes. Village cricket was booming, as a glance at the literature of A. G. Macdonell, Hugh de Selincourt and Siegfried Sassoon will testify. While country house cricket flourished in the south, a harder version evolved in the disadvantaged north – the Birmingham

Lunchtime at Lord's during the Varsity match in the early years of the twentieth century. How did the authorities ever manage to clear the playing area in time for the post-lunch session?

The Scarborough Cricket Festival of 1913. The full house underlines the appeal of first-class cricket in an exclusively domestic season, without any Test

The England team in the nets before the 1912 Leeds Test

League was formed in 1888, followed by the Lancashire league two years later. By the dawn of the twentieth century, there were trophies to be won by endless clubs in Durham, Yorkshire, Cheshire, Staffordshire and Northumberland. Interest in county cricket was massive: in 1906, no less than 80 000 attended the Surrey *v.* Yorkshire match at the Oval, the benefit game awarded to Walter Lees. The county championship was shared around the country – in the last fifteen seasons before the Great War, it was won six times by Yorkshire, four times by Kent and once each by Surrey, Lancashire, Nottinghamshire, Middlesex, and Warwickshire. In the Golden Age, county cricket still held the public's attention. The Australian tourists came once every three or four years and it was not until 1907 that South Africa became the second country to play a Test in England. As a result, it was commonplace to have an English season without Test matches, with the Gentlemen *v.* Players game played out against the backdrop of a vibrant, exciting county championship.

Although the Golden Age is characterized as a time of striped blazers, straw boaters and amateur dominance, it has to be said that the professional played his part in the entertainment. In the last fourteen seasons before the Great War, they won sixteen matches to the Gentlemen's eight and in their ranks could be found some of the greatest players of any period. They included Jack Hobbs and Frank Woolley – destined to make their indelible mark on later generations – the marvellous bowler S. F. Barnes, the great Yorkshire all-rounders, George Hirst and Wilfred Rhodes, the dazzling Lancastrian batsman Johnny Tyldesley, the mercurial George Gunn and great wicket-keepers Dick Lilley and Herbert Strudwick.

Daring creativity was not the sole preserve of the amateur, although his chivalrous captaincy invested cricket with an air of challenge. It was up to the professional to make a positive contribution in such a dynamic atmosphere and they were rarely found wanting for long. The Australians, with Trumper, Noble, Hill and the others in their ranks, were always popular visitors, with the quest for the Ashes as diverting as it is now. Yet cricket supporters in the Golden Age did not have to wait for the sight of an Australian cap before the pulse could quicken. The batting of Gilbert Jessop – who scored at an overall rate of 79 runs an hour – kept the most exacting critic enthralled without longing for an Ashes encounter.

H. D. G. Leveson-Gower (*left*) and Pelham Warner bidding bon voyage to J. W. H. T. Douglas (*right*) before the England party leave for their triumphant tour of South Africa in 1913/14

It must have seemed that this galaxy of talent, this commitment to entertainment would never be halted. When an obscure archduke was murdered in a sleepy Balkan country in 1914, the news was greeted by an indifferent English public. The sun was beating down in late July, the wickets were perfect and Surrey looked set to wrest the championship from Kent. A month earlier, that benevolent despot Lord Hawke had stood up at the Lord's centenary dinner and expressed the conviction that Lord's and the MCC would continue to flourish for the next hundred years, whatever the state of the world. Like many influential figures of that self-confident age, Lord Hawke could not conceive a society with no time for the off-drive, a generous bonus for the perspiring professional bowler and a turn on the dance floor after a spot of country house cricket.

Many of that carefree generation of country house cricketers perished in the mud of Flanders. *Wisden* for 1916 devoted eighty-two pages to the deaths of cricketers, and a further seventy-five pages the following year. Clifton College alone lost more than five hundred former pupils. It was sad enough to lose W. G. Grace, Victor Trumper and A. E. Stoddart in

1915, but man's inhumanity to man claimed some illustrious cricketers:

Colin Blythe – One of the best slow bowlers of his time. More than 2500 wickets for Kent and England. He played the violin and suffered epileptic fits. Killed in France in 1917.

K. L. Hutchings – Dashing, handsome batsman for Kent and England. Killed in France in 1916.

Albert Cotter – Australian fast bowler of great heart and speed. A sniper's bullet cut him down in Arabia in 1917.

Percy Jeeves – One of the best all-rounders in England and the inspiration for P. G. Wodehouse's famous butler. Killed in 1916.

Major Booth – Named after the Salvation Army leader, he performed the 'double' in 1913 and played against South Africa that winter. He died on the Somme in 1916.

The world – and cricket – would never be the same. 'Never glad, confident morning again.' It had to be serious when W. G. Grace spent the last few months of his life exhorting cricketers to don the uniform of war. While the lights were going out all over Europe, the game of cricket began yearning for an era that would never return.

Jack Hobbs

Jack Hobbs was the nearest to batting perfection that the game has known. W. G. Grace may have been the more creative, moulding a technique to dominate the emerging game of first-class cricket, and Don Bradman was certainly more acquisitive in run gathering – but over a thirty-year period, Jack Hobbs adapted to every new bowling test, every technical problem. He met and mastered all types of bowling – swerve, fast cutters, seamers, leg-spin, off-break and googlies – and prospered on every kind of wicket all over the world. Even in early middle age, he was still blessed with that uncanny knack of knowing instinctively where the ball was going to pitch, and what stroke to play.

Hobbs's career spanned thirty years. He made his debut for Surrey on Easter Monday 1905 in a match captained by the first two men to reach a hundred hundreds – W. G. Grace and Tom Hayward. Eighteen years later, Hobbs became the third batsman to reach the target. The man who opened the batting with C. B. Fry lasted long enough to grace the same cricket field as Don Bradman and Walter Hammond. When he first batted for Surrey, the ball had to be hit clean out of the ground to count six runs and slow bowlers used to open the bowling, rubbing the ball in the dirt to eliminate the shine. Before he died in 1963, Hobbs had seen the abolition of the amateur status and the start of limited overs cricket. Few cricketers can have witnessed such revolutionary changes in their lifetime and certainly no one adorned it with greater distinction.

Jack Hobbs was the very last man to worship the statistical Holy Grail – indeed he always said that cricket would be a better game if the newspapers did not

Masterclass from Hobbs at the Duke of York's Barracks, Chelsea, 1936

publish the averages. Yet the roll call of his achievements is awesome. He made more runs and centuries than anyone else in history. His technique was so ageless that he scored ninety-eight hundreds after reaching forty. He was still good enough to score 221 in just over six hours against Griffith and Martindale in 1933, when the two West Indian fast bowlers intimidated the flower of English batsmanship. Hobbs was rising fifty-one at the time. Before Bradman, he was the most consistent run-scorer of all time – 35 017 runs and 131 centuries in his last fifteen years – yet he cared little for big scores just for the sake

of it. He would often give away his wicket to a deserving bowler after reaching his century – he was out fifty-one times between 100 and 110. He missed five seasons through illness, injury and war, declined several overseas tours for family reasons and did not play first-class cricket until the age of twenty-two; otherwise his final career record would have been even more astonishing.

In his modest way, Jack Hobbs did more for the professional sportsman than any other man. In 1953 he became the first professional games player to be knighted, an honour bestowed on him for his personal qualities as much as for his batting. He lifted the status of the professional after the Great War, even though he still called amateurs 'Mr'. Hobbs received the princely sum of £1671 from his benefit in 1919 and with the money he bought a sports goods shop in Fleet Street. That gave him security, something vital to the eldest of twelve children who had been born into a poor Cambridge family.

Quietly, and always with dignity, Jack Hobbs made sure that he and his fellow professionals were treated with respect. In 1924 he initially refused to tour Australia because he would not be allowed to take his wife with him. Hitherto, only the amateurs had been allowed that privilege – with the exception of that stormy petrel S. F. Barnes in South Africa a decade earlier – and even then the ladies had to stay in separate hotels at the expense of their husbands. Hobbs stood his ground, won the day and his wife accompanied him on his last two tours to Australia. In 1926, when Arthur Carr was ill, he captained England at Old Trafford and he and Wilfred Rhodes were co-opted on to the selection committee that year.

Above : Jack Hobbs's impeccable defence in the Adelaide Test, 1925

Country house cricket – Penshurst Castle, Kent, in 1935

Right : Lord's 1932 and for the Eton v. Harrow match, a comfortable cushion is almost as essential as the topper

The 1926 Ashes series. Arthur Carr leads out the England side but professional Jack Hobbs is close behind, alongside amateur Percy Chapman

Twenty years earlier, when Hobbs had joined Surrey, the relationship between club and professionals still retained a semi-feudal touch: he was paid thirty shillings a week in the summer and a pound in the winter. Incredibly the registration rules at that time were so stringent that he had to spend two winters in lodgings in south London to qualify for Surrey – he was not even allowed to go home to Cambridge to see his mother. In those days a professional cricketer would end up a groundsman, publican or umpire if he was lucky, yet when Jack Hobbs retired, the professional could afford to drive a motor car, grateful that his sporting prowess had led him into cricket, rather than soccer, where the rewards were less attractive.

The special elevation of the professional cricketer was inspired by the example of Hobbs but galvanized by the increasing publicity afforded to the game. Press interest was great enough in the days of Grace but after the Great War, the electronic age affected cricket, as it affected all other areas of society.

The dawn of radio commentary, and the popularity of the cinema put extra pressure on newspapers and this competitive element spurred journalists in the direction of 'exclusives'. The personal 'quote' became desirable, and the 'star system' evolved. In the 1920s, with his stature and his popularity undimmed, Jack Hobbs was a national institution. He endorsed fountain pens, cricket bats and other equipment, cocoa and soft drinks; he was filmed demonstrating his matchless batting art and, with the aid of loyal 'ghost writers' he published no less than eleven books, including a thriller called *Test Match Surprise*. He was even asked to play the lead in a feature film. As he toppled one batting record after another, Hobbs came to accept the travelling caravan of reporters, cameramen and feature writers with a degree of equanimity: he was never a materialistic man, but security for his family came top of his list of priorities. The adulation of the twenties assured him of that, but not at the expense of his batting, his integrity or enduring public appeal. His gentle, wry sense of humour was no doubt tickled at the values of a world which saw him feted at a civic dinner at Cambridge and offered honorary membership of the MCC for something as simple as batting prowess – but his fellow professionals would not begrudge him the laurel wreaths.

Jack Hobbs always asserted that he was a far better player before the Great War, and certainly his contemporaries waxed lyrical about his brilliant strokeplay. He was the first to master the quartet of South African googly bowlers; many famous batsmen were perplexed by the googly, playing their usual off-drives, and watching horrified as the ball drifted in from a leg-break action.

R. E. Foster wrote in *Wisden* that the googly would kill offside play, the glory of the Golden Age, but the young Hobbs simply took stock and adapted. On the matting wickets of South Africa on the 1909/10 tour, he averaged 67 in Tests, twice as much as any other colleague – by the simple expedient of playing back as far as possible to combat the extra bounce and pushing forward to a ball that could be smothered. Two years earlier, Hobbs had revealed astonishing maturity in his first series against Australia. At Melbourne, he gave an early indication of his genius on a 'sticky' wicket: an innings of 57 out of 105 all out, with only one other player reaching double figures. Such virtuosity was to be displayed countless times. Hobbs could always be replied upon in desperate circumstances.

It is a measure of the strength of English cricket in the Edwardian Age that Hobbs only made the 1907/08 tour to Australia because of the absence for various reasons of batsmen of the calibre of Tommy Hayward, J. T. Tyldesley, R. E. Foster, C. B. Fry, F. S. Jackson, Pelham Warner, R. H. Spooner, Archie MacLaren and Gilbert Jessop. Characteristically Hobbs seized his chance and never looked back. He played in ten series against the Australians – four won by England, six by Australia – and his wicket was always the prized one. When the 1921 Australian touring party blitzed English cricket, it was universally agreed that England would have fared better if Hobbs had not been ruled out with a ruptured thigh muscle, then appendicitis.

The fearsome fast bowling of J. M. Gregory and Ted McDonald and the spinning wiles of Arthur Mailey and Warwick Armstrong would have tested the great man, but he had met and mastered enough great bowlers in his time to still any doubts. That Australian team stands out as one of the most powerful in Test history. The solid batting of Warren Bardsley and H. L. Collins, the genius of Charlie Macartney, the all-round ability and ruthless captaincy of Armstrong, the peerless wicket-keeping of Bertie Oldfield and that relentless fast bowling – no wonder Australia won eight Tests in a row against England just after the Great War ended. England took longer to recover from the war, and the Australian Forces team that came over in 1919 gained valuable experience of English conditions. The pattern of slow recovery by England was to be repeated after the Second World War: in both cases a single victory at the Oval won the Ashes back after a 4/1 defeat in Australia a couple of years earlier. The initial feat in 1926 owed much to Jack Hobbs and his great opening partner, Herbert Sutcliffe. The match was evenly poised until a thunderstorm flooded south London during the night. The sun shone in the morning and play began on time, with Hobbs and Sutcliffe having to face the spinners on a wicket that would tax the most skilful technique. Somehow they added 161 before lunch and both made hundreds. The pitch was so bad that the great Oldfield allowed 37 extras in the total of 436, but the two openers were unperturbed. Australia, needing 415 to win, were demoralized and they

Above: Jack Hobbs being immortalized by sculptor John Tussaud in 1930

Left: Johnny Douglas. Jack Hobbs considered him to be the best new-ball bowler he faced throughout his career

collapsed to lose by 289 runs. It was a famous victory for an England team of rich talent:

Hobbs
Sutcliffe
Woolley
Hendren
Chapman (captain)
Stevens
Rhodes
Geary
Tate
Larwood
Strudwick (wicket-keeper)

Percy Chapman, glamour boy of the Roaring Twenties, had taken over the England captaincy at the tender age of twenty-five for this match and he relied heavily on the tactical sagacity of Hobbs and Rhodes, who returned to the England fold at the age of forty-nine and bowled beautifully. Larwood was just starting out on his famous career, Tate was the best fast-medium bowler in the world and George Geary and the young Middlesex amateur Greville Stevens were top-class all-rounders. The batting was a mature mixture of great players, but for Hobbs and Sutcliffe it was the high summer of their wonderful understanding. For good measure they showed Australia how it had been done at the Oval when they toured two years later – a stand of 105 on a pig of a wicket when England ought to have been bowled out for less than a hundred. Instead they won by three wickets, chasing a total of 332. At the age of forty-six, Hobbs averaged 50 in the series.

Eighteen months later, he bowed quietly out of Test cricket at his beloved Oval in the series that was dominated by Don Bradman. Hobbs was still a wonderful player, although his demise may well have been symbolized at Leeds when the young master ran him out with a direct throw from deep mid-off. The ability of Jack Hobbs to steal a single from

anywhere in the field had always been as matchless as his glorious versatility, his calmness under pressure. He was exceedingly lucky in his choice of opening partners. For England, Wilfred Rhodes was his staunch prewar partner – thirteen stands of a hundred and tough, Yorkshire common sense at the other end. After the war, it was Herbert Sutcliffe – twenty-six partnerships of a hundred and more – and an imperturbable presence. For Surrey, the majestic Tom Hayward (forty century stands) – Hobbs's mentor and confidant. Then Andy Sandham kept him company in sixty-six century partnerships for the last fifteen years of his great career. Hobbs shared in first wicket stands of a century no less than 166 times – a rate of

Left : Charles Macartney off to lunch in the midst of his famous 151 at Headingley, 1926. England captain Arthur Carr, who dropped him off the fourth ball of the innings, was to lose his place

Below : A 1926 pitch invasion at the Oval as England regain the Ashes

Above: Herbert Sutcliffe during the 555 partnership with Percy Holmes, Leyton 1932

Right : Jack Hobbs selecting the willow for his bats in 1922. His choice was unerring; he made another hundred hundreds before retiring

one per eight innings – and although he would be the first to acknowledge his invaluable partners, there were no doubts about his pre-eminence.

In common with Grace and Bradman, Hobbs was the dominant batsman of his halycon period – roughly twenty of his twenty-two years in Test cricket. In the last two Ashes series, Hammond and Bradman eclipsed him, but it was purely relative. Gargantuan scores on shirtfront wickets may have impressed sports editors in Fleet Street, but the intrinsic worth of J. B. Hobbs could never be gauged from the scorebook. His durability was remarkable: from the hansom cab era to the rise of Hitler. He saw West Indies, New Zealand and India admitted to Test status between 1926 and 1932 and lasted long enough in the game to captain a Surrey side which contained eleven professionals.

He watched the balance of power move from ball to bat after the Great War and considered it a poorer game as a result. Although uncovered wickets could always yield a 'sticky' wicket if the elements decreed, there were far too many pluperfect batting surfaces in the 1920s and 1930s. In 1930, Ashes Tests in England were extended from three to four days – an acknowledgement that the pitches were too good and that an extra day was a commercial desirability. Don Bradman had no complaints about the extra day – it simply made him hungrier for vast totals. At the age of forty-eight, Jack Hobbs had nothing to prove in that direction. Four years later he was still demonstrating the value of an impeccable technique in county cricket, even if the feet did not quite take him into the perfect position any more.

This was the man who batted better under pressure than any other player – yet laughed out loud when his great friend Arthur Mailey bowled him with a full toss in the crucial Oval Test of 1926. To Jack Hobbs, cricket was always a game: it simply happened that he was better at it than any of his contemporaries.

Frank Woolley & Maurice Tate

Frank Woolley and Maurice Tate were two of the greatest professional cricketers in a period where the amateur became a more peripheral figure. Both played before the Great War, when a county game could often feature up to fifteen amateurs, but Woolley and Tate were particularly dominant in the 1920s. One was generally acknowledged to be the greatest left-hand batsman the game had yet seen, while the other the best fast-medium bowler in the world. Only S. F. Barnes and Alec Bedser can rival Tate for controlled variety at fast-medium pace, and only Garfield Sobers among left-handers could seriously dispute the claims of Woolley. Above all, Woolley and Tate were marvellous entertainers and superb all-round cricketers who brought joy to a cricketing age that began to take itself more and more seriously. They were lucky enough to play for two counties who consistently tried to entertain during the period between the wars. Although Lancashire and Yorkshire usually won the county championship, the style of Woolley's Kent and Tate's Sussex was immeasurably more attractive. Kent had a spectacular batting side – Woolley, Les Ames, Percy Chapman, Brian Valentine – and a genuine commitment to spin bowling. No wonder the canny county player usually chose Kent for his benefit match: they would always ensure a large crowd, in the days when takings at the benefit match were the major source of income for the beneficiary. Sussex were equally appealing, with graceful batting from Melville, Duleepsinhji, Bowley and all-round talents of Tate, Arthur Gilligan and James Langridge. Neither Sussex nor Kent achieved the highest prize during those years, but they always brought colour and human fallibility to a cham-

Frank Woolley. 'Here comes the lion-tamer' commented Patsy Hendren whenever Woolley stalked in to bat

pionship battle usually won by the more solid, utilitarian cricketers of the north.

It would be wrong to paint too gloomy a cricketing canvas of that inter-war period. Spin bowlers were still plentiful, tail-end batsmen invariably tried to slog a few sixes, rather than potter around, and spinners like 'Tich' Freeman reaped a rich harvest. Freeman took more wickets than any other bowler apart from Wilfred Rhodes, and although he rarely succeeded in Tests, he was a terror for Kent. He bowled high-tossed leg-spin, googlies and top-spin to an accurate line and length and countless batsmen perished through over-ambition. He picked up hundreds of wickets through catches in the deep and 'stumped Ames bowled Freeman' was a regular mode of dismissal – 259 times in fact. Les Ames collected no less than 418 stumpings in his wicket-keeping career for Kent and England (52 alone in 1928). Indeed *Wisden* remarked of Ames that he needed more practice at standing back to the fast bowlers – a salutary corrective to the modern wicket-keeping lament, where he is little more than an athletic long-stop.

Spin bowling remained important at that time because the pitches were so benign. A bowler had to toil or experiment, otherwise he would be hammered out of sight. Some, like Fred Root, would experiment with inswing to a leg-trap, others would try intimidation. Gregory and McDonald had shown what could be done on perfect, fast wickets in the dry summer of 1921, and over the next decade the likes of Larwood, Voce, Bowes, Constantine and Martindale all demonstrated that accurate, fast bowling designed to intimidate a batsman could succeed. Yet the increasing use of pad-play and the placid wickets generally meant it was a batsman's game between the wars.

The 1928 season epitomizes this batting dominance. Five men scored more than 3000 runs that summer – including Frank Woolley, who was not even picked for the Australian tour that winter! No less than 414 hundreds were scored and 72 of the season's matches produced aggregates of

Left: Maurice Tate's glorious action. Only Alec Bedser has matched his ability to extract speed off the pitch from such a short run-up

Below : County cricket at Blackheath in 1933. The knotted hankies were necessary to ward off the sun's rays – especially when jackets remained stoically donned in a heatwave! Fifty years on, a streaker would be negotiating with a Fleet Street photographer in such weather

more than 1000 runs. Runs were compiled at speed – when Phil Mead scored 180 in 3½ hours at Maidstone, the press said he batted 'stolidly'. *Wisden*'s editor talked about the need to 'reduce run-getting to reasonable limits' and he deplored the excessive use of pad-play, with even the great Jack Hobbs coming in for some trenchant criticism. There were calls for larger stumps, a fourth stump, a smaller ball and a reform of the lbw rule. The latter came to pass in 1935, but not before further subjugation of the bowlers. Apart from the matchless aspect of the wickets, it was a time of great batting quality. In the period 1925–35, the game was dominated by men who could score a hundred almost at will. Nine of the twenty-one batsmen who have scored a hundred centuries in their career were in their high summer at this time – they were Hobbs, Woolley, Mead, Hendren, Hammond, Sutcliffe, Sandham, Ernest Tyldesley and Ames. All of them professionals.

Some of these professional batsmen were wonderful entertainers. Hobbs, Hammond, Ames and Hendren would bat like carefree amateurs whenever possible, but only Woolley consistently played like a survivior of the Golden Age. Gradu-

ally the amateur was fading from the full-time cricketing scene: the Great War and the economic slump of the late 1920s had ushered in a new era of realism. The Flapper was replaced by the Jarrow marcher and this harsh new world was reflected in English cricket.

Amateurs such as R. W. V. Robins, G. O. Allen, I. A. R. Peebles and A. P. F. Chapman could not devote their talents full-time to the game for any great length due to business reasons, and the game was poorer for the absence of their dynamism and unselfish captaincy. The amateur who could devote his talents to the game was usually a 'professional amateur' – the county secretary or the fortunate recipient of largesse from a philanthropic supporter of the county side. Within a decade of the Great War, the convention that amateurs and professionals should walk out on the field of play from separate gates had been quietly dropped. The only tangible difference between the two groups of cricketers was now found in the Gentlemen *v.* Players games. By 1939, the social revolution in

Tate playing 'shove ha'penny' in his pub after retirement

Phil Mead displaying the kind of generosity he rarely showed to perspiring bowlers. An obdurate left-hander of little finesse, he scored more runs for one team (Hampshire) than any other cricketer in history. He took a practical view of his batting and enjoyed the talent-money available for scoring fifties and hundreds. 'That's another bag of coal for the winter,' he would mutter whenever he reached the target
Below: Elias ('Patsy') Hendren pictured in characteristic mood. One of the most popular cricketers of any era, Hendren scored prolifically between the wars; only Jack Hobbs has surpassed his 170 centuries

cricket was almost complete, with the England captain, Walter Hammond, a recent recruit from professional to amateur rank. He could now captain England because he had security from a job with a tyre company, and did not need to be paid for his cricketing labours. The age of the 'shamateur' was upon us.

Players like Frank Woolley and Maurice Tate helped the professional cricketer establish his prominent status, as the amateur came to terms with earning a living outside the game. They were both splendid all-rounders: each did the 'double' eight times and, between them, they played 103 times for England. When England regained the Ashes at the Oval in 1926, it was fitting that Woolley and Tate were there for the historic occasion. Tate had carried the England bowling on his broad shoulders for two Ashes series, while Woolley had adorned the traditional contests with his own languid charm since 1909. When Gregory and McDonald scattered the English batting in 1921, they were checked by a supreme display of gallantry under fire by Woolley.

Frank Woolley's timing, like David Gower's, was an aesthetic delight

In the Lord's Test, he scored 95 out of 187 and 93 out of 283 in circumstances that deserved a double hundred in both innings. It was a legendary performance, one that could only have been accomplished by a cricketer of genius.

No one has hit the ball harder for a longer period of time than Frank Woolley. Among modern players, only Ian Botham can rival him for clean, long hitting, but Woolley was still driving fast bowlers straight back over their heads in his last season, at the age of fifty-one. One cannot visualize Ian Botham handing out such treatment in his middle age! Even Harold Larwood, one of the fastest bowlers of all time, suffered so much at Woolley's expense that he normally had a fielder out straight on the boundary when he bowled at him. Patsy Hendren used to shout 'here comes the lion-tamer!' when Woolley walked out to bat and certainly it was Woolley rather than the bowler who usually cracked the whip. His method was disarmingly simple – feet slightly apart, hands at the top of the bat handle and a long, easy sweep of the bat. He could play equally well off front- and back-foot and his sense of timing was uncanny. Woolley had a stiff angularity in his movements, but that disappeared when he

batted. Neville Cardus was often enraptured by his grace. He wrote, 'His cricket is compounded of soft airs and fresh flavours. The bloom of the year is on it, making for sweetness. And the very brevity of summer is on it too, making for loveliness.' Heady stuff indeed, guaranteed to be read out to a blushing Woolley by his whimsical team-mates, but there is no doubt that Woolley's batting was consistently lyrical. He never really suggested permanence in the way of a Hobbs or a Bradman – he made 89 noughts in his career and got out 35 times in the nineties – but that was part of his charm. Woolley never seemed to care about statistics or the grind of a chanceless hundred. The ball needed to be hit in the air and the spectators entertained. Woolley batting on a sunlit, golden day at Canterbury between the two wars remains the abiding memory of many an octogenarian cricket-lover.

Woolley's batting record is remarkably impressive, considering the dashing way he approached the job. Only Hobbs has scored more runs, only five batsmen have topped his tally of 145 centuries and he shares with Grace the record of 1000 runs in a season twenty-eight times. For good measure he also took more catches than

anyone in cricket history and picked up more than 2000 wickets with classical slow left-arm bowling. It is true that Woolley played a long time – from the age of nineteen to fifty-one – but he was no Boycott in his approach to statistical prowess. He stands out as one of the greatest all-round cricketers but more important, as one of the most dazzling entertainers. Bill Bowes, the shrewd unemotional Yorkshire fast bowler summed up Woolley's enduring charm thus: 'To see a hundred by him would keep you going for years.'

When Frank Woolley entered county cricket in 1906, a disillusioned Sussex bowler had just left the game at the comparatively early age of thirty-eight. Poor Fred Tate had never recovered from the traumas of the Old Trafford Test in 1902, when, to all intents and purposes, he lost the Test for England. His form tailed off and he retired three years later, hoping that one day his son, Maurice would prove a more durable cricketer against the Australians. Yet Fred never encouraged Maurice to be a cricketer, even though Sussex gave him a trial and took him on the staff in 1911, at the age of sixteen. The son was a carbon copy of the father as a bowler: slow-medium offspin.

He seemed to lack the ability of Fred who, after all, had taken over 1300 wickets in first-class cricket. When war came, there seemed every reason to suspect that Maurice Tate had been consigned to cricketing oblivion. To his surprise, he was taken on again in 1919 and he continued his plodding, mediocre progress. Maurice Tate was twenty-seven before he bowled the ball that turned him into the greatest bowler of his generation. In July 1922 he was trundling away at the inscrutable Phil Mead on a batting paradise at Eastbourne; Mead was on his way to another laborious hundred that seemed to be his trademark throughout the twenties. Tate, exasperated by Mead's obduracy, suddenly delivered the ball at the fastest pace he could manage: it pitched off stump and hit leg stump. Exit Mead, enter a great bowler. Arthur Gilligan, the wise and inspiring Sussex captain, implored Tate to work on this new style and the following season he took 219 wickets. In 1924, the tally was 205 and in 1925, a little matter of 228. In each season, he also scored over a thousand runs; the batsman began to flourish along with the bowler. At the age of twenty-nine, he played in his first Test, took a wicket with his first delivery and helped Arthur Gilligan to bowl out South

Africa for just 30. Almost overnight Tate had become a devastating bowler and he proceeded to confirm this in Australia. On the 1924/5 tour, he took thirty-eight wickets in the series – as many as the next three English bowlers put together. A man of great heart and unquenchable optimism, he bowled over 300 overs, more than any other two bowlers combined. All this on splendid batting wickets, against Ponsford, Ryder, Bardsley, Kippax, and Collins, with England losing the series by 4/1. Like Alec Bedser, Tate had to carry the English bowling almost single-handed against an Australian side that had quickly regained its strength and vitality after a war. Both English bowlers were heroic in Ashes series that were lost 4/1 and both were on hand eighteen months later at the Oval to play a part in a joyous English victory. Between 1924 and 1928, Tate held the English fort until Larwood reached maturity and Bedser did the same for Trueman, Tyson and Statham from 1946 to 1953. It was entirely appropriate that Maurice Tate lived to enjoy that second English revival after a world war.

Like Bedser, Tate had wide-shoulders, with thick legs, large feet and a big heart – ideally equipped for long unrewarding

Maurice Tate batting against Australia in 1926. Good enough to score a Test hundred, Tate also performed 'the double' eight times

The R101 floats over the Lord's Test Match in 1930 – a spectacular sideshow to one of the most spectacular Tests of all time

spells on perfect batting strips. Both had perfect actions from short run-ups, and both could bowl with such masterly control that they preferred the wicket-keeper to stand up to the stumps to pressurize the batsman. Bedser's forte was the leg-cutter (those massive hands could manipulate the ball at will) while Tate used the seam to bowl a superb outswinger. When Tate was in his prime, every young player was told to play forward to him: informed opinion was that he was fast-medium through the air and fast off the pitch. The amount of bruises he inflicted on batsmen's thighs and the frequency with which he hit the stumps were due testimony to his lethal prowess. For a decade, no bowler was more consistently dangerous on wickets that overwhelmingly favoured the batsman.

This batting supremacy was first confirmed at Test level in England during the 1930 series against Australia. Increasing concern at the easy-paced pitches had led to the introduction of a

fourth day for the Tests of that year: the feeling was that the extra day would produce a definite result, rather than a dull draw.

Unfortunately the groundsmen over-compensated by preparing wickets that were even more placid. As a result, Bradman set new batting records and the balance of power shifted even further away from the ball. At least the unde-manding batting conditions produced one classic Test that summer. The Lord's Test was a spectator's delight throughout; it was played in gorgeous, sunny weather and 1601 runs were scored at a rate of 69 an hour. More than 110 000 watched the game, which Australia won by seven wickets amid great excitement. Both teams fielded players of great distinction, charm and variety.

England	Australia
Hobbs	Woodfull (captain)
Woolley	Ponsford
Hammond	Bradman
Duleepsinhji	Kippax
Hendren	McCabe
Chapman (captain)	Richardson
Allen	Oldfield (wicket-keeper)
Tate	Fairfax
Robins	Grimmett
White	Hornibrook
Duckworth (wicket-keeper)	Wall

Australia just had the edge in batting – wonderful opening batsmen, a genius at number three, the classic poise of Kippax and McCabe – while England had the greater variety in bowling. There was the speed of Allen, the fast-medium Tate and Hammond, with White and Woolley to bowl slow left-arm and the leg-spin of Robins. All were put to the sword when Australia rattled up 729 for 6 declared. Bradman made 254 in just 339 minutes, with just one false stroke and that got him out – beautifully caught at cover by Percy Chapman. On the second day, Australia

Maurice Tate en route to Lord's in 1932 to learn he had been selected for his final England tour. The precaution of walking around the ladder did not bring him good fortune on the tour to Australia. Douglas Jardine had no room in his Bodyline strategy for the greatest fast-medium bowler of the age

scored 255 in the last 160 minutes of play, as Bradman asserted his rapacious genius. He has always acknowledged this to be his greatest innings, because he placed every ball where he wanted it. Endearingly England continued to attack him: it was not in the nature of either Percy Chapman or his proud bowlers to seal up the game. They continued trying to get Bradman out, setting attacking fields. The Australians had used the same tactics on the opening day, as Woolley rattled to a gorgeous cameo innings of 41 in the first half-hour. Duleepsinhji, nephew of the great Ranji, played in the same charming vein to make 173 on his Test debut before getting himself out trying to accelerate the already impressive scoring rate. England 401 for nine at the close of the first day; how could they lose a match from that position of security? After the Australian blitzkrieg, England were 304 behind. They started the final day on 93 for two and in these more ruthless times, it seems incredible that they could lose on such a perfect batting strip, with so much batting available and just six hours left to negotiate. The leg-spin of Clarrie Grimmett hustled them out (six for 167, splendidly old-fashioned figures), although not before a dashing hundred from Percy Chapman had staved off the innings defeat. Australia, needing just 72 for victory, slumped to 22 for 3 (including Bradman for a single, caught brilliantly again by Chapman), but the match was over by five o'clock and the sun-bronzed

spectators wandered off into the golden evening, still chattering about the vicissitudes of a spectacular match.

It was the manner in which the game was played that made it so memorable. A bowling rate of 21.50 an hour and a glut of spin bowling from either side contributed to the air of challenge. Compare the Centenary Test between the two sides fifty years later at Lord's – just 122 overs of spin, a bowling rate of 15.82 an hour and 48.4 runs every hour. By 1980, field placing and its overall standard were immeasurably higher, but the prevailing toughness of the age could never be preferable to the naive charm of the 1930 Test. By the end of that series, it looked as if the England selectors had agreed that the approach had to be less Corinthian: the gallant, chivalrous Percy Chapman lost the captaincy, to be replaced by the unspectacular deep thinker, R. E. S. Wyatt. The battle lines were being drawn up for the Bodyline series two years later, when Wyatt was second in command to Jardine, an amateur captain from an entirely different tactical planet to Chapman.

There was no place for Frank Woolley or Maurice Tate in Douglas Jardine's blueprint for the future. Tate was taken on the Bodyline tour as insurance, but the success of the strategy did not depend on a bowler who always liked to hit the stumps, rather than the batsman's body. Apart from a Test in New Zealand, that was the end of Maurice Tate's wonderful

England career. Woolley only played in three Tests after the 1930 series. He was snubbed unforgivably by Jardine, who sent a great slip fielder down to fine leg and third man in the 1931 Test at Lord's against New Zealand. Jardine clearly felt Woolley's expansive talents were unsuited to the relentless pragmatism of modern Test cricket. The amateur clearly distrusted the dashing professional. The admirable, solid virtues of Maurice Leyland, the Nawab of Pataudi and Bob Wyatt were preferable, so Woolley slipped back into county cricket amid the bunting, the tents and the intimate atmosphere of those lovely Kentish grounds.

As Woolley and Tate eased themselves towards honourable retirement, they could reflect on many changes in the game during their glorious careers. There had been a Test every summer since 1928; 1925 remains the last time an English season passed without a touring team. In the 1920s some county captains had complained that Australian visits distracted public attention from the real business of county cricket. Arthur Gilligan, a former England captain, even suggested that the county championship should be suspended or curtailed whenever the Australians toured. He would never win that battle: Test cricket was becoming too important. In the winter of 1929/30, England played two series at the same time – in West Indies and New Zealand – while the following winter saw Test action in Australia and South Africa. By the end of the 1930s, county cricket was undeniably the poor relation as huge newspaper coverage and massive scoring by superstars fanned the Test Match flames into a roaring inferno. In 1938, when the television cameras covered a Test for the first time, the pre-eminence was complete.

Woolley in particular had spanned a remarkable length of time without any real diminishment in his powers. He first played at the height of the Edwardian Age of attacking cricket, and he continued to play in the same fashion throughout the restrictive thirties. The youngster who made his debut in the season that W. G. Grace scored 74 against the Players on his fifty-eighth birthday was still charming spectators in the year of Chamberlain's famous piece of paper after his trip to Munich. As for Maurice Tate, he was still cheerfully accepting his lot on perfect wickets until 1937, fully thirty-five years since his humiliated father had shed tears of frustration in the Old Trafford pavilion. In the interim, the Tate family had made a happier impact on cricket history.

Walter Hammond

Walter Hammond was the best English batsman in the decade that led up to the Second World War. Yet Hammond had more than supremacy to offer; as a majestic stylist, he stamped himself on the memory of three generations. Forty years after his retirement, contemporary players and spectators still assert that Hammond was a rare sight to behold on the cricket field. Everything he did was out of the top drawer – he was poised, assured, a devastating mixture of power and elegance. In county cricket the bowlers measured their success against him by the number of times they beat the bat. Leonard Hutton, who played several Tests with Hammond, summed up the man's charisma aptly: 'Whenever I saw him bat, I felt sorry for the ball.'

Anyone who ever saw Hammond play will state unequivocally that it was worth being there just to watch him walk out to bat. He was a thoroughbred in all he did – whether bowling with a graceful, classical action, or standing at first slip or murdering the bowlers. The physique was perfect: just over medium height, deep-chested, broad-shouldered with an ease and grace of movement that marked him out as a natural games player. In his last season as a first-class player in 1946, *Picture Post* wrote, 'See him while you can. Your grandsons will feel you have let them down if you haven't seen Hammond on their behalf.' Hammond was forty-three at the time and dogged by fibrositis – yet the allure was still as strong as it had been twenty years earlier, when Neville Cardus wrote, 'I tremble to think of the grandeur he will spread over our cricket fields when he has arrived at maturity.'

Hammond's charismatic presence on the cricket field was so powerful that

Hammond's majestic on-drive at Lord's in the Victory Test, 1945

it was easy to overlook his magnificent statistical prowess. He made 167 hundreds (more than all but two batsmen), scored just over 50 000 runs, took 732 wickets and held 819 catches with calm detachment at slip. His detractors in

the game said that he should have taken more wickets, that Gloucestershire would have won two championships if he had stirred himself to bowl more. Certainly he had the kind of natural ability and glorious action to rival Maurice Tate as a fast-medium bowler, but Hammond felt he was more useful as a batsman. Hard to argue with that, but now and again, he would give tantalizing glimpses of his all-round prowess. In 1928, during the Cheltenham Festival, he made 362 in three innings, took sixteen wickets and made ten catches. Even C. B. Fry, a critic loath to praise later generations at the expense of the Golden Age, conceded that 'Hammond would have been a bright light in their company.'

Hammond's record would have been even more awesome if he had not been robbed of eight seasons by a combination of war, illness and the kind of administrative dogmatism that was only too typical of the doctrinaire instincts of Lord's in the 1920s. Hammond played a few games for Gloucestershire in 1921, even though he had been born in Dover. Lord Harris, that wilful martinet at Lord's, heard about the young man's promise and expressed his anger that he had not chosen to play for Kent, the county of his birth and the love of Lord Harris's life. The noble Lord insisted that Hammond should serve a two-year residential period in Gloucestershire before he could play for that county. So a great young talent had to fester in club games for two years, the same fate suffered by Jack Hobbs twenty years earlier. It is good to know that consistency remained one of the salient points in attempts by Lord's to keep the professional under the heel. Mercifully the amateur county captains of that time were rather more enlightened in their dealings with the professionals. They made sure that the professionals were reasonably paid and to a great extent they succeeded. While Hammond was qualifying for Gloucestershire the manager of Southampton begged him to devote his talents to football, but Hammond viewed the offer dispassionately and came to the correct conclusion that he would be better paid by cricket. Forty years later, after the good offices of

Mr Jimmy Hill helped lift the footballers' maximum wage, the young Hammond would probably have taken a different course. Cricket lovers can only be grateful for the strength and vitality of the county game in the 1920s, otherwise we might have lost an immortal. The experience of an established professional cricketer like Roy Kilner must have impressed the ambitious Hammond to stay with the summer game – in 1925 Kilner's benefit

raised the sum of £4016, a total that was not surpassed until after the Second World War.

It was to be 1928 before Hammond played for England against Australia, and he immediately established himself as the greatest batsman in the world. That touring party which carried off a 4/1 victory in Australia was one of the strongest squads England ever sent abroad. The happy, lucky captaincy of Percy Chapman led batsmen such as Hobbs, Sutcliffe, Hendren, Leyland and Jardine, while the bowling was in the hands of Larwood, Tate, Geary and White, with Ames and Duckworth to contest the wicket-keeping duties. The Ashes tide had turned with a vengeance, as England completed the postwar recovery. For the first time in seventeen years, England won a series in Australia and amid the galaxy of talent, one man stood out: Walter Hammond. He scored 905 runs (average 113.12) in the series, an unprecedented total. The manner in which he scored those runs was even more impressive. He realized the wickets were so good that there was no need to take any undue risks; the hook, the glance and the cut were usually eschewed and he played primarily 'through the V', in the arc between extra cover and midwicket. His awesome power off front- and back-foot was sufficient to punish the slightest deviation in length. His ruthlessness had been fortified by an illness that kept him out of the entire 1926 season – when he had been expected to be playing against the visiting Australians – and his frustration at Lord Harris's blimpish attitude also found an outlet as he churned out gargantuan scores. Test cricket had seen nothing like this: scores of 251, 200 and 177 in a series by one man were unbelievable.

So at the age of twenty-five, Hammond stood head and shoulders above anyone else in the world. He had taken over the mantle of Jack Hobbs, as that great player eased himself gently towards his retirement. The young lion was going to dominate world cricket for at least twenty years. In fact Hammond's supremacy lasted little more than a year. In the 1930 series, Don Bradman surpassed him, making 973 runs in frighteningly clinical fashion. Hammond averaged 34 to Bradman's 139, a decline as astonishing as Bradman's ascent to the slopes of batting greatness. Thereafter, Bradman's phenomenal achievements gnawed away at Wally Hammond for the rest of his career. If he made a hundred, Bradman would make it a double; if Hammond

The Tonbridge cricket festival, June 1932 – the enduring appeal of county cricket is reflected in the vantage point claimed by two spectators up that emerging symbol of the electronic age, the telegraph pole

scored a double hundred, Bradman would get two of them later in the series. In 1934 Hammond had another inexplicable lapse, averaging just 20; Bradman made a triple century, a double hundred and averaged 94. Two years later, England stormed to a 2/0 lead in the series, after Hammond had scored a wonderful 231 not out at Sydney – only to see Bradman make scores of 270, 212 and 169 as Australia triumphed 3/2. Even when it came to saving a match, Bradman's example was crucial. At Lord's in 1938, Hammond made 240 in thrilling, masterful fashion to set up the push for victory. He was now the England captain and desperately wanted to go one-up in the series against his rival captain, the little man who had tormented him for eight years. It was not to be: on a damp pitch, Bradman made an unbeaten

Hammond returns from his triumphant first tour of Australia in April, 1929. He was almost 26 and at the peak of his athletic powers, even though this unflattering picture is a salutary corrective to the fulsome prose employed by Neville Cardus about the noble charisma of the great batsman

Below: Before the run-gorged Oval Test, 1938. Walter Hammond about to win the toss, as 'Bosser' Martin, the legendary groundsman, and a dapper Don Bradman look on

hundred to save the match. When England amassed 903 for seven declared that same year, Hammond would not declare the England innings closed at the Oval until he had received medical assurances that Bradman's injured ankle would prevent him from batting. Hammond knew better than anyone the capabilities of the man.

After the war, the two masters were again opposing captains and the relationship between them was never cordial. On the first morning of the opening Test in the 1946/7 series, Hammond was appalled when Bradman did not 'walk' after he seemed to have snicked a ball to Jack Ikin in the slips. The Australian stood his ground and Hammond was furious. At the end of the over, he passed Bradman and hissed, 'That's a fine bloody way to start the series!' and Bradman went on to score 187. He slowly recovered his mastery after the wartime break and led Australia to a 3/0 victory in the series. After that incident, Hammond only spoke to Bradman when they tossed the coin at the start of each Test.

That was Hammond's last England tour. He announced his retirement when he returned home, amid great public sympathy that he had not given many nostalgic glimpses of his greatness to a young generation that had only heard about his grandeur. His decline was sudden – in the 1946 English season, he had topped the averages with 84, 16 ahead of his nearest challenger – but personal problems took their toll while he was in Australia. Fibrositis crippled him and the publicity over his private life drove him deeper and deeper into his shell. When the team landed in Australia, it was announced that he had fallen in love with a South African beauty queen, that he was set to divorce his wife of seventeen years' standing and then remarry. Hammond simply could not understand why his personal problems should be of any interest to a curious media: surely the resumption of the ancient Ashes rivalry after the horrors of war was a preferable subject? To the newshound, the England captain and a messy divorce was a meatier subject. Ian Botham was not the first cricketing superstar to be angered by media fascination in his private life.

Such was the stature of Walter Hammond that it caused little interest that he would leave his team-mates to travel on their own during that tour. While he and the manager journeyed by expensive car, the rest of the touring party sweltered on interminable train journeys across Australia. The media seemed to think

this irrelevant as they concentrated on Hammond's divorce and occasionally pondered why England was being thrashed out on the cricket field. Today the vanquished England captain would be thoroughly grilled and turned over by the press, television, and radio, with the inevitable conclusion that a better man must be found while the self-esteem of our national sport could still be salvaged. No such public ordeal faced Hammond when he returned home in the spring of 1947: the BBC invited him on to the nine o'clock radio news to give his version of the disastrous tour. He made an impressive debut on peak-time radio, praising the goodwill engendered by the series, commenting on the food parcels that were coming over to austerity Britain from a sympathetic Australia and the fact that the game of cricket was still the paramount consideration. No probing interviewer on hand to question the captain's role in the defeat, his continual absences from the company of his fellow-players, or the row with Bradman at Brisbane. Beleaguered England captains of later vintage must have wished they could simply read a prepared statement on BBC radio and retreat to a cosy drink with a grateful producer.

Yet Hammond always seemed above vulgar considerations such as criticism. Even his rare struggles at the crease were invested with an air of nobility. When Bill O'Reilly troubled him throughout the 1934 Ashes series, it was never suggested that the great man should be dropped. An England side without Hammond was unthinkable; a decade later, on his retirement, it was still a shock to think he was permanently lost to the Test scene. Unwittingly Hammond cultivated this air of superiority by his aloofness. He never played to the gallery, never cultivated the common touch, and from early on in his career, he kept himself apart from his Gloucestershire team-mates. His prowess at soccer earned him some money in the winter and he cultivated personal tastes that were denied to the other professionals: a night at the theatre, the company of attractive ladies. Hammond bought a motor car within a year of joining the Gloucestershire staff and he always aspired to the grander things in life. Just after his first triumphant tour of Australia, he married the daughter of a wealthy Yorkshire textile merchant and life was comfortable for a time. Like Herbert Sutcliffe, his great England contemporary, Hammond flitted easily between the world of the amateur and the professional cricketer. The social attrac-

tions of country house cricket came smoothly to both men – secure in their national stature, confident that their elegant clothes marked them out as men of the world. They spoke well, mingled happily with influential businessmen and enjoyed the flattering attentions of society hostesses who did not know a googly from a square cut. Unemployment in the thirties may well have been horrendous, poverty still laid its deadening hand on communities in the major cities and a megalomaniac in Berlin continued to flex his dictatorial muscles – but high achievers like Herbert Sutcliffe and Walter Hammond had no intention of plodding along with the rest of their fellow professionals.

Wally Hammond refreshes the appropriate parts, August 1946

Right: Hammond in 1946 just prior to divorce, defeat and desolation

When the chance presented itself, Hammond had no qualms about taking the England captaincy after he had landed a good job with a tyre company. The secure post now meant he could play as an amateur in the summer, thus saving the honour of a grateful Establishment who would give him the England captaincy. He did not worry about the status of the professional cricketer in the way of Jack Hobbs; the goal had to be attained, the initials had to be in front of the surname, rather than bringing up the rear. It did not matter that the world was changing, that postwar egalitarianism

BAR OPEN
11.15 – 2.15
4.15 – 7.

DANGER
DO NOT THROW
LIGHTED CIGARET
THROUGH WINDOW
OR OVER RAILING

Above : St Pancras Station, 1932 – Herbert Sutcliffe (in light suit) and Walter Hammond prepare to leave for another successful trip to Australia, while the amateur Errol Holmes prepares to join belatedly the languid action at Penshurst Castle in Kent (left), in August 1934. Errol Holmes, an attractive batsman for Oxford University and Surrey flitted effortlessly between social and realistic cricket in the best amateur tradition. Later in 1934, he played four times for England in the West Indies and the following season, he was a good enough player to be one of Wisden's Five Cricketers of the Year. To many of his admirers, Errol Holmes was an anachronism; he would have thrived in the social whirl at the turn of the century

would usher in a professional England captain. It mattered little that by temperament and tactical ability, Hammond was totally unsuited to the task; the social cachet was infinitely more desirable.

If Hammond must accept his fair share of blame for the growth of 'shamateurism', he cannot be held responsible for the other great change in the thirties – the lbw law. By the early thirties, the game's legislators were worried about the preponderance of pad-play; many were masters at padding away deliveries pitched outside the off-stump, even though the ball might have broken in to hit the wicket. The glories of off-side play were being muted as batsmen chose the safe option. Invidious comparisons were being made with the Golden Age, when Victor Trumper was lbw just five times in

eighty-nine innings for Australia and the dashing Archie MacLaren batted sixty-one times for England, with just three lbw dismissals. It has to be said that Walter Hammond was the last batsman in the 1930s to bother with pad-play – he had too many off-side shots and too much justifiable confidence in his ability to play them – but along with all the other great batsmen of the period, he had to come to terms with a change in the lbw law.

From 1935, a batsman could be given out if the ball pitched outside the off-stump and the obstructing leg was in line with the wicket. The supporters of the new legislation believed it would restore off-side play to its former glories by making the batsman play a shot, rather than just padding up. Yet after a season or two, the shrewd, resourceful professional player worked out how to combat the new rule, by thrusting out the front leg to meet the ball pitching outside the line of wicket and wicket. Not to be outdone, the frustrated bowlers began to place their line of attack on the leg-side, to stop the front-foot lunge outside the off-stump. As a result, an undue emphasis has been placed on bowlers who can swing or spin the ball into the bat, rather than make it go away on the outside. The off-cutter, inswinger and offspinner have prospered since the 1935 legislation and batsmen have learned to play more and more on the leg-side.

Even Walter Hammond had to get used to playing more leg-side shots in the last few years of his career, as bowlers stopped feeding his favourite off-side strokes. Yet he was so powerful off the back-foot that he could wait for the loose delivery and whip it away through the leg-side with as much ease as the off-drive of his pristine youth. Like all great players, he was as masterful off back- as well as front-foot. If everyone had put bat to ball in Hammond fashion, there would never have been any need to tinker about with the lbw law. The slow left-arm bowler and the leg-spinner would still be a force in the game today if more batsmen had tried to develop their off-side shots.

Players like Hammond turn up just once every generation, but inferior batsmen who scorned the use of pad and tried to play like him would have been a boon to the genuine slow-bowler, who relied on flight and turn away from the bat. A halcyon age of attacking bowling would have been a fitting tribute to the glorious example of Hammond, but it was not to be: the solid accumulator held sway on somnolent pitches as the thirties stumbled towards another world war.

Don Bradman

Don Bradman was quite simply a phenomenon. He influenced the result of a cricket match more than any other player and his amazing deeds led to a form of bowling that almost ruptured diplomatic relations between Australia and Great Britain. The 'Bodyline' experiment under Douglas Jardine's control remains the only tactical innovation aimed at a single cricketer: the aim was to thwart Bradman and, in attempting this, Jardine was paying Bradman the biggest compliment he would ever receive.

Don Bradman was the third of the batting immortals to exercise a profound influence on the game. Grace evolved the principle of playing back and forward against the bowlers, while Hobbs adapted that technique to later variations in bowling styles – then Bradman perfected those principles by scoring more runs than anyone else, at a faster pace and with complete certainty. Bradman remains the only great batsman in history who was never really out of form. Grace and Hobbs had their lean seasons, their times of fallibility, but not Bradman: even in the Bodyline series he averaged 56, more than Sutcliffe and Hammond on the other side.

Players like Hobbs, Trumper, Woolley, Hammond and Macartney were more attractive to watch, but Bradman was compelling in the ruthless way he battered the opposition bowlers into submission. He was just under medium height, slim and wiry with athletic, co-ordinated movements. His footwork was dazzling and he seemed to read the ball faster than anyone else. Thus he had that split second longer to execute his stroke. When he first came to England in 1930 some critics felt he was mechanical, a calculating machine solely dedicated to amassing huge scores. Certainly English crowds had been used

Bradman, pushing 40, slaughters the Essex bowling at Southend in 1948. The Australians scored 721 in a day, to which the Don contributed 187

to seeing great Australian batsmen playing with the charm and flair of a Trumper or a Macartney – indeed Alan Kippax and Archie Jackson of the 1930 side were in that tradition. Yet English spectators soon warmed to Bradman, despite the mayhem he caused over the next two generations. His utter certainty could never stir the emotions like an innings from Woolley, or Compton, but his quality was ruefully acknowledged. Bradman was a genius, a cricketer to savour and when he made his last tour to England in 1948, the tributes and admiration were heartfelt.

His detractors sometimes maintained that Bradman was not a team man, that he was more interested in personal aggrandisement. That may well be true of Geoffrey Boycott, but cannot be held against Bradman. He scored too fast to be accused of putting himself before the course of a match: the slowest of his 117 centuries took just 253 minutes, a perfectly respectable rate for any batsman in these days of superb fielding and slow over rates. Bradman always ensured his bowlers had plenty of time to bowl out the opposition by the simple expedient of getting massive scores at remarkable speed. Only Gilbert Jessop among Test batsmen ever surpassed Bradman's astonishing speed of scoring – and with respect to Jessop, a solitary Test hundred cannot compare with twenty-nine by Bradman.

From 1930 to 1948, Don Bradman was the world's greatest cricketer and the rest were nowhere. His presence in the side was almost a guarantee against defeat – of his 117 centuries, only eight were scored for a losing team. In Test cricket Bradman played in eleven series and Australia lost just two of those – the Bodyline series and in 1928/9 when he made his debut, played four games, and watched Australia lose 4/1 to an immensely strong England side. After 1933, Bradman never played in a losing Test series, and invariably he was the man who constituted the difference between the two sides. Against England, his match-winning performances were the stuff of legend – an average of 94 in 1934, when his health was breaking, an average of 90 in 1936/7 when he helped turn a 2/0 deficit into a 3/2 win by a string of huge scores, and in 1938, with a resurgent England pressing hard, he held them at bay with an average of 108. After the war, he was his usual indomitable self under pressure – an innings of 187 in the first Test of the 1946/7 series that set up a 3/0 victory. It is true that Bradman's come-back innings was shrouded in controversy (was he caught early on at slip?), but the way he battled through poor health and little practice was remarkable. On his last tour to England in 1948, he scored two more Test centuries and inspired a powerful side to win the series by 4/0. He ended his Test career with a

nought that brought his average tumbling down to 99.94 – the nearest challengers are Graeme Pollock, George Headley and Herbert Sutcliffe with averages of 60. No one can approach his record of thirty-seven double hundreds, nor his tally of a century every third innings. No wonder Sir Pelham Warner, a man of vast crick-eting experience said of Bradman, 'Bowling to him is like casting pebbles at the Rock of Gibraltar.'

Wilfred Rhodes, statistically the best bowler of all time, and a man who studied

first-class cricket for eighty years, was convinced that Bradman was streets ahead of anyone else. Jim Laker first bowled at Bradman in 1948, when the great man was forty years of age and not at his peak any more: Laker's verdict was, 'He was the only batsman to give me an inferiority complex.'

Bradman's impact on England in 1930 was phenomenal. England held the Ashes after Percy Chapman's triumphant progress through Australia eighteen months earlier and the first Test at Nottingham was also easily won. There seemed every prospect that England's supremacy would be maintained; their batting was rich in class and maturity, the damp weather would surely test the techniques of young batsmen like Bradman, McCabe and Jackson, and Larwood and Allen were blossoming as genuine fast bowlers. At Lord's Bradman gave warning of his mastery with a wonderful innings of 254 and the mammoth Australian total of 729 for six declared set up a seven-wicket victory. Some believed that Bradman's perform-ance at Lord's would be just a one-off, that he would abruptly return to the earth inhabited by ordinary mortals – but then came Leeds.

That day, 11 July 1930, was one of the most important in cricket history. Don Bradman made 309 not out at Leeds and in the process he unwittingly forged the chain of events that led to the infamous

Above: Outside Lord's in the 1930s: gargantuan scores brought in the crowds

Right: Cricket fans on the Isle of Wight in the summer of 1934 were able to keep in touch with the events at Old Trafford, courtesy of an enterprising whisky firm. For some inexplicable reason, the name of the most famous cricketer of that time was not included on the board – but Don Bradman played in all five Tests, scoring a double and a triple hundred. Perhaps the manipulators of the board were fantasising on behalf of England's bowlers!

Bodyline series 2½ years later. On a fast outfield, and placid pitch, Bradman scored a hundred before lunch, to take his place alongside Trumper and Macartney. He added 115 in the second session, hit the last ball of the day to the boundary and skipped up the pavilion steps, fresh as a daisy. He had averaged 52 runs an hour, against bowlers of the calibre of Larwood, Tate, Geary, Hammond and Dick Tyldesley.

Bradman was helped by some immobile fielding and the attacking inclinations of the English bowlers. When Maurice Tate was asked why he had not tried to tie down Bradman, he replied, 'Pin him down? Of course not! I was trying to get the little devil out!' Admirable sentiments and England kept attacking fields and bowled 22 overs an hour to that end. Yet it proved impossible to stem the tide, a tide that was to sweep Percy Chapman from the captaincy and bring in the tactically superior Bob Wyatt before the end of the series. At the Oval Bradman made another huge score – a little matter of 232 – but not before he suffered some discomfiture against a hostile Harold Larwood when the wicket was drying out after a shower. Larwood tested him out with short-pitched deliveries and Bradman looked unhappy for a time. Wyatt noticed Bradman's unease and the seeds of Bodyline were sown. Something had to be done about the kind of batting butchery seen at Leeds – and Douglas

Above: Bradman displaying his formidable powers of concentratrion as he works on his speech at a dinner to mark the 1930 tour to England

Left : Bradman devotes his single-minded attention to a different ball game – at Leicester Square, London, in 1934

Jardine proved to be just the man to cut Bradman down to human dimensions. After the 1930 series, Test cricket was never quite the same; we would never again see 650 overs of leg-spin in a series, courtesy of Ian Peebles, Walter Robins, Dick Tyldesley and Clarrie Grimmett. From now on, containment was the general tactical aim and leg-spin faded in its influence, despite gallant efforts from Wright, O'Reilly, Benaud, Chandrasekhar, Gupte, Intikhab and Abdul Qadir. Attacking fields were no longer automatically adopted, unless a new ball was available, the wicket was unreliable – or Bodyline was being implemented. After Bradman's dominance in 1930, the average Test captain's message to opposition batsman was 'come and fetch it'.

Bradman's fabulous deeds inevitably

placed him in the goldfish bowl of publicity, in an age where the electronic wonders were bringing the game to a massive audience. The newsreels in cinemas beamed out his latest exploits, the early radio commentaries were full of excited chatter about Bradman and he captained Australia during the first televised match, at Lord's in 1938. Newspaper editors and book publishers vied with each other to drum up a new Bradman angle if they had failed to sign him up on an exclusive contract for themselves. Bradman soon demonstrated the business acumen that was to serve him so well; he published a book of his 1930 tour, though that led to a £50 fine by the Australian Board of Control for alleged breach of contract. Relations between the Board and Bradman were further strained at the start of the Bodyline series, when Bradman was refused permission to comment on the game in a daily newspaper. Bradman quite properly pointed out that some of his team-mates were allowed to broadcast their views daily on radio, so why should he be treated differently? Happily the matter was resolved when the relevant newspaper released him from his contractual obligations, but the episode demonstrates not only Bradman's mental clarity and business sense, but also the huge interest that had been created by his deeds and an increasingly influential media.

In Britain, the obsession with Bradman was as all-consuming as in his own country. In 1930, a newspaper placard had a simple message, 'Peebles Does It' – a reference to the dismissal of Bradman by Ian Peebles for just 14 at the Old Trafford Test, the next game after Leeds. No reference on the hoarding to the great batsman; the newspaper presumed, probably rightly, that Peebles and Bradman were more interesting to the public than Ramsey MacDonald or Stanley Baldwin.

Four years later, another revealing placard, 'Bradman Bats and Bats and Bats', as he picked off another double hundred against England. On the rare occasion that Bradman made nought, the newspapers were beside themselves with frothing emotion. It happened twice in 1934, when Jack Davies did it at Cambridge and Giles Baring followed him at Southampton. Was Homer nodding? These were genuine media events at that time and the press wrung every ounce of drama out of each dismissal – even to the extent of debating why Baring had not won a Blue when he was up at Cambridge. More illustrious names than Davies or

Baring have had the pleasure of bowling Bradman for nought. Bill Bowes did so at Melbourne and Alec Bedser at Adelaide; decades later, both men are still being asked about it, an indirect tribute to Bradman's enduring fascination. After all, he made nought on only sixteen occasions.

When Bradman came to England, he was mobbed when he got into a car outside his hotel, and trailed on the rare occasions he chanced to go for a walk. No wonder he usually preferred the solitude of his hotel room and his piano. The newspaper stunts became sillier. In June 1934 the *Bath and Wiltshire Chronicle and Herald* boldly announced, 'If D. Bradman comes to Stone's Garage, he can have a second-hand Austin Seven for a present.' One assumes that Bradman managed to cope with his own modes of transport on that England tour.

In 1948, public interest in Bradman was just as devouring when he paid his last visit to England as a player. Bradman was the man everyone wanted to see, despite the brilliant side he captained. Early on it was apparent that England would be no match for such a powerful juggernaut, so the public settled down to will Bradman to a valedictory orgy of runs. At the age of forty (old for an Australian cricketer) he was not quite as dominating, taking rather longer to settle into an innings than in his pomp. Now he needed to take a look at the pitch, the line and length of the bowling before he took them apart – in other words, he was almost human. Two Test hundreds – the 173 not out at Leeds in the classic ruthless mould – meant the vast crowds were not disappointed, and his anti-climactic nought in his farewell Test innings at the Oval could not possibly dim his lustre. The Australians took home with them a remarkable profit of £75 000 from that tour and there is no doubt that the presence of the game's most amazing cricketer was largely responsible.

Forty years after his retirement, the flame of publicity still licks around Don Bradman. In 1972, his son John changed his surname to Bradsen, so that he could make a success out of his career on his own merits, rather than as Don Bradman's son. In 1980, his absence from the Centenary Test celebrations in London attracted ill-founded, unfavourable comment. It was later revealed that Bradman was worried about the health of his beloved wife, Jessie, and could not bear to be parted from her or his daughter, who is a spastic. With any other illustrious cricketer, there would be no need for friends to give the background to a decision not to come to London. It is laughable to suggest that

Bradman did not wish to share the limelight with other famous cricketers – he never went out of his way to court publicity for himself. More significantly, the story underlines the enduring attraction of Don Bradman's name to the media. Even in his eighties, he remains compelling – busloads of tourists occasionally turn up and gawp at his house in an Adelaide suburb.

The only caveat to claims for Bradman's pre-eminence as a batsman lies in his performances on bad wickets. He always maintained that a batsman should not be expected to display his art on damaged wickets and for that reason many judges still consider that Jack Hobbs was the

Right: August 1930 and at the age of 22, Don Bradman was experiencing his first taste of public hysteria. Here he is driven out of the Oval at the end of a series in which he had scored 974 runs and established himself as a phenomenon. Bradman had to come to terms with the glare of publicity for the rest of his astonishing career; indeed for the rest of his life, he has had to endure public obsession

Below: Bradman takes a walk down the Strand in 1938. By now he had become used to the kind of awe and hero-worship etched on the faces of his young acolytes

greatest batsman of all time. Certainly Bradman cut a sorry figure at Lord's in 1934 when Hedley Verity tempted him into an ill-judged slog on a turning wicket. From that day, the legend of Bradman's unreliability on dubious wickets was born. Yet he made four trips to England, scored more than 2000 runs each time and, on wickets that were uncovered, he totalled 110 innings. In that time – more than a third of all his career innings – he encountered a host of wickets that were far from perfect to bat on, and he fared well, particularly in 1938. One would have thought that the man who could improvise so impressively against the frightening Bodyline assault would have been well able to dominate the spinners on a wet wicket – if he put his mind to it. Whenever Bradman put his mind to anything – batting, captaincy, writing, commerce, golf, public speaking – he was ahead of the rest. Sunil Gavaskar recognized this when he was being lionized for passing Bradman's record of twenty-nine Test centuries in 1984. The little Indian was amused to hear cricket buffs trying to compare his achievement with that of Bradman – even though it took him 166 innings to equal Bradman's tally, set up in 79 innings. Gavaskar would have none of it: 'Don Bradman was a superman,' he said. Not every player from the cynical eighties is blind to the great deeds of the past. Gavaskar got it just right. The range of tributes to Bradman's dominance from rueful and admiring contemporaries brooks no argument.

Douglas Jardine & Bodyline

'In a battle, on a cricket field or anywhere else in the world, I should always want Jardine on my side.' That tribute from the tough Yorkshireman Herbert Sutcliffe encapsulates the qualities that made Douglas Jardine such a successful England captain. It also explains why he was such a public relations disaster, a man who could see no further than ruthless victory on the cricket field. For Douglas Jardine, the end categorically justified the means – even if it led to the most unpleasant Test series in the game's history. The Bodyline series still rankles in Australian hearts. Fifty years after the climactic events, and amid the welter of dramatized plays and films, the revelations of veteran cricketers, the thundering newspaper editorials, one salient fact glows ever brightly: without Jardine there would have been no Bodyline. His supporters may well point out that Bradman was indirectly responsible for Bodyline because of his batting supremacy, but that is rather like blaming the citizens of Poland for Hitler's invasion, which led to the Second World War. It was not Bradman's fault that he and his Australian team-mates were subjected to a barrage of short-pitched deliveries aimed at speed at their bodies; it was Jardine's obsession about the master batsman that forced him into expediency.

Admittedly Jardine's tactics were not illegal: the spirit rather than the letter of the law was ignored. That is something which never perturbed Jardine on the Bodyline tour; he had been selected to regain the Ashes and as far as he was concerned that could only be done by reducing Bradman's performance to human dimensions.

Such clear-sightedness had long been a characteristic of Douglas Jardine. He was

The familiar Harlequin cap – Jardine in 1951, walks out to bat in a charity match

born in India, into a family of lawyers who dedicated themselves to streamlining the administration of that country. Young Douglas was sent back to England, to study at Winchester and then at Oxford. His father had won a cricket Blue at Oxford and it seemed natural that he would follow the family footsteps into cricket prestige and later legal eminence. The spartan conditions at Winchester hardened an already flinty persona and he had enough self-confidence to debate tactics with two eminent cricket masters, E. R. Wilson and H. S. Altham, two men with deep knowledge and practical experience of the game – Wilson an England all-rounder and Altham one of the great coaches and gurus of cricket history. Jardine, displaying a maturity beyond his years, had no qualms about disagreeing with Wilson and Altham and, together with his cricket ability, he was marked out as a natural leader of men. Yet the temperamental rigidity was already noticeable: several years later, on the eve of the Bodyline tour, Wilson commented sagely, 'He will probably win us back the Ashes, but he will also lose us a Dominion.' Such a depressing forecast almost proved correct.

Jardine's character and attitude to cricket were both poles apart from his predecessor as England captain, Percy Chapman. They may have shared the same public school and Oxbridge background – indeed they played against each other in the Varsity match – but Jardine felt that Chapman was a feckless dilettante as captain. He had toured under Chapman in Australia in 1928/9, and even though the series was triumphantly clinched, he disapproved of Chapman's fondness for the social whirl and his readiness to mix easily with the professionals. On top of

Above: Douglas Jardine guides Amar Singh to third man at Lord's, 1932

Left: Bill Voce (*left*) and Harold Larwood relax on the 'Orontes' en route to Australia in September, 1932. Within six months they were world famous and their deeds on the cricket field divided the sporting world. A fondness for cigarettes did not seem to affect Voce's stamina with the ball, nor his longevity – he lived for 75 years

that, Jardine loathed Australia and most of its populace, whom he found coarse and ill-mannered. When Bradman conquered England in 1930 and Chapman's captaincy style was deemed naive and lightweight, the way was cleared for Jardine's remorseless leadership. He was a better batsman than Wyatt, Chapman's immediate successor, and provided he gave a season or two to the Surrey captaincy, the job was his.

All the while, Bradman loomed large in Jardine's tactical consciousness. He called for films of his great exploits in 1930; finally he spotted Bradman's discomfiture against Larwood's pace at the Oval. After consultations with Larwood's county captain, Arthur Carr, the plan started to germinate in Jardine's keen brain. The perfect Australian pitches meant that a split field (five on the off-side, four on the on, or vice versa) would be useless against someone of Bradman's footwork and rapacity – far better to concentrate on a 7/2 field, restricting him to just one side of the wicket. To accomplish that, he needed fast bowling of extreme accuracy. Arthur Carr had just the men in his Nottinghamshire side – Harold Larwood and Bill Voce. Larwood was just about at his peak, the fastest bowler in England. He would be able to push the ball into the batsman from the edge of the crease at high speed, while his partner Bill Voce, would bowl fast left-arm to provide variety. Larwood had a score to settle with Bradman; not fully fit in the 1930 series, his four wickets had cost 73 runs apiece and he relished the chance of revenge. He and Voce would do what they were told; they were professionals and the authoritarian Jardine would brook no deviation from his master plan.

Although the leg theory tactic caused a stir in the early days of the 1932/3 tour, it did not become an emotive issue until the second Test at Melbourne. Bradman had dropped out of the first Test through illness and without him Australia was helpless against fast bowling aimed at the off-stump. If Bradman had played, perhaps the line would have been altered sooner to the leg-side. The term 'Bodyline' was then coined by an Australian journalist and the emotive undertones of that term inflamed the Australian fans, who were already angry enough at being one down to the Englishman in the fancy Harlequin cap who clearly hated the sight of all things Australian. When Bradman was bowled first ball at Melbourne – getting the bottom edge to a delivery from Bowes – the atmosphere was starting to

Two Australians suffer a familiar fate at the hands of Larwood on the Bodyline tour – Woodfull (the right-hander) and O'Brien

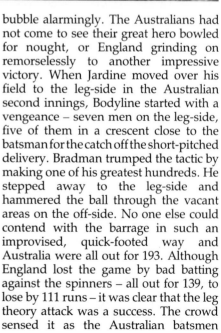

bubble alarmingly. The Australians had not come to see their great hero bowled for nought, or England grinding on remorselessly to another impressive victory. When Jardine moved over his field to the leg-side in the Australian second innings, Bodyline started with a vengeance – seven men on the leg-side, five of them in a crescent close to the batsman for the catch off the short-pitched delivery. Bradman trumped the tactic by making one of his greatest hundreds. He stepped away to the leg-side and hammered the ball through the vacant areas on the off-side. No one else could contend with the barrage in such an improvised, quick-footed way and Australia were all out for 193. Although England lost the game by bad batting against the spinners – all out for 139, to lose by 111 runs – it was clear that the leg theory attack was a success. The crowd sensed it as the Australian batsmen hopped around or turned their back on the ball, and the press frothed at the mouth. Ten days later, at the start of the Adelaide Test, emotions were running dangerously high, with the press exploiting the tensions by a combination of injudicious 'quotes' and unashamed jingoism.

The Adelaide Test of January 1933 ranks as one of the most distressing and unpleasant in history. England won it by 338 runs, but that was subsidiary to the injuries, crowd disturbances and a flurry of cables that seriously threatened diplomatic relations between Britain and Australia. When Bill Woodfull, the Australian captain, was hit over the heart at the end of Larwood's second over, the crowd feared the worst. They were further inflamed when Jardine changed to a Bodyline field at the start of Larwood's third over, with Woodfull on strike after his painful recovery. Later in the innings, Bertie Oldfield was struck in the mouth by a ball from Larwood and taken to hospital. It mattered not that Oldfield admitted on the field of play that it had been his own fault: the implacable hostility of Jardine had caused the assault, in the opinion of the crowd. Genteel Adelaide, the cathedral city, had never seen an atmosphere like it – mounted police were lined up behind a stand in case the crowd jumped over the pickets to get at Jardine and the England players. In retrospect, if the incidents on the field had taken place in a more rumbustuous city like Brisbane or Sydney, the crowd would probably have stormed the pitch.

The press had a field day. Woodfull's comment to the England manager that only one side was trying to play cricket was leaked to the newspapers amid a righteous conviction that something had to be done. The Australian Board of Control sent a cable to the MCC accusing the England team of unsportsmanlike behaviour. This was a tactical error by the Board, although one can understand how its members would be affected by the prevailing passions. The solid denizens at Lord's would never countenance an English gentleman being dubbed 'unsportsmanlike'. The MCC fired back a cable that was a masterpiece of diplomacy, deploring the use of the word 'unsportsmanlike' and wondering what all the fuss was about. Jardine was given the full support of Lord's and the tour would continue. There is no doubt that Jardine would have packed his bags and taken the team home with him if the MCC had not supported his tactics. The Australian Board also faced pressure from the Prime Minister, Joe Lyons. He was a cricket-lover and equally appalled by Bodyline, but he pointed out that unless the Board withdrew the word 'unsportsmanlike', several vast Australian loans due for conversion in London might be at risk and the national economy threatened. All because an Englishman's honour was being impugned.

After Adelaide, the diplomatic storm blew over, the tour proceeded uneasily and England won the final two Tests comfortably. The Australian batsmen were demoralized by now – clearly some of them had little physical relish for the fray. There were some honourable exceptions – Woodfull, Vic Richardson and above all, Bradman, the main target. He carried on trying to play the ball through the off-side area and he still looked head and shoulders above any other Australian batsman, even if he looked frenetic and unbalanced, compared with his cool mastery of 1930. Bradman was only hit once in the series – on the elbow by Larwood in the last Test – even though the English bowlers clearly aimed at his body, rather than the stumps. Eye-witnesses and players recall watching Bradman moving at least a yard away from his leg stump while the bowlers followed him, rather than the exposed wicket. In later years, Les Ames, the England wicket-keeper in the series, admitted, 'It wasn't in my view the best way to play cricket – ' a view that is hard to challenge.

It seems obvious, in these days of player power, to ask why the England players took part in something they all knew to be inherently distasteful? The dominating character of Jardine is relevant: at the height of the furore he called a team meeting and asked for support and was given it by sixteen of the seventeen players. The odd one out was G. O. Allen, a fine fast bowler who had refused to bowl 'Bodyline' when asked by Jardine at the start of the Melbourne Test. Allen – Eton and Cambridge – symbolized the code of sportsmanship that had been drummed into generations of athletes at the English public schools and would have nothing to do with the tactic, to his eternal credit.

G.O. Allen (*left*) and R.E.S. Wyatt leave Waterloo station in September 1936 for Australia, on a goodwill mission designed to repair the breaches over Bodyline

Yet Allen was on safer ground than the rest of the team; he had influential friends at Lord's and was unlikely to be black-balled out of the Test arena because of his genuine principles. R. E. S. Wyatt, Jardine's vice-captain, has said he was uneasy about the tactic, but his respect for Jardine was profound, he admired his qualities of leadership – and his success as captain. The other amateur, the Nawab of Pataudi, was a peripheral figure, and would not have exerted any influence on the ethos of England's bowling strategy. The rest of the touring party were the professionals, men of vast experience who wanted nothing better than to clip the wings of the young upstart Bradman and regain the Ashes. They were never really part of the discussions as Bodyline took shape. Three of the survivors from that touring party – Ames, Allen, Wyatt – are convinced that the plan slowly evolved when they had arrived in Australia. Jardine had decided to curb Bradman by bowling at his legs but the precise area of attack had not been delineated; the conversations with Larwood and Voce before the tour had not touched on deliberate assaults on the batsman's body. It seems that the uneven bounce on the Australian wickets caused a major problem. Modern cricketers talk about uneven bounce as if it was the creation of contemporary groundsmen, but on the Bodyline tour, one delivery would be at chest height, the next at the hip and the third would threaten the head. The combination of Larwood's speed and accuracy added to fast pitches of uneven bounce against a leg-trap that was still within the law – all these factors combined to assist Jardine.

Bob Wyatt says that the ball soon stopped swinging in Australia, so that very little went to the slips. As the Australians were so adept at playing through the leg-side, it was a sensible tactic to plug the gaps. Larwood and Voce agreed; they said they bowled short at Bradman to unsettle him, not to cause him any physical danger. In his book on the tour, Larwood said he was simply bowling leg-theory: 'The mere use of the word "body" was meant to damn me, and damn me it did.' He pointed out that only two batsmen were seriously injured by Bodyline – and one of them, Bertie Oldfield, admitted his head injury was his own fault. Certainly the tactic was stunningly successful: Larwood was the first genuine fast bowler to spearhead a successful quest for the Ashes in Australia since Tom Richardson in 1894/5. His thirty-three wickets in the Bodyline series were fitting

testimony to his fitness, accuracy and speed. How fast was Larwood? George Geary had no doubts; in the Oval Test of 1926 he took two slip catches off Larwood and the bruise came out on the back of his hand. Since 1926, he had become even faster and certainly more controlled. Even without Bodyline, he would have been a hostile proposition on the 1932/3 tour.

After that historic tour ended, the three main English protagonists enjoyed contrasting fortunes. Larwood had damaged his foot in the final Test and an operation put him out of half the 1933 season. He returned in 1934, operating off a short run and, despite continued success, he was never the same bowler. The foot injury never really cleared up and he needed to operate on soft grounds. Larwood never played for England again – partly through injury but mostly due to some ill-judged remarks in books and newspaper articles. His dogmatic assertion that he had done nothing wrong, that he would bowl the same way against the Australians if the need arose, outlawed him at Lord's. Certainly Larwood was only acting under orders – but the post-Bodyline mood was one of eagerness to paper over the cracks in Anglo-Australian cricket, to restore the rivalry to its former status. *Wisden* for 1935 refers to the desire of the press 'constantly to stir up strife' over the Bodyline issue, and certainly Larwood's flirtation with the printed word did not help his prospects of England rehabilitation.

For three years, Bill Voce refused to apologize for the Bodyline tour. When the Australians came to Trent Bridge in 1934, Voce bowled Bodyline at them, taking eight for 66 and upsetting the tourists. They had been led to believe that such tactics had been outlawed and it was rumoured that they complained officially about Voce's tactics. When Voce was absent with an alleged leg strain in the second innings, the Trent Bridge crowd booed the tourists heartily when they took the field. In the same summer Voce also injured two young Middlesex batsmen and soon Nottinghamshire found itself isolated amid the general revulsion at Bodyline. Finally Voce had to accept reality in 1936. G. O. Allen was named England captain for the forthcoming tour of Australia, a tour that would need formidable powers of diplomacy to be a success after Jardine's exploits. Allen insisted that if Voce were picked, the bowler had to express his regret over Bodyline in writing – otherwise a new captain would have to be found. Voce withdrew his earlier statement that he would only play first-

class cricket for Nottinghamshire and he toured Australia, with no ill-will displayed on either side.

The constructive part played by G. O. Allen in the immediate after-match of Bodyline cannot be underestimated. He helped open the reactionary eyes of the hierarchy at Lord's, men who had huffed and puffed at the temerity of the Australian Board. Allen's forthright, honest remarks, the intimidatory bowling of the West Indians in 1933 and the continuing hostility of Voce's bowling all helped convince the authorities that Bodyline must have been as bad as the Australians had alleged. In the winter of 1934/5, the Bodyline tactic was officially banned, and umpires were instructed to stamp down on its practice. If Australia had not been assured that Lord's was trying to put the house of intimidation in order, there would surely have been no tour of England in the summer of 1934. The Australians had threatened to bring four fast bowlers over to England if necessary and feelings still ran high. Finally, in December 1933, the invitation to tour was extended to Australia by the MCC committee by a margin of eight to five. Without the plain speaking of G. O. Allen and smooth liaison work by Dr Robert MacDonald, an Australian dentist, the hostility between England and Australia would have been prolonged. When Allen took the next England side to Australia, his admirable efforts on and off the field helped heal the breach.

The absence of Jardine from the 1934 Test series was equally beneficial. One can only wonder at the consequences if Jardine had made himself available for the series. After all, he was the man in possession – captain against the West Indies in the English summer, then leading the side to India in 1933/4. Suddenly in March 1934 Jardine announced he would not be available for Surrey in the forthcoming summer. Moreover, he said, 'I have neither the intention nor the desire to play against Australia this summer.' Instead he was to be found in the press box, giving his learned opinions to a newspaper. Perhaps Jardine realized that influential figures at Lord's were slowly turning against him, even though they had supported him initially by renewing his captaincy after Bodyline. Perhaps his greatest innings in Test cricket sealed his fate, when, at Old Trafford, he batted for almost five hours to score a courageous hundred against Constantine and Martindale, who bowled Bodyline at him. Jardine scorned thigh or chest protector, refused to rub the injured

Plus ça change. A handful of months after he captained England successfully in India, Douglas Jardine joins the queue filtering into the Oval for the last Test against Australia in August, 1934. Jardine had earlier announced he would not play that year against the Australians and he took to the press box to comment on their performances – in the process experiencing the frustrations of every press man who has ever tried to jump an elephantine queue

the curbing of Bradman's dominating influence was the sole aim. According to the laws of cricket at that time, he was advocating nothing illegal. To a trained lawyer, that would have been anathema.

Fifty years after Bodyline, the cricket world braced itself for the inevitable media coverage. We were not disappointed – a flood of books, learned articles, new documentary evidence, interviews with survivors from that fateful series, and, most bizarrely, television soap opera. Almost half the British population watched a 7½-hour treatment of the Bodyline saga that was unintentionally hilarious. It was meant to be a combination of *Brideshead Revisited* and *Chariots of Fire* with a dash of the anti-imperialist sentiments of *Gallipoli*, but it fell between every available cinematic stool. The technical and historical errors were as bad as the one-dimensional attempts at characterization. It was soon realized that the film was a soap opera, with just a tenuous connection with reality. The views of Sir Donald Bradman were no doubt solicited; he wisely kept his counsel, but a teammate from that series was a good deal more trenchant. Bill O'Reilly pushed the 'off' button soon after the start and told everyone it was rubbish.

If that television fantasy told us nothing new about Bodyline, at least several fascinating sidelights emerged from the rash of interest in the phenomenon. Many old players took the opportunity to set the facts straight on a few old chestnuts that have lingered on the fire for decades. The English players deny that Jardine hatched a plot over the previous two years – they say that all he wanted to do was restrict Bradman's attacking range, but he was still unsure about the means as they travelled to Australia. Other fascinating vignettes emerge – Jardine telling his team that they must learn to hate the Australian players, the total lack of complaint from the opposition, the request by Jardine to Les Ames that he must make sure that Larwood and Voce did not drink too much beer in case their fitness was affected. G. O. Allen has confirmed that he warned Jardine he would make a full statement to the MCC if he was left out at Melbourne for refusing to bowl Bodyline. It seems that Jardine and the tour manager, Pelham Warner, were barely on speaking terms by the second Test, and that Larwood would not speak to his captain during that Test because Jardine was furious that his main fast bowler was having trouble with his boots, and had to go off the field on occasions. The role of the hapless Warner was remarkable. As

areas and battled through in admirable fashion. He would have been the last man to complain at the tactics, but the crowd and the press were disturbed. So this was Bodyline? What must it have been like out in Australia, on faster wickets, with Larwood, Voce and Bowes no doubt bowling it more accurately than these West Indians?

After the Indian tour, Jardine never played again for England. He was at his prime, but prudently he chose to concentrate on his legal career, no doubt reflecting on the irony of a series that saw a great triumph of captaincy, but eventually brought him international opprobrium.

When *Wisden* remarked of the 1934 season, 'the whole atmosphere of cricket in England was utterly foreign to the great traditions of the game', it was clear that the Establishment was pointing its accusing finger at a man who never buckled on a pair of pads in first-class cricket that season. Events had caught up with the captain whose record – just one defeat in fifteen Tests – is unrivalled. He never publicly apologized for his role in the whole unhappy episode and no doubt maintained that he had done what he set out to do and that single-mindedness is a vital human trait. Without Bradman, there would have been no need for Bodyline – to Jardine's clear, analytical mind,

Last rites on Sydney Hill, 1932. England won by ten wickets

chairman of selectors, he had helped pick the touring party and its captain – yet he was also reporting the tour for the *Morning Post* and as editor of the *Cricketer*!

Warner was one of just three writers on the Bodyline tour – the others were Jack Hobbs's ghost writer, and Reuter's Bruce Harris, a man who knew little about cricket and was soon under Jardine's spell. No wonder the British public (and Lord's for that matter), were slow to believe that the colonials might have been justified in their complaints. The lack of Fleet Street representation is astonishing: on the next tour, the *Evening Standard* alone was represented by four writers, including the comments from home of one D. R. Jardine. Perhaps that was the safest place for him to make his assessments.

Apologists for Bodyline point to the devastation caused by Thomson and Lillee in 1974/5. The feeling is that the two Australians were more dangerous than Larwood and company, because the ball stayed hard for around 50 overs, instead of going soft too quickly, as in 1932/3. Certainly the English batsmen who suffered at the hands of Lillee and Thomson ruefully admit the ball kept its shape and shine for a long time, that the wickets had uneven bounce and that they were physically frightened. Yet Thomson and Lillee did not bowl specifically at the batsmen's legs, with a ring of fielders close up on the leg-side. They were allowed just two men backward of square on the leg-side, and most of the catches came in the slip area, with wicket-keeper Marsh equally prehensile; Les Ames, in contrast, picked up just eight catches in the Bodyline series.

Jack Fingleton, that courageous opening batsman who suffered as much as anyone in the Bodyline series, says, 'The people to blame for it were those who

Above: Jardine marrying Margaret Irene Peat, September 1934
Below: Larwood's Bodyline field at Brisbane in 1933. The unlucky batsman is the Australian, Bill Woodfull

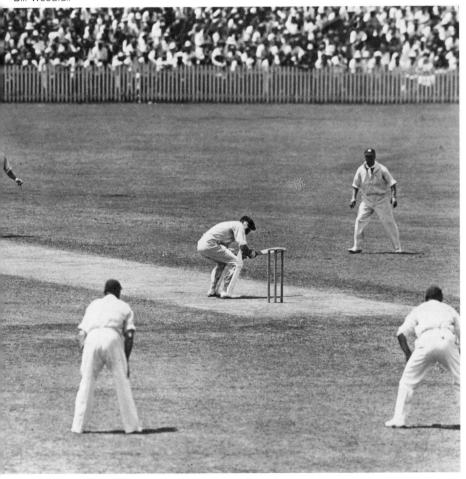

could see no further than huge scores, doped wickets and limitless Tests.' It was a time of bowling purgatory and on that basis Bodyline was a product of its age. So were the individual characters of Jardine and Bradman: they were both ruthless men, survivors in a tough period, where the false prosperity of the 1920s had slid into a time of mass unemployment and human misery. To the Australian struggling in a time of crippling recession, Bradman was a symbol of hope – the poor boy made good through his own talents, without a helping hand from any paternalist source. Bradman's comparative eclipse in that series hurt the Australian nation deeply – and not just because the tactics used were unsavoury. Warwick Armstrong, the Australian captain of the previous decade, was straight out of the Jardine mould and no one vilified Armstrong in his own country. He was a winner and they loved him for it, even though he would have happily adopted Bodyline tactics if the need had arisen. It was the country's sense of pride that was violated when Bradman was nullified by Jardine. Australia was starting to cut itself away from the mother country and it wanted to stand on its own economic feet. The massacre of young Australians at Gallipoli in 1917 had not been forgotten and there was a strong feeling that Britain – and more pertinently, the First Lord of the Admiralty, Winston Churchill – bore responsibility for the carnage. Australia could just about stomach charming amateurs of the old school like Arthur Gilligan and Percy Chapman when they captained an England tour, but Jardine was something else.

Jardine was also representative of his class and upbringing. An education at Winchester uniquely fits a man with a sense of rectitude; that finely tuned lawyer's brain was only interested in the goal, rather than the merits of its attainment. The man who insisted that all his players had a clean bill of health from a dentist before touring Australia would leave nothing to chance. In contrast, Percy Chapman would hope that his side would eventually come out on top amid all the social distractions. For Douglas Jardine there would be no social distractions.

A postscript to the Bodyline series comes from Jack Fingleton: 'I do not think there was one single batsman who played in those games who ever afterwards recaptured his love for cricket.' That remains the most damning indictment of the obsessive nature of Douglas Jardine.

Denis Compton

Denis Compton will be remembered above all for bringing glamour and an infectious gaiety into a period starved of such diversions. He was, of course, one of the great batsman of any age, with a record over a twenty-year career that will stand up to the severest examination. Yet it was the way Compton played the game that transcended any statistical niceties. For a few short years after the Second World War Denis Compton was the supreme entertainer. Even now, the mention of his name to a middle-aged cricket fan will induce a mellow smile: 'Ah, Denis,' they will murmer and their thoughts are transported back to the days of ration books and postwar austerity. Denis Compton did not deal in short rations when he batted. He symbolized postwar optimism, the conviction that a better world was emerging from the ravages. To the crowd he was always 'Denis'; Hutton, Evans, Washbrook, Edrich and Bedser were all greatly respected, but Denis was one of us. He made us care for him by his unfettered genius, his knack of communicating the boyish pleasure in his gifts.

Compton was just twenty-one when war came, slowing his inevitable progress towards cricketing greatness. Six years later Compton and the rest of the cricket world started to inch towards some form of normality. For the next five years the standard of English cricket was poor – a generation had been lost, fast bowlers were scarce and the best players remained of pre-war vintage. In contrast the Australian side that triumphed 3/0 in the 1946/7 series comprised confident, athletic cricketers. It was really no contest but resumption of the traditional Ashes rivalry was then more important to a world that craved for the comforting

Denis Compton relaxing at home in 1956, the penultimate year of his great career

traditions. Under Bradman's relentless captaincy, Australian hegemony was confirmed in 1948: the side which decimated England that summer was a devastating amalgam of ruthless fast bowling, high-class batting and dazzling fielding. Defeat by such a unit was no disgrace to England, but events over the next two summers were even more depressing. England's bowling was too mundane to disturb the serenity of the 1949 New Zealanders, in a summer of fine weather and benign pitches. All four Tests were left drawn; never again would they be confined to just three days. Thereafter all Tests in England would be played over

five days, as the newer Test countries caught up on their elders. The point was underlined the following year, when England were routed 3/1 by the West Indies. The spin bowling combination of Ramadhin and Valentine and the brilliant batting of Weekes, Worrell and Walcott were too much for the England of 1950. The bowling was cannon fodder for brilliant batsmen while England's batsmen lacked positive footwork and intent against the two 'mystery' spinners.

When England lost the first four Tests of the 1950/1 Ashes series, it seemed the rot would never be stopped. At last victory came at Melbourne through the inspirational captaincy of F. R. Brown, the majestic batting of Reg Simpson and Len Hutton and the indomitable seam bowling of Alec Bedser. A margin of 4/1 may seem emphatic enough, but England's overdue recovery was imminent; the return of the Ashes two years later confirmed the trend. Appropriately Denis Compton hit the winning runs at the Oval in 1953 to bring back the Ashes after nineteen years. Along with Hutton, he had stood foursquare against Lindwall and Miller as the rest of the English batting was blown apart in the immediate years after the war.

Yet if 1953 was the crowning glory of Compton's career, the year of 1947 will always be associated with him. No one in the game's history has scored more runs or centuries than Compton in that season, but it was the manner in which those runs were scored that burns brightly in the memory. His great friend, Bill Edrich was almost as prolific – between them they scored over 7000 runs – and their daring exploits helped Middlesex win the county championship. The sun seemed to shine every day as Compton and Edrich gorged

Above: The push off his legs. Compton was devastating on the legside

The young left-winger with Arsenal in 1937

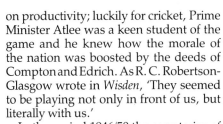

themselves that summer. Bowling and fielding standards may have been mediocre and the field-placing may have been stereotyped, but nothing can dilute the pleasure that Compton and Edrich gave us. At one stage during that summer, the Labour Government was worried that cricket was hampering the production drive. Some sports had been suspended altogether in midweek as the Government tried to launch a massive rebuilding programme. It was estimated that 3 million man-days were lost to cricket in 1947 as the crowds flocked to the marvellous entertainment. No less than 75 per cent of county matches yielded a definite result. The secretary of the MCC, Colonel R. S. Rait-Kerr was summoned to Downing Street to discuss cricket's effect on productivity; luckily for cricket, Prime Minister Atlee was a keen student of the game and he knew how the morale of the nation was boosted by the deeds of Compton and Edrich. As R. C. Robertson-Glasgow wrote in *Wisden*, 'They seemed to be playing not only in front of us, but literally with us.'

In the period 1946/50 the secretaries of county cricket clubs were happy men, as they watched the huge crowds fill their grounds. There was no lack of cricketing interest – the charming, talented South Africans of 1947, Bradman's Australians the following year and the glamorous West Indians of 1950 – and the glorious summers of 1947 and 1949 were ideal for the spectator. The social context also favoured cricket. Clothes, petrol and food were rationed throughout the late forties and it was still a luxury to own a car. Foreign currency was difficult to acquire and holidays abroad were an exception.

Above: Appropriately, Compton makes the winning hit at the Oval in 1953 to bring the Ashes back to England after an interval of 19 years. Happily, his batting partner is Bill Edrich. The bowler is Arthur Morris

Right: Partners Compton and Bill Edrich — 1947 belonged to them

Many spent their holidays at home and public transport would obligingly ferry the interested parties to the sporting arenas. Television was still in its infancy. All such social deprivations meant cricket could not fail at the turnstiles: people were aching to get outdoors again after years of skulking in air-raid shelters or fighting the enemy on foreign fields. It was fun to be part of a genial crowd again, to experience that special brand of sporting excitement. In later eras, cricket's superstars became remote from the public, but in the unsophisticated days of the late forties, our heroes were less fastidious. None more so than Denis Compton. His face beamed out at us from countless newspaper hoardings, extolling the virtues of Brylcreem. For the princely sum of £200 a year, the Brylcreem Boy helped to usher that familiar small white jar into countless bathrooms.

It was not in Denis's carefree nature to make large financial killings out of the game, but his legendary vagueness had far-reaching effects on star cricketers who were not even alive during his 'annus

mirabilis' of 1947. At the end of his benefit year in 1949, Denis admitted to a friend that his accounts were as haphazard as every other aspect of his life. His friend offered to help sort out his business affairs and in the next few weeks he was appalled to discover that sportsmen were poorly paid in relation to the pleasure they gave to millions. The friend was called Bagenal Harvey and he helped improve the financial lot of many cricketers. Harvey became the first agent for sportsmen and drove a hard bargain with the business community. Before Bagenal Harvey, cricketers of a certain eminence could rely on occasional endorsements but little else, unless they had the rare genius and the hard-nosed commercial enterprise of a Grace or a Bradman. The players were conditioned to gratitude for whatever small pickings came their way, while hoping for a benefit after years of loyal county service. They did not realize they were being exploited in an age of increased media attention, when cricket was playing a major role in reviving the nation's morale. Forty years later, Test

stars are seen in huddled conversation with their agents, discussing lucrative trips abroad or wondering if the appropriate company will pay them in cash, rather than alert the taxman. Almost every player who now comes into the England side has an agent, or at least a financial adviser. No doubt the change in status would have come about in due course, but it took an accountant from County Cork and an absent-minded England batsman to set the wheels in motion.

Glamour after years of austerity. The Brylcreem Boy with Anna Neagle

A bird's-eye view of the Nottinghamshire v. Surrey match at Trent Bridge in 1949. Most young boys of that generation will recall those heavy shoes with something less than affection

While Denis Compton's labyrinthine personal affairs were being regulated, the same transformation was coming to English cricket. Yet it took fully a decade after the war before English cricket could claim to be strong. By then social conditions were changing: full employment meant greater spending power and increased leisure options, while the influence of the motor car and television became more and more profound. Crowds began to dwindle in the early 1950s, despite the increasing professionalism of the players and the emerging success of the England side. Jack Hobbs wrote in *Wisden* that he preferred to watch village, rather than county cricket, while Neville Cardus proclaimed that 'safety-first' tactics would ruin the game. Too many county captains were grasping the option of a draw too eagerly and invidious comparisons with the cricket of the 1940s were being made. It did not matter that English cricket had been weak just after the war; the crowds had savoured the entertainment and the exuberance of men like Denis Compton.

By the time Compton played his last Test in 1957, England were the unofficial world champions. The tyro who had batted against Maurice Tate in his first county game twenty years earlier had thickened out into a mellow maestro with chronic knee trouble. He had lasted long enough to see England unearth a string of fast bowlers fearsome enough for any batting line-up, and spin bowling of class and variety. It was no fault of Denis Compton that English cricket in the mid-fifties was perceived to be dull by the public. As Godfrey Evans, another great entertainer of that period, put it, 'He played cricket for fun and made it look fun.' Only Bobby Charlton and Henry Cooper among postwar British sportsmen can even approach the depth of affection that Denis Compton inspired.

Len Hutton

Len Hutton was one of England's greatest opening batsmen but his influence on the game was far greater than just scoring runs. He was the first professional to captain England and he was knighted for services to cricket. In Victorian England, Arthur Shrewsbury had started the process of grafting self-respect into the ranks of the professionals; Lord Hawke did his utmost in the same direction and Jack Hobbs carried it on. By the time Hutton was being mooted for the England captaincy, many social barriers were being dismantled after the Second World War; the special bond created by wartime service had chipped away at the concept of class distinction. A Labour Government laid the foundations of the British welfare state from 1945 to 1951 and gradually the vision of a classless society took shape. It was no longer heinous to suggest that a professional cricketer had powers of leadership superior to that of an amateur. Within a year of Hutton's appointment as England captain, Jack Hobbs became the first professional games player to be knighted. The professional had finally arrived at the gates of respectability.

It was fitting that the fates of two great opening batsmen should be so entwined. Hutton had made his first-class debut in 1934, the year that Hobbs retired. The young Yorkshireman became the latest in the line of dependable, outstanding opening batsmen – from Shrewsbury to Hayward to Hobbs to Sutcliffe, then to Hutton. All professionals, all utterly respectable on and off the field. Within a year or two of Hutton's debut, it was abundantly clear that England had unearthed another in the grand tradition. In 1935, Herbert Sutcliffe forecast he would play for England and the Yorkshire coach, George Hirst, told the youngster in the

Len Hutton obliges the autograph hunter at Arundel in 1956, the year he was knighted

nets, 'Booger off, there's nowt we can teach thee' – a handsome tribute from the man who had bowled at Trumper, Hobbs and the other giants of the Golden Age.

When he was twenty-one, Hutton first played for England. He made nought, but more than compensated over the next two decades. Only three batsmen have scored more runs for England than the impeccable stylist with the lovely off-drive; this

despite the loss of six years to the war, an injury to his left arm that hampered his postwar batting, and early retirement at the age of thirty-nine. During Hutton's career, the Test arena broadened and gained depth. England *v.* Australia remained the major attraction, but the other countries toughened up and passed through the psychological barriers of defeatism. South Africa won a series in England for the first time (1935), West Indies did the same (1950), and for good measure defeated England twice in the Caribbean (1934/5 and 1947/9), while India beat England in a series for the first time in 1951/2. Astonishingly, Pakistan became the first country to win a Test in England on its first visit, in 1954. In some of these series, England was not at full strength because several senior players declined to tour, but there was a levelling-off process at work, a precursor of the 1970s when every Test country was perfectly capable of beating the others.

In Hutton's early years in Test cricket, the bat was still monotonously on top of the ball. The 1938 series against Australia was an obscenity for those who feel there is more to cricket than batting largesse. The statisticians loved it: Paynter 216 not out, McCabe 232, Hammond 240, Leyland 187 and, most memorably, Hutton 364. At the Oval, England ground Australia down until even that bonny band of fighters collapsed. Hutton batted for 13 hours 20 minutes, through eight sessions of play on a perfect wicket against only three Test-class bowlers. He would have liked to have played his shots but Hammond, the England captain, quietened him down when he reached the 140s, and he settled for batting in perpetuity. Hutton beat Bradman's score of 334 at Leeds – an innings watched by

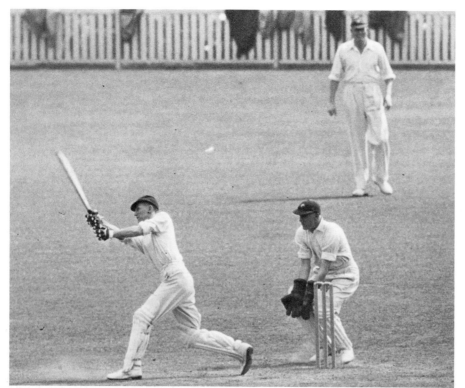

the fourteen-year-old Hutton in 1930 – and Bradman was the first to congratulate him when he passed the figure. Inevitably Hutton was the man of the hour in the eyes of the media and those sections of the cricketing public who slavered at the welter of statistics – yet he is realistic enough to admit that, as an innings, it was hardly the stuff of history. Hutton maintains that he played far greater knocks in more difficult circumstances and he is right to keep the Oval 1938 in proportion. It is a measure of the ruthless approach to that game that Hammond would not declare until he was certain that the injured Bradman could not bat. One could assume that a score of 903 for seven declared was immunity against defeat, but the spectre of Bradman on a plumb wicket dogged every England captain throughout the acquisitive thirties.

Left: The classic off-drive. Hutton's historic 364 at the Oval, 1938

Below: Dawn chorus – waiting to get in the Oval, 1938

The Bedser twins. Eric (*left*) was a splendid all-rounder for the excellent Surrey side of the 1950s while Alec was the rock of England's bowling for a decade. When England won the Ashes in 1953, Bedser's 39 wickets were crucial. For the next 30 years, he gave great service to English cricket as a great bowler, conscientious Test selector and voluble upholder of the game's traditional virtues

A few months later came the ultimate comment on the batting dominance of that decade – the Timeless Test at Durban. The match lasted for ten days and yet it was still drawn, as England ended at 654 for five, still 42 short of victory. The England party had to catch the ship that was taking them home, so a game that had lasted ten days was still unfinished. No wonder American tourists expressed bewilderment at the curiosities of cricket; it was impossible to defend such a bias against the bowler.

Within six months of the Timeless Test, the battle for civilization put other matters into perspective. War came at a particularly frustrating time for Len Hutton; after Bradman, he was the best batsman in the world. The Oval innings had not been typical. In six years in first-class cricket, he had become established as a glorious strokeplayer, with an immaculate technique that served him nobly if the wicket ever turned sour. Good judges were mentioning him in the same bracket as Hobbs. Hutton says he was never quite the same player after the war: the disability in his left arm led to technical adjustments and he felt the weight of

responsibility on his shoulders. The England batting was weak for the remainder of Hutton's career and he came to believe that if he was dismissed early, the innings would crumble. Perhaps that is a little unfair on Cyril Washbrook, his regular opening partner, or the indomitable Bill Edrich and the brilliant Denis Compton – but there is no doubt that England relied heavily on Len Hutton until Peter May and Colin Cowdrey blossomed under Hutton's captaincy.

It was Hutton who bore the brunt of the Australian attack in the first four series after the war. On the first tour to Australia in 1946/7, England lacked a genuine quick bowler, while the opposition had two great performers in Lindwall and Miller. Hutton was the obvious target as he tried to come to terms with the lifting ball on hard, lively wickets. It was the same in 1948, when the new ball was available after every 55 overs and Lindwall, Miller and Johnston took full advantage. Hutton lost his nerve temporarily and was left out for one Test, but he soon returned and played several brave innings against overwhelming odds. At the Oval he made 30 out of 52 all out and only he looked like a

Test batsman. Hutton had come through the pace ordeal with dignity and with his reputation intact: the four half centuries he scored in that 1948 series were more meritorious than 364 easy runs chiselled out on a batting paradise.

When England next toured Australia in 1950/1, Hutton had worked out his technique against the fast bowlers. The left shoulder pointed slightly towards mid-on in deference to the growing trend towards inswing, and to the fast bowlers he would play half-forward with the weight easily balanced so that he would not get out of position, or be vulnerable to late movement. Using the lightest possible bat to compensate for his shortened left arm, Hutton had become a master at the deft deflection and the dead bat in defensive play. He would play the ball exceptionally late, with perfect balance. As a result, his batting on bad wickets was the best of his generation, greater even than that of Compton, who relied on genius as well as a fundamentally sound technique. Hutton remained a fascinating batsman to watch, even when batting slowly: that beautiful cover drive would invariably compensate for the reflective periods when he was coming to terms with the bowling and the wicket.

Although England lost heavily to Australia on the 1950/1 tour, there were signs that recovery was on its way. The bowling of Bedser and the wicket-keeping of Evans remained inspirational, but the batting of Hutton was outstanding. His 62 not out in an all-out total of 122 on a foul Brisbane pitch was reminiscent of Hobbs or Trumper in similar circumstances and his Test batting average of 88 in a beaten side was remarkable. He was now the best batsman in the world. What other horizons lay open to Hutton?

In retrospect it would seem that Hutton was the obvious man to take over the captaincy from the 41-year-old Freddie Brown. Hutton's tactical acumen was widely acknowledged – on the Australian tour he had stood in the slips alongside Brown and contributed many sound tactical suggestions. He was also the best cricketer in England, an attribute which has often been rewarded by the England captaincy in later years. Yet Hutton was a professional and some reactionary voices were heard in the area of St John's Wood

to the effect that the great amateurs of yesteryear would turn in their graves if such a thing ever came to pass. They trotted out Lord Hawke's famous dictum ('Pray God no professional ever captains England!'), without bothering to check the context of that remark. When Lord Hawke uttered those heartfelt words, he was still presiding over the Golden Age of cricket, when the game was brimful of talented amateurs with a flair for attacking captaincy. The noble Lord was simply expressing the opinion that it would be a sad day for cricket's entertainment prospects if the amateur faded out of the game. No man of the Establishment ever did more for the professional cricketer than Lord Hawke and if he had lived to see the state of English cricket in 1952, he would have lined up alongside Len Hutton without hesitation.

In the space of two years, England had lost series against the West Indies, against Australia and against India and the time for rebuilding was certainly nigh. A strong leader with a clear conception was vital. It would also help if he was good enough to be picked on merit as a player. With

Norman Yardley and Freddie Brown past their best, with Bill Edrich lacking support in the corridors of power, there was only one logical choice. Even then it took some powerful backstage lobbying at Lord's before the historic announcement was made. It was a blow to some sections of the Establishment – no professional had held the post of England captain since the MCC took over responsibility for the game. James Lillywhite, Alfred Shaw and Arthur Shrewsbury had led some of the 'mercenary' sides to Australia in the nineteenth century, but they were never truly representative of English cricket. Since the war, there had been several straws in the progressive wind: the election of twenty-six professionals to honorary life membership of the MCC, the appointment of Les Ames to the England selection

Right: The England side after their Ashes triumph. Back row: T.E. Bailey, P.B.H. May, T.W. Graveney, J.C. Laker, G.A.R. Lock, J.H. Wardle, F.S. Trueman. Seated: W.J. Edrich, A.V. Bedser, L. Hutton (captain), D.C.S. Compton and T.G.Evans
Below: A nation yearning for the Ashes. The Oval in 1953

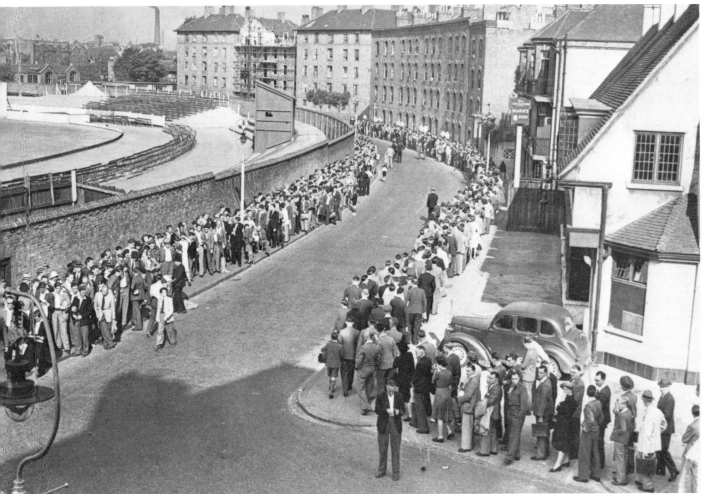

Full house at the Oval with thousands locked outside the turnstiles and others standing on their seats watching the historic England versus Australia Test in August 1953

committee in 1950, and the vice-captaincy of Denis Compton on the Australian tour later that year. Yet Hutton's appointment still ruffled the reactionary dovecotes. He of all people knew that he had to win Test matches to still the criticism.

Hutton made a good start – a 3/0 victory in the home series against India, and a batting average of 79. His strategy was firmly fixed on the visit of the Australians the following year, and in his customary clear-headed fashion, he decided to have a balanced attack. He believed in pace as a weapon when the conditions were right and to that end he played Brian Statham in the Lord's Test and Freddie Trueman at the Oval. Both were young fast bowlers of immense promise, who needed to be nurtured for future hard tours and Hutton only used them when it was right. Trueman, in particular, repaid him handsomely with four for 86 in the first innings at the Oval. Apart from sheer speed, Hutton relied on the marvellous, enduring bowling of Alec Bedser (thirty-nine wickets in the series), the spin of Jim Laker, Tony Lock or Johnny Wardle and the emerging seam bowling of Trevor Bailey. Bailey's all-round ability was crucial to the balance of the side: his epic stand at Lord's with Willie Watson saved

the game from an apparently hopeless position. They stayed together for more than four hours and showed that there was steel at last in the England middle order. Just to even things up, England had the better of the draw at Old Trafford, with Laker and Wardle almost winning it on the last day on a turning wicket. Leeds was also a draw so the fate of the Ashes rested on the final Test at the Oval. An extra day was added for a conclusive finish, but it was not needed. Laker and Lock bowled Australia out cheaply, taking nine wickets between them and England needed just 132 to win. Happily, Compton and Edrich were together in the middle when the winning runs were made and the Ashes returned to England after a gap of nineteen years. Significantly, Hutton was the only man on either side to average more than 50. He had captained the side with calm assurance, conducting a holding operation until he could get Australia on a wicket that suited his spinners. His modest good nature had also contributed to a happy, relaxed atmosphere between his opposite number, Lindsay Hassett, and the two sides. The cricket had been hard and unyielding, but always free of rancour. As Len Hutton acknowledged the crowd's cheers on the Oval balcony, he could reflect that he had won the first major battle against the reactionary forces of English cricket.

He nearly lost the second battle a few

months later in the West Indies. The tour started disastrously, with England two-down early on, and a host of extraneous aggravations took their toll of Hutton. Political disturbances, crowd riots, ill-discipline by some English players and some ludicrous umpiring decisions all added up to a nightmare period for the captain. By his own example he pulled England round; innings of 169 and 205 helped square the series. Bailey's seven for 74 on the first day of the final Test gave England the required stranglehold but if Hutton had not played so nobly when it was so vital, the series would have been lost by the third Test. Once more the immense strain of captaincy did not affect his batting.

One would have thought that Hutton's marvellous influence on that West Indies tour would have secured the captaincy for as long as he wanted it – but the Establishment had one more cruel shot in its locker. David Sheppard, a veteran of six Tests, captained England in the Second and Third Tests against Pakistan, and let it be known that he would delay his ordination if it meant leading the side to Australia later that year. With respect to Sheppard – a man who had led Sussex with skill and daring – it seems amazing that the selectors could treat Hutton in such a callous way. His knowledge of first-class cricket stretched back twenty years, he was still one of the greatest batsmen in the world, he had the respect of his team after two tough winning series – yet he was still on trial. No wonder Hutton became more and more introverted during his period as England's captain.

Eventually Hutton was asked to take the side to Australia for a momentous series. The tour finished him as a cricketer, but he had the satisfaction of getting almost everything right. Some of the selections seemed odd: the omission of Jim Laker in favour of the Glamorgan off-spinner, Jim McConnon, the absence of Tony Lock and the choice of Frank Tyson and Colin Cowdrey. The young Cowdrey was picked for his abundant class and the hope that his natural gift of timing would serve him well on fast Australian pitches, while Tyson was picked ahead of Fred Trueman because of his extra pace. This is not to demean Trueman's genuine speed, but Tyson was a shade faster; he relied on outright pace and brute strength and his inability to do anything with the new ball would not matter, because the shine would not last very long. Cowdrey and Tyson were to prove inspired selections.

Hutton was convinced that speed would win the series and he nursed Tyson and Statham through the early stages. The omens were terrible after the First Test. Hutton put Australia in, watched them amass 601 for eight and England lost by an innings and 154. The recovery after Brisbane was remarkable: Tyson shortened his run-up and bowled frighteningly fast. He and Statham took forty-three Test wickets after the Brisbane debacle and the Australians, unused to such pace in recent years, capitulated. To Hutton, it was sweet revenge after the ducking and weaving at the hands of Lindwall and Miller in previous years. Victory was achieved at a cost to Hutton's health. He became so wrapped up in the job, so sensitive to press criticism, so worried about his own form that he behaved bizarrely. On the morning of the Melbourne Test he refused to get out of bed and Godfrey Evans and Bill Edrich had to plead with him to come to the ground. He even forgot to have a consoling word with Alec Bedser, when that great bowler was dropped for the Second Test. By the end of the tour, Hutton was a sick man, suffering from blackouts and plagued by fibrositis. After a few uncomfortable games in 1955, he announced his retirement. A knighthood a year later was a deserved reward for a man who gave so much of himself to the game.

His record as England captain is impressive – just four defeats in twenty-three Tests, and he never lost a rubber.

Sir Len Hutton on the day he was knighted in 1956 'for services to cricket'. With him are his wife, his younger son John, and Richard, who was to play for England

Some criticized him for his emphasis on fast bowling, but he realized better than most that Test cricket after the war was generally dominated by the side with the best fast bowlers. He had been battered enough by Lindwall and Miller to know that every batsman dislikes genuine speed; to Hutton it was a case of waiting till the English saviours came along, and then utilizing them properly. No one can say he failed to do that. It must also be said that Hutton won the Ashes in 1953 with a balanced side, that spin bowlers such as Laker, Lock, Wardle, Tattersall and Appleyard all played under him during his period as captain. Hutton's attitude to the over-rate is more relevant: he took the view that the batsmen could be winkled out by frustration as much as by fear. As a great batsman himself, he knew that the well of inspiration could run dry if the bowler took an inordinate amount of time to deliver the ball. On the Australian tour of 1954-5, Hutton unashamedly slowed down the over-rate, to keep his fast bowlers fresh. Melbourne was the nadir: 54 eight-ball overs in five hours, to a storm of booing from the crowd. Although the Board of Control at Lord's agreed that something had to be done about over-rates, the influence of Len Hutton extended through later generations. England could hardly complain about the tardiness of the West Indies fast bowlers under Clive Lloyd's captaincy when the prototype had been impressively assembled in Australia twenty years earlier. Hutton's legacy on over-rates remains the only blot on an impressive escutcheon: he was one of the select band of great batsmen who really cared about the side, a man who rarely put personal aggrandisement above the exigencies of the game.

Keith Miller & Ray Lindwall

Keith Miller and Ray Lindwall hand-somely exemplified the axiom that great fast bowlers win Test Matches. For a decade they were a magnificent bowling combination for Australia, and in the immediate postwar years, they were devastating. Undoubtedly England was immeasurably weaker than Australia in every department at that time, but the main difference between the two sides lay in the quality of fast bowling. In England's case, it was non-existent: it was Australia's good fortune to possess one of the best pair in Test history.

Lindwall and Miller were totally different bowlers, but their varied attri-butes made the perfect combination. Lindwall was a beautifully controlled bowler – a master of changes of pace, with the ability to swing the ball at speed from a beautiful action. In short, an artist: only Dennis Lillee can be mentioned in the same breath among later Australians. Miller, in contrast, was unpredictability itself. His run-up would vary in length, he would sometimes bowl a googly, an off-break and a bouncer in the same over and he gave the general impression that bowling was a chore. When roused, he was magnificent; his great height gave him lift and bounce and his work with the seam was high class. Lindwall was the better bowler, but Miller's flair for the unorthodox often undid the best batsmen. They were the natural successors to Ted McDonald and Jack Gregory, who plundered England in 1920/1 – McDonald the artistic thinker, Gregory the dashing all-rounder. That partnership was short-lived, with McDonald opting to play for Lancashire and Gregory developing muscular troubles: a quarter of a century later, their successors inflicted long-term damage.

A social function, 1956. Miller arrives with customary flair

The word 'charisma' might have been invented with Keith Miller in mind. There cannot have been a more popular over-seas cricketer in the eyes of English spec-tators. The nearest analogy is a combi-nation of Gary Sobers and Ian Botham, with an innate sense of fair play backing up his natural aggression. He was tall – well over six feet – with the physique of a superb athlete and he wore his black hair long when it was hardly fashionable in those days of national service. Miller would casually toss back that black mane after bowling a fearsome bouncer at Len Hutton or pouching a difficult slip catch with casual ease. He had a flair for communicating with the crowd and his duels with Denis Compton were memor-able for their gusto, chivalry and daring. To Miller, cricket really was just a game. He had seen the darker side of life as a fighter pilot in wartime Britain and like Bill Edrich, such an experience taught him to relish the joy of playing sport supremely well. In the decade after the war, relationships between most Australian and English players were genuinely warm and much of that stemmed from the wartime bond and the efforts of dedicated partygoers like Miller, Edrich and Compton. Miller's com-manding officer considered him 'the bravest and most willing pilot under my command', and such a man could take no pleasure from the ruthless nature of Don Bradman's captaincy, as English cricket was laid waste in 1948. Miller cared little for statistics: when Australia scored 721 in a day against Essex, he allowed himself to be bowled first ball. On the same tour, the Lancastrian Jack Ikin had got to 99, with the game almost over and a draw inevitable. Ikin had been dismissed for 99 in the previous match and when Bradman called for the new ball with just six minutes left, Miller refused to bowl, suggesting a medium-pacer would be suitable. Bradman gave the new ball instead to Lindwall, who bowled Ikin for 99. To Miller, that was pointless; he was a member of one of the great touring sides, and one more run to a popular player such as Ikin would not destroy Australian invincibility. No wonder English cricket loved him – he may have looked like the tough macho Aussie but he never lost sight of the human touches. Life was hard enough in the Britain of ration books and austerity measures without getting carried away on the cricket field. In Miller's case, the business out on the pitch often seemed a mere diversion to more important matters like getting to a nearby racecourse or wondering where the next hangover was coming from. If Miller bowled like someone nursing a hangover – a shade grudgingly, a trifle irritated if hit to the boundary – that was often the reality.

Keith Miller was at his best in a crisis. That was obvious in his very first Test against England in 1946. After just 12 overs, Lindwall was ruled out with chickenpox, and Miller had to soldier on: he took nine wickets. At Adelaide in 1955, England was on the point of retaining the Ashes, needing just 94 to win. Miller galvanized himself to dismiss Hutton, Edrich and Cowdrey in the space of twenty balls. England got home nervously, by five wickets, but not before Miller had shown his true worth. On his last tour to England in 1956 he won the Lord's Test with ten wickets and scores of 28 and 30 in a low-scoring game. Miller bowled 70 overs in the match after Pat Crawford pulled a thigh muscle in his fifth over. Crawford did not bowl again in the game and, at the age of thirty-seven, Miller responded wonderfully. Two incidents from that match typify his approach to cricket. When Peter May drove him straight to the boundary, Miller applauded, took off his second sweater and whizzed the next two deliveries past May at chest height. Then he raised his bat in acknowledgement to Fred Trueman for a fine piece of bowling that saw Miller caught behind by Godfrey Evans. At the end of the Test, the reception for Miller was emotionally affectionate; typically, Miller threw the bails into the crowd, in the manner of a golfer throwing away his ball after winning a tournament. Keith Miller never missed a public relations trick, never forgot that cricket should involve the spectators as well as the men in flannels.

Right: Ray Lindwall: only Lillee among Australian fast bowlers can be measured alongside him since the war

Below: Keith Miller attacking the ball in his usual style at Hove in 1956

His batting was the embodiment of that principle. He played like an Englishman, rather than an Australian, with a high backlift and a fierce front-foot drive. He was too tall to be an effective hooker, but his straight hitting was a joy. Many thought he should have been a truly great batsman, because he had all the attributes – apart from a killer instinct. He scored seven Test hundreds and would have doubled that in a weaker side with more pressure on the middle order. As a bowler he could transform any game. He was such a natural athlete – occasionally he would drop the ball absent-mindedly while running up to bowl, retrieve it in one effortless movement and complete the delivery as if nothing had happened. Such was the flair of Miller that no batsman could ever think he was really 'in' when he was bowling. A record of 170 wickets in Tests only hints at the rich variety of his talents.

It is a mystery why Keith Miller never captained Australia, unless it was simply a case of a lack of trust in a mercurial character who did not set out to win at all costs. Richie Benaud, no mean judge of captaincy talents, said he was the best skipper he ever played under: 'No one sized up a situation more quickly and no one was better at summing up a batsman's

weakness.' After becoming captain of New South Wales in 1953, Miller launched the state on a string of nine successive championships and the style that Benaud brought to the job owed much to the example of Miller. He was no great theorist, he preferred a hunch to long-term strategy. He was hardly a rigid disciplinarian. Once he led out the New South Wales side, only to be told that for some reason he had twelve players on the field. Miller carried on walking out to the middle and shouted over his shoulders, 'One of you bugger off, and the rest scatter!' Hardly the kind of tactical insight you would expect from a Hutton or a Bradman.

If Miller was the flair cricketer 'par excellence', Ray Lindwall was the thinking man's bowler. Neville Cardus once wrote, 'He has so many brains it's a wonder why he ever went in for fast bowling.' Pelham Warner, England captain at the start of the century, said he had never seen a better fast bowler, or one more blessed with all the necessary ingredients. Apart from a low arm at the point of delivery – which meant he lacked bounce with the old ball – Ray Lindwall was the genuine finished product. At just under six feet, he would glide in off a sixteen-pace run-up, a glorious fusion of power, control

and athleticism. Trevor Bailey, a man who suffered enough at the hands of Lindwall, wrote, 'Watching him bowl was one of the most satisfying spectacles the game has ever produced.' Apart from the aesthetics, he was exceptionally skilful. His change of pace was subtle, his yorker deadly and he could move the ball in the air at the very last moment – the type of delivery that traps the best players. Of his 228 Test victims, 67 of them were openers: Lindwall was invariably the man for the early breakthrough. His battles with Hutton were epics – master technicians trying to outthink each other. Lindwall could influence the whole tenor of a day's play with a single over. At Leeds in 1953, Lindwall bowled Hutton second ball with a classic yorker and the crowd seemed to go into mourning, stunned at the demise of their favourite player. England laboured to 142 for seven in a complete day and the shadow of that dismissal hung over the proceedings like a shroud.

Lindwall kept himself very fit. He would prepare physically months in advance for a new season and like Lillee in later years, he would train in great detail. He used to limber up in the dressing-room before play started and then go through some calisthenics while waiting to bowl. As a result, Lindwall was primed

for action from the very first ball: he never gave away runs while easing into a bowling stint. He thought deeply about his technical armoury and played in the Lancashire League to develop his skills – the result was a controlled inswinger to supplement his natural away swing. He used the bouncer sparingly, but to telling effect, and it was never apparent from his run-up that a sharp bouncer was on its way.

The need for deep tactical thinking had been drummed into Lindwall before he ever played first-class cricket. He was lucky in his choice of mentor: Bill O'Reilly, scourge of English batsmen in the thirties, and one of the greatest triers the game has seen. O'Reilly captained the St George club in Sydney and he took the young man under his wing, taking photographs of his bowling action and dissecting the weaknesses. By the time Lindwall was ready for Test cricket, he was twenty-five, with a broad chest, wide shoulders and a wiry fast bowler's physique in the Harold Larwood mould. His first Test, against New Zealand, was the last for Bill O'Reilly but the old maestro knew he would not need to be at Lindwall's shoulder any longer. Lindwall and Miller took thirty-five wickets in that 1946/7 series and at last Australia had a winning combination.

A selection of action photographs from the 1948 tour to England showing the controlled grace of Ray Lindwall's bowling action – one of the classic actions of all time

Miller's sense of showmanship was never far away from the surface and his last appearance at Lord's did not disappoint his many admirers. After taking 10 for 152 in the match to bring Australia victory by 185 runs, Miller tosses the bails to the crowd

The havoc wrought by Larwood and company a decade earlier still rankled; the nation wanted genuine fast bowlers to repay the humiliation. Interest in the series was massive – 340,000 for the Melbourne Test, a new world record – and with Bradman rehabilitating himself, the juggernaut rolled on. The Australians had been worried at the start of the series, with only Bradman, Sid Barnes and Lindsay Hassett having any experience of Ashes battles. Almost overnight, the team of young, strong, fit hopefuls gelled into a formidable unit. There was the batting of Barnes, Morris, Bradman and Hassett, the great wicket-keeping of Don Tallon, a variety of spin bowling, the stock bowling of Ernie Toshack and above all, the bowling of Lindwall and Miller. The batting had great depth – even Lindwall buffeted a fast century in the Melbourne Test – and only one player could be dubbed a tail-ender. England could not compete with such youthful talent, and the contrast was even more painful when the Australians came over in 1948. The team was further bolstered by Neil Harvey, destined to become one of the game's great left-handers, and Bill Johnston added his varied left-arm swing and cut. Lindwall, Miller and Johnston took sixty-seven wickets between them in the series and the fielding was brilliant. Seven Australian batsmen had Test averages over 44. They were fortunate to take advantage of a regulation that played right into the hands of the team with superior fast bowling – the availability of the new ball after just 55 overs. Bradman simply relied on Toshack or Johnston to keep things quiet until the new ball became available and then he would set Lindwall and Miller loose. No wonder England was bowled out for 52 on a damp Oval pitch, no wonder the series was lost by a 4/0 margin – two by an innings, the others by seven and eight wickets. England only once had a chance of victory – at Leeds when Australia needed 404 on a dry, turning pitch. But England lost their nerve, the spinners bowled badly, catches were dropped and the old master, Bradman, guided the youngster Harvey to a famous seven-wicket victory. England lacked the self-confidence, the dynamism and the fast bowling of the Australians. Of Lindwall's eighty-six victims on that tour, half were clean bowled, eleven lbw and fourteen caught by the wicket-keeper, a fitting testimony to Lindwall's control and line.

Australia's dominance in Test cricket lasted for several years after that famous 1948 tour. South Africa was hammered 4/0, England by 4/1 and the West Indies – fresh from their victory in England – went down 4/1 in Australia. Even without Bradman's massive batting ability and sagacious captaincy, they were still too powerful. England won back the Ashes in 1953, but not before some doughty Australian fighting. Even in defeat, Lindwall and Miller were still a force, taking thirty-six of the seventy English wickets to fall. Over the next few years, the balance of power tilted towards England, as a succession of young fast bowlers made inroads, but Lindwall and Miller did not fade dishonourably from the Test scene. Lindwall was still playing for Australia at the age of thirty-nine; the pace may have gone but the tactical ploys were still subtle. When Australia blooded some fast bowlers with distinctly dubious actions against England in 1958, it was a pleasure to avert the eyes from the bent elbows and feast on the purity and beauty of Lindwall's action. As for Miller, he bowed out in 1956, at the age of thirty-seven. The charismatic looks were still there – he adorned the pages of the *Cricketer Magazine* in July 1956, extolling the virtues of a certain electric shaver and Brylcreem within the space of four pages. Brylcreem. Denis Compton. Keith Miller. Evocative words, though the two great entertainers of their age had more in common than a jar of hair cream.

Sonny Ramadhin & Alf Valentine

Sonny Ramadhin and Alf Valentine will always be associated with the English summer of 1950. They were the 'mystery' bowlers who became an overnight sensation, making experienced English batsmen look like novices and thereby setting up the first West Indies triumph in England. The year 1950 is a watershed in the history of Anglo/West Indian cricket: never again would England dismiss the Caribbean cricketer as an undisciplined, brittle, calypso-singing failure. That West Indies side crept up on England and took it by surprise, in the same manner as the Hungarian foot-ballers in 1953. In its naiveté, English cricket thought the only consistent threat would come from those tough, sun-bronzed Australians. Teams like the West Indies could be indulged, encouraged to improve, but eventually given a good thrashing; after all they had not won a single Test in three visits to England since 1928. Why should this 1950 team be any different?

Yet the writing had been on the wall for a few seasons. In 1947, G. O. Allen took England to the Caribbean and lost the series easily enough. It was a weakened unit and Len Hutton had to be flown out to supplement the squad, but there were obvious signs that the West Indies team was beginning to do itself justice. In Frank Worrell and Everton Weekes, they possessed two young batsmen of the highest class and another called Clyde Walcott was ready to make an equally impressive impact. By the time of the 1950 tour, England was ripe for plucking: demoralized by Australia, thwarted by strong New Zealand batting in 1949, the postwar recovery was still an illusion. The batting relied far too much on Hutton and Compton – and Compton's injured knee

Alf Valentine practises at Lord's on the eve of the 1950 tour. Note the choice of footwear

was beginning to plague him – and the bowling consisted of Bedser and little else. A collection of bright young men from Oxbridge looked a promising bet for the future, but they were not ready for the unique pressures of Test cricket. It seemed that it would at least be a high scoring series: without authentic fast bowlers, England looked likely to suffer at the hands of the powerful West Indian batsmen, while the visitors could only offer the undemanding seam attack of Jones, Johnson and Pierre, with support from Gomez, Worrell and Goddard. Surely England's honest journeymen could profit against that little lot?

Little was known of two young slow bowlers, Sonny Ramadhin and Alf Valentine. They had played just four first-class matches between them and they were on the trip mainly for experience, to learn their trade on soft English wickets. The sages did not expect either to play in the Tests. Valentine in particular bowled impressively in the early games and so when they came to Old Trafford for the First Test, the West Indies took notice of the wicket's spin potential and picked them both. In England's first innings, Valentine took the first eight wickets and he finished with eleven in the match. An innings of genius from Evans, staunch support from Bailey and superior bowling from three English spinners all contrib-uted to victory for England by 202 runs. Ramadhin and Valentine took fifteen wickets in the match, but the tourists' batting lacked judgement against the turning ball. It seemed that England's greater experience of spin bowling would be decisive in the rubber and that West Indies would continue to flatter to deceive.

The following Test at Lord's shattered

Sonny Ramadhin comes to terms with the placid pitch at Fenner's in May, 1950, as Cambridge University pile up 594 for 4 declared. The non-striker is a youthful Peter May, who missed out on the run feast. Ramadhin finished with 0 for 86, but by the end of the summer he was hailed as a genius

England's smug assumptions – and the agents were the two young spinners who had been patronized by the experts just a few weeks before. Ramadhin and Valentine took eighteen of the twenty England wickets: victory by 326 runs was deserved and celebrated in carnival style by thousands of exuberant West Indian supporters. A calypso record was rushed out and soon every cricket lover in England knew all about 'those little pals of mine, Ramadhin and Valentine'. The next two Tests saw crushing victories – by ten wickets and an innings. The two spinners took fifty-nine wickets in the series and all the other bowlers managed just eighteen. They were a contrasting pair: Valentine may have been categorized as a slow left-arm bowler, but he did not give the ball much air and could spin it greatly, while Ramadhin was very difficult to figure out. He delivered a mixture of off-breaks and legspin from between the third and middle finger and his busy, cartwheeling action gave no clue which way the ball would break.

Valentine's nagging accuracy and Ramadhin's mysterious technique were too much for English batting that remained passive and crease-bound. Denis Compton, the one batsman guaranteed to try attacking the spinners, was restricted to just one Test and the younger batsmen found that Ramadhin and Valentine were too quick through the air, even if they could trust their footwork out of the crease. The selectors did not exactly impress in the series, either – the England side for the final Test contained just three players from the previous one.

None of this can detract from the impact of Ramadhin and Valentine. After the pace barrage from Australia two years earlier, it was a delight to see spin bowling take centre stage again in a Test series in England. The two spinners would be the first to acknowledge that their batsmen gave them wonderful support, with six of them averaging over forty in the series. Allan Rae and Jeff Stollmeyer were a splendid pair of openers and Gerry Gomez a reliable number six, while at number three, four and five in the batting order, the '3 Ws' reigned supreme. No side in the world could match the versatile brilliance of Frank Worrell, Everton Weekes and Clyde Walcott. They were different types of players but their strokeplay and hunger for runs were common ingredients. The '3 Ws' came from

Barbados, that island which seems to have produced more great cricketers per square mile than anywhere else. They were born within two years of each other and tales of their precocious brilliance had been filtering back from the Caribbean for a year or two before they conquered England in 1950. At the age of nineteen Worrell scored 308 not out against Jamaica; then two years later, the Jamaican bowlers again suffered, as he and Walcott added an unbroken 574 for the fourth wicket. He averaged 147 against England in 1947/8 and 89 in 1950, charming everyone with a relaxed grace. Worrell played beautifully straight – he used to pepper mid-on and mid-off when going well – and his late cutting of the fast bowlers was a delight. Everton Weekes was probably the most complete batsman of the illustrious trio – remarkably quick on his feet, with a vast array of shots on either side of the wicket. His partnership of 283 with Worrell at Trent Bridge was an outstanding example of textbook batting; they scored at 80 an hour with seemingly no exertion. Weekes's brilliant footwork and his audacious strokeplay meant he was the best of that West Indian generation on a bad wicket: his 90 in 1957 at Lord's, with a broken finger, lingers in the memory. While Worrell batted with sublime elegance, and Weekes rattled along with darting efficiency, Clyde Walcott bludg-

Left: August 1950 – and Sonny Ramadhin waits to phone home with news of a tour that made him an overnight sensation
Below: Weekes and Worrell take the field at Fenner's in May, 1950. No wonder they looked happy – Weekes made 304 not out and Worrell 160

eoned the bowlers with awesome power. At 6 feet 2 inches and weighing about 15 stone, Walcott had a massive physical presence and this was epitomized by his batting. His high, looping backlift may have offended the purist but England bowlers of the fifties still wince at the memory of his powerful driving. Off either foot he would bombard the off-side cordon and his square cut was savagely effective. He murdered slow bowlers with evident pleasure, and for a big man his footwork was surprisingly nimble. As a result, he was usually in position for the hook shot against fast bowlers.

Worrell, Weekes and Walcott were marvellously effective as a unit, and they also typified the way all West Indians want to bat – at speed, with the bowler a subsidiary part of the tactical equation. This tremendous trio of batsmen continued to adorn Test cricket for a decade. At one stage, Walcott made twelve centuries in twelve successive Tests, while Weekes scored four hundreds (and a 90) in one series against India. Their Test averages vary between 49 and 58, and they share 39 Test hundreds. When their playing days ended, their contributions to the good of the game were rewarded with two OBEs and a knighthood.

The knighthood came to Frank Worrell, a man of exemplary principles, quiet diplomacy and great distinction. Frank Worrell was much more than a great cricketer: by his outstanding personal qualities, he raised the status of the black West Indian in the same way as Jack Hobbs did for the English professional. When Worrell came into Test cricket in the late forties, the convention decreed that the West Indies would be captained by a white man. It was felt that the deep divisions in Caribbean cricket could be papered over more easily by someone used to a more sophisticated lifestyle than the average black West Indian. With Jamaica fifteen hundred miles from Barbados, the difficulties in unifying the disparate islands into a corporate force were many and varied: parochialism was rife in selections and local supporters were unrelentingly biased in favour of their familiar heroes. Worrell's background fitted him for the unifying task. He had an admirably broad perspective on life, having played in the Lancashire League and studied sociology at Manchester University. Yet he was thirty-six before being entrusted with the captaincy of his country; the social divisions still ran deep in the Caribbean. Worrell became the first black man to captain the West Indies on a tour when he took the side to Australia in 1960/1, and the impact he made was astonishing. His calm, subtle captaincy fused the exciting yet unreliable talents of

the side and the rapport he established with his rival, Richie Benaud helped create one of the greatest ever Test series. The immortal Tied Test at Brisbane owed much to Worrell's attacking inclinations and although he lost the series by 2/1, he had helped revitalize interest in the game in Australia. When Worrell's team left for home, more than half a million thronged the streets of Melbourne to say farewell – a significant gesture from a country that had never been the spiritual home of the black man.

Two years later, Worrell captivated England in similar circumstances. The inter-island prejudices were submerged into a genuine team effort as Barbadian encouraged Jamaican. The fast bowling of Hall, Griffith and Sobers, the spin of Gibbs, the batting of Kanhai, Hunte and Sobers – all these contributed handsomely to the 3/1 victory, but the key was the tactical sophistication and calm authority of Frank Worrell. At the end of that 1963 tour, as Worrell retired from Test cricket, he could reflect that he had helped give the black man a measure of self-respect as he came to terms with life in England. Worrell simply wanted the black man to have the right to claim equality – a concept he stressed with his usual dignity after being elected to the senate in Jamaica and then the post of Warden of the University College of the West Indies. He seemed set for a distinguished career in world affairs until his tragic death from leukaemia at the age of forty-three. A memorial service was held at Westminster Abbey to honour a fundamentally good man; such an honour to a black cricketer would have been unthinkable just a few years earlier, a measure of the influence of Frank Worrell.

Worrell's achievements on and off the cricket field were followed with delight by two men who had performed wonders for West Indies cricket in previous eras. Learie Constantine and George Headley both lived to see the West Indies dominate the Test scene after their personal and cricketing qualities had sustained the black man since the 1920s. Headley must rank as one of the greatest of batsmen, because of the massive responsibility he shouldered. He played in the first Test to be staged in the Caribbean, in 1929, and until 1948 he was the backbone of the side's batting. His bowlers never had enough runs to bowl at during that period, but that was rarely the fault of

George Headley. After an impressive first tour of Australia, he was dubbed 'the black Bradman', although his supporters felt that the Australian was really 'the white Headley'. Like Bradman, he never failed in a Test series and his average of 60.83 is only surpassed by Graeme Pollock and, of course, Don Bradman. He scored a hundred every four innings against England and Australia, when the odds were always stacked against the fledgling West Indians and there were no cheap runs to be had. A proud man, he wrote 'African' on his immigration form before the 1930 tour of Australia and was appalled when a team-mate wrote 'European' on his form. Fittingly, Headley was the first black man to captain his country in the West Indies and his stature remains undiminished.

Learie Constantine's character was as impressive as his charismatic cricketing ability. The grandson of a slave ended his life as Lord Constantine, Baron of Maraval and Nelson, and his career was an object lesson in self-improvement. As a cricketer, he batted, bowled and fielded in the archetypal West Indian way: volatile hitting, cyclonic fast bowling and dazzling virtuosity in the field. A statistical assessment of Constantine's career is unrewarding. He was an inconsistent batsman, with an uncontrollable and occasionally fatal zest for sixes. He was an

erratic fast bowler, capable of high speed but often expensive. For all that, Constantine was one of the most magnetic, compelling cricketers of his time, an automatic choice for a place in any All-Time Entertainers eleven. He was the greatest all-round fielder in the 1930s – in the Hammond class at slip and as athletic and sharp as Bradman away from the bat. Constantine was the first to impart the unique Caribbean flavour to English cricket and he had Keith Miller's flair for getting English supporters on his side.

Like Frank Worrell, Constantine's worth to the West Indies extended beyond the narrow parameters of cricketing expertise. He worked very hard to better himself intellectually and socially. During the Second World War, he devoted himself to welfare work for coloured people in England and in 1944 he went to court on a matter of principle

Right: the bludgeoning power of Clyde Walcott, by common consent one of the most powerful strikers of the ball in the postwar game

Inset: Everton Weekes, the most complete batsman of the famous triumvirate

Bottom right: Learie Constantine batting against Middlesex in 1939. An erratic batsman, but a remarkable striker of the ball when his luck was in

Below: Frank Worrell displays his lordly offside play at Cambridge in 1950

Learie Constantine in London on the 1939 West Indies tour. His team-mate K. H. Weekes stands behind. Constantine did much for the West Indian cause, both by his spectacular cricketing ability and a mature intelligence that led to a shoal of honours and towering political achievements

and won the case. A London hotel had refused to give him a room, even though one was available. After the war, he studied law and was called to the Bar. He became Trinidad's Minister of Works and Transport, then High Commissioner of Trinidad and Tobago in England. In the last years of his multifarious life, the honours came thick and fast – rector of St Andrews University, a knighthood and significantly, membership of the Race Relations Board. When he died in 1971, the principle of racial equality was established in English law. Tragically neither Constantine or Worrell lived to see whether their struggle to raise the black man's status proved to be a transient success or a solid social evolution.

As for Ramadhin and Valentine, they were never again as fabulously successful as in 1950, although they harvested 297 Test wickets over the next decade. Valentine was eventually plagued by illness and injury and in his last tour to England in 1963, he was kept out of the Test side by a certain Garfield Sobers. Ramadhin's story is altogether more poignant. He continued to be an effective performer until the Edgbaston Test of 1957. In the first innings he took seven for 49, and to the English batsmen it looked as if the horrors of seven years earlier were about to be visited on their hapless shoulders again. Peter May and Colin Cowdrey took the significant decision to play Ramadhin purely as an off-spinner, to forget all about the possibility of the ball turning away from the right-hander. The result was a partnership of 411 by May and Cowdrey and Ramadhin was broken: two for 179 off 98 overs. No one has ever bowled as many balls in a Test (774 of them), and it was hard not to feel some sympathy for Ramadhin during that epic stand. Cowdrey used his pads to intercept the ball just outside his off-stump, without playing a shot, and this frustrated Ramadhin. He must have appealed at least fifty times for lbw, but under the existing law the verdict had to be 'not out'. May and Cowdrey, the finest English batsmen of their generation, set out to obliterate a fascinating, dangerous bowler and they succeeded resoundingly. Ramadhin played in ten more Tests after Edgbaston, but he was never the force of that first innings. At the age of thirty, when the slow bowler is not yet in his prime, he was finished in Test cricket. With the honourable exceptions of Lance Gibbs and Gary Sobers, that has been the case for all West Indian spinners in the last quarter of a century.

Fred Trueman, Brian Statham & Frank Tyson

Fred Trueman, Brian Statham and Frank Tyson restored virility to England's proud tradition of fast bowling. For a decade, from 1952 onwards, they ensured that England could always retaliate in a pace barrage; no longer would Hutton, Compton and the others take all the flak without the consolation of knowing they also had bowlers who could repay the intimidation. Time after time the fast bowlers rescued England after batting disasters and Trueman, Statham and Tyson were unquestionably the finest of their type, since Harold Larwood dominated the Bodyline series.

They were all born within eight months and 60 miles of each other, a remarkable concentration of fast bowling talent. Only the '3 Ws' can rival such a coincidence – they were born within seventeen months of each other in Barbados. There was little else in common between Trueman, Statham and Tyson apart from their ability to bowl quicker than anyone else. Statham was amazingly accurate for his pace: loyal, undemonstrative and tireless, he was one of the most popular cricketers of his time. Tyson was simply breathtakingly fast for a couple of years; a cool, detached person, he took a university degree and aimed no higher than a few years of making batsmen duck and dive. Fred Trueman, suffering more from the nervous stresses of cricket than the others, was the most complete English fast bowler of this century: hostile, resourceful, astonishingly strong, he had the rare ability to swing the ball at speed. No other fast bowler lasted at the top as long as Fred Trueman, and subsequently only Bob Willis and Dennis Lillee have surpassed his span in Test cricket. Even then, Lillee and my co-author suffered many more injuries than Trueman.

The young Fred Trueman. On his first team debut in 1949 Trueman was described by *Wisden* as a spin bowler!

For various reasons – form, injury, the whim of selectors – Trueman, Statham and Tyson only played in one Test together (at Adelaide in 1959), and Trueman and Tyson took the field as England bowlers just four times (again in 1959). In the early fifties, Trueman was the sole striking force, then it became Tyson and Statham, and finally, for a glorious five years, Trueman and Statham carried the flag of English fast bowling. As a result, England could never be ruled out of contention in any Test series: the West Indies had better batsmen, while Australia possessed players of equal talent to England, but the edge provided by the English fast bowlers was often decisive. When supplemented by the quality of English spinners, it was often an irresistible bowling line-up.

Brian Statham was the first to make his mark in the Test arena, when he was flown out to join Freddie Brown's side in Australia and New Zealand in 1951. He was just twenty, raw and short of stamina but England was desperate for someone who could at least approach the pace of Lindwall and Miller at that time. While Statham developed pace and strength, a young bull from Yorkshire was battering at the Test selectors' door. At the age of nineteen, Fred Trueman had been picked for a Test trial, with just sixty-odd first-class wickets to his credit. Word had filtered down from Yorkshire that they had someone genuinely fast; some experts thought he was too wild, others believed him to be an ephemeral presence, but he was undeniably quick. By 1952, the press – and as a result, the public – were ready for 'a new Larwood'. It did not matter who fitted the bill, but it was time that the slow postwar recovery yielded someone who could hand back some of the rough treatment suffered by England's batsmen. The dark-haired Yorkshireman with the ideal physique fascinated the public. At the age of twenty-one, he was ideally built for a fast bowler – 5 feet 10 inches tall, massive chest, immensely strong legs – and his flair for the dramatic, his beautiful bowling action and his willingness to

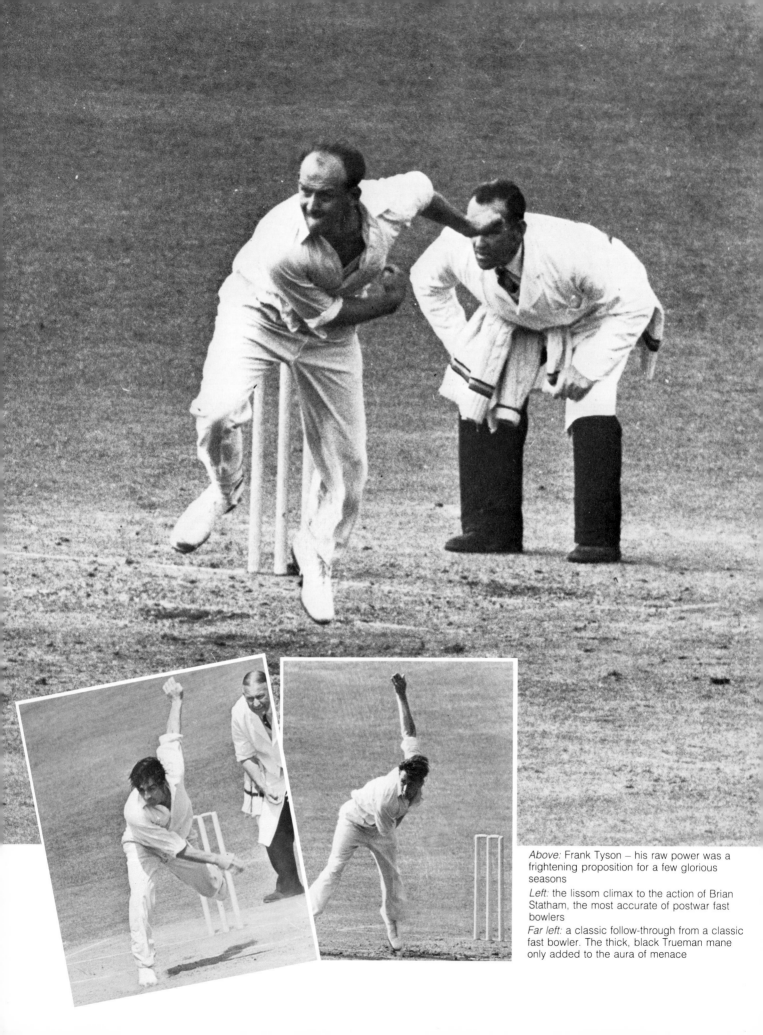

Above: Frank Tyson – his raw power was a frightening proposition for a few glorious seasons

Left: the lissom climax to the action of Brian Statham, the most accurate of postwar fast bowlers

Far left: a classic follow-through from a classic fast bowler. The thick, black Trueman mane only added to the aura of menace

intimidate batsmen were all the answer to Fleet Street's prayers. He was thrown at the Indian tourists and they had no stomach for the fight. Trueman took twenty-nine wickets in the series and, along with Alec Bedser, reduced them to nought for four wickets at Leeds. At last England had a fast bowler! It was a stirring sight to see this truculent specimen tear in at timorous Test batsmen, with three slips, three gullies, a silly point and two short legs there for the kill. Surely the scene was set for an Ashes triumph the following year, with the Australians at last getting their just desserts from a genuine fast bowler?

The Australians did lose the Ashes, but a balanced attack, rather than a fast bowling blitzkrieg, was responsible. Trueman only played in the final Test because Len Hutton wanted accuracy from all his bowlers. At that stage, Trueman was undeniably fast and dangerous, but erratic. Hutton had sagely remarked in 1952 that Trueman would not be at his peak for another five years, and, much to the young tearaway's frustration, he entered a limbo period. The tour to the West Indies was deeply disappointing for Trueman: his relationship with Hutton was strained and a host of apocryphal stories began to circulate about Trueman's alleged unsocial behaviour. No doubt he contributed in part to the image of the brash, blunt-speaking Yorkshireman, but he could not have perpetrated every social peccadillo attributed to him. Trueman was the only player whose good conduct bonus was withheld and he was refused an explanation. That tour damaged his Test career: he never played in any of the remaining eleven Tests under Hutton's captaincy and when Peter May took over in 1955, Trueman missed twelve of the next fifteen Tests.

Over the next couple of years, Trueman had to depart centre stage while Tyson and Statham forged a spectacular partnership. By now Statham had become a model fast bowler. His beautifully smooth action enabled him to move the ball both ways off the seam. He was impressively fit for such a lean man and his remorseless accuracy was summed up when he said, 'If they miss, I hit.' He was a wonderful foil for Tyson or Trueman because he would uncomplainingly bowl uphill or into the wind and drive the batsmen to distraction with accurate bowling at high pace. At the other end, the faster bowler could afford to slip himself, knowing that the overall run rate would never become too disturbing.

Tyson and Statham won the 1954/5 series in Australia by the devastating combination of nagging accuracy and overwhelming speed – and yet it could easily have ended in disaster. The selectors were criticized for ignoring Trueman in favour of Tyson and for taking Peter Loader on tour. One can only assume that Hutton did not vote for his county colleague's inclusion. Along with other sound judges, he knew the likely impact of Tyson's high pace on fast Australian pitches. When he first played for Northants in 1952, Tyson's first ball forced the slips to move back another 5 yards. His run-up started 70 yards from the wicket-keeper. The press quickly dubbed him 'Typhoon Tyson' and for a time the sight of Tyson evoked gasps from spectators who were seeing him for the first time. Fred Trueman may have believed he was faster than Tyson, but from 1954 to 1956 this was not the case. Tom Graveney stood at slip to both bowlers and says, 'I cannot believe any bowler could be faster than Tyson at that time,' and he swears that Godfrey Evans stood back 50 yards to take him when his tail was up on that Australian tour. Jock Livingstone, a Northants team-mate of Tyson's, and a fine batsman for New South Wales, is certain: 'When really firing, Tyson was the quickest of all over a period of three or four overs.' This from the man who saw Larwood bowl on the Bodyline tour and experienced the splendid fast bowling of Lindwall and Miller at first-hand in Sheffield Shield cricket.

Tyson simply bowled as fast as he could. He was intelligent enough to know that he was putting excessive strain on his powerful frame by his long final stride, that his action was not particularly fluent and that bowling on the unresponsive, slow wickets at Northampton would truncate his career. He had his one marvellous period in the sun on that Australian tour and Hutton's sympathetic captaincy must take full credit. He and Tyson made a nightmare start to the series. Hutton, the first England captain to insert the Australians in that country for more than forty years, saw England drop twelve catches and lose by an innings. Tyson, labouring under an immensely long run-up, took one for 160. He then took the crucial decision to shorten his 38 yard run-up by 10 yards, reducing it to eighteen running strides. It made an immediate difference and everything clicked into place. At Sydney, Ray Lindwall made the great mistake of hitting Tyson on the head with a bouncer. Suitably stung, massively determined to

avenge Brisbane, he swept aside the Australians, and he took ten wickets in the match to bring England victory by 38 runs. At Melbourne, Tyson was even faster: he took seven for 27 as England won by 128 runs. On a pitch of uneven bounce, Statham probed away with his usual intelligence while Tyson simply swept the batting away. Suddenly a star was born, as is often the case with a fast bowler. Tyson ended the series with twenty-eight wickets, Statham with eighteen and the Australians at last had a taste of their 1940s medicine.

Although Tyson continued to frighten Test batsmen after that tour, he was never quite as consistently fast again. He played in only two Tests against South Africa in 1955 – taking an impressive fourteen wickets and showing the Trent Bridge crowd what he must have been like at Melbourne – but he was beginning to be dogged by a sore left heel and other assorted strains. By this time, Statham was the established, admirable foil to anyone else at the other end, but Trueman could not regain his England place. He managed one Test against South Africa and two against Australia the following summer – but only because Tyson or Statham was injured. At the Leeds Test in 1956, G. O. Allen, the chairman of selectors, took out Trueman to the nets, placed a handkerchief on a good length and asked him to hit it. Trueman, aware that a large crowd was observing his discomfiture, did not take kindly to the incident, and when he was not picked for the tour to South Africa later that year, he was even less impressed. The selectors chose the pace of Tyson, Loader and Statham with the invaluable fast-medium support of Trevor Bailey. The MCC secretary, Ronnie Aird, took the unusual step of stating that there was no discrimination against Trueman, that the selections had been made on current merit.

Trueman at last showed his true colours in the 1957 season and forced England to pick him regularly. He reduced his run-up to eighteen paces, managed to lose the distressing side-strain that had dogged him for three seasons and bowled consistently well. With Tyson in decline, he seized the chance and played in all five Tests against the West Indies that summer. In the process he established a rapport with Brian Statham that was a source of enduring happiness to both men, on and off the field. Their first success as a partnership came in the Trent Bridge Test: in sweltering humidity, with Bailey unable to bowl, the pair sent down 135 overs in the match, and took fifteen wickets. This against the '3 Ws', Rohan Kanhai, Garfield Sobers and the precociously brilliant 'Collie' Smith. It was not the fault of Trueman and Statham that the game was drawn on a Trent Bridge featherbed.

By 1959, Fred Trueman was a happier individual. Frank Tyson's recurring injuries meant Trueman was now the fastest bowler in the world. His partnership with Brian Statham was good for both men – batsmen were never settled against Statham's reliability and Trueman's flair – and he at last had a satisfactory understanding with his Yorkshire captain. Ronnie Burnet cajoled Trueman with a mixture of flattery, cunning and genuine respect and Trueman responded by bowling with wonderful consistency. In four of the next five seasons, the championship was won by Yorkshire and Trueman began to revel in the public acclaim. He even acceded to a position of responsibility when he was appointed senior professional on the England tour to the West Indies in 1959/60. It did not matter that the job fell to him only because Brian Statham had to fly home because his son was ill: the poacher had turned gamekeeper, if only for a brief period. Trueman and Statham picked up thirty-one wickets in that series (won against all the odds) and they shared fifty-two South African wickets the following summer. They were a marvellous pair, with the experience to capitalize on a green pitch and the stamina to cope with long spells on placid pitches under a blazing sun. Trueman lost nineteen pounds in weight on the West Indies tour, and he bowled more than a thousand overs each season from 1959 to 1963. This from the man who was supposed to be England's shock, rather than stock bowler.

As they entered their early thirties – supposedly the final curtain for fast bowlers – Trueman and Statham showed few signs of eclipse. After a bad match at Old Trafford, Statham was dropped against the West Indies in 1963, but he came back in 1965 to show the old reliability, taking seven wickets against South Africa in his last Test. By now, he was the captain of Lancashire, a richly deserved honour. He had captained the Players against the Gentlemen in 1960 and when Ken Grieves resigned the Lancashire captaincy in 1964, it seemed that Statham was the obvious successor. The Lancashire committee revealed a characteristic insensitivity by advertising for a captain. After a poor response, they gave the job rather grudgingly to Statham. Typically Statham said it would be an

honour, that he wanted to repay the generosity of Lancashire's supporters after a successful benefit three years earlier: not the prevailing attitude of the modern county beneficiary, who often retires within a year of a benefit. For the next three years, Statham's shrewd yet genial captaincy was instrumental in restoring Lancashire cricket to a position of strength after the horrors of the early sixties. When he retired in 1968, Statham

made the grand exit – six for 34 to bowl out Yorkshire in the Bank Holiday Roses Match. He could always be relied upon to do the right thing on and off the pitch.

Fred Trueman also retired from first-class cricket that season. It was hard to accept that the engine could no longer coax top speed out of the vehicle, but it had been a stimulating journey over twenty years. In the early sixties, he still turned in some marvellous performances

for England. At Leeds in 1961, he switched to off-cutters on a dusty pitch and bowled out Australia with five for 0 in 27 balls. In 1963, he reacted to the speed of Hall and Griffith with characteristic panache, taking thirty-four West Indian wickets in the series. Throughout his career, he had always been in conflict with someone, often other fast bowlers: only Brian Statham among rivals ever aspired to friendship. It was the same with the West Indian fast bowlers in 1963 – when Trueman read that Hall was now the world's fastest, he summoned up the necessary willpower to dominate the series. He was equally single-minded a year later, as he chased the total of 300 Test wickets. Trueman knew that his England days were almost over – not even his marvellous constitution could keep him at the highest level forever – and his self-respect and fierce pride in performance drove him onwards. After being dropped for the Old Trafford Test, he came back at

Left: One of Trueman's 307 Test wickets – Neil Harvey caught behind at Lord's in 1961

Below: A sight many batsmen would have loved to witness in the mid 1950s . . . the fearsome Frank Tyson asleep during a charity match

Trueman approached fast bowling and yarn-spinning with the same irrepressible gusto

the Oval and advanced on the magic 300 figure with his usual high-profile aplomb. The wickets of Ian Redpath and Graham McKenzie in successive balls gave him 299 wickets; it also coincided with the lunch interval, so Trueman and his many supporters had to wait forty minutes to see if he could create the record with a hat-trick. He failed, but eventually Neil Hawke snicked an outswinger to slip and Trueman revelled in the full-throated emotion of the moment.

The tension associated with that spell of bowling was a microcosm of Trueman's career. While Statham went about his job with admirable professionalism and philosophical detachment about umpiring and fielding fallibilities, Trueman was cricket's moth to the flame of notoriety. It was typical that on the eve of his triumphant 1963 series against the West Indies he should lose £50 of his good conduct bonus from the winter tour of Australia. It was equally typical that he announced he would no longer play for England, secure in the knowledge that he was needed, that a compromise would be cobbled together. He was – and remains – larger than life, a character about whom masses of untrue allegations have been made. Yet he never denied that he loved being called 'Fiery Fred'; he was born to be a fast bowler. Even at birth he weighed a massive 14 lb 1 oz. He relished the essentially dramatic contest between batsman and fast bowler, the mental intimidation he could exert over a player he knew instinctively did not relish the fray. As a fast bowler, he was in the

Lindwall class for craftsmanship – indeed his action was purer than Lindwall's. Like the great Australian, he had the control of a fast-medium bowler, but bowled at the speed of a fast bowler. Only Lindwall could rival Trueman's yorker and when conditions demanded it, Trueman used the seam brilliantly, controlling his natural outswing. He had the body action to dig the ball in and get bounce on unresponsive wickets. His memory for batsmen's frailties was razor-sharp; he knew what to bowl at which player. No one of Trueman's pace has taken more wickets and his strike rate of over $4\frac{1}{2}$ wickets per Test is tremendous. An average of 18 for each first-class wicket is also impressive when one considers that he invariably bowled with an attacking field and that a snick usually meant a wicket or four runs.

England played 118 Tests from the start of Fred Trueman's England career to its close – yet he played in only 67 of them, despite a phenomenal record of physical fitness. He missed two Australian tours, two trips to South Africa and declined two Indian tours. He was also dropped several times during a home series. A number of factors combined to rob Trueman of around thirty Test appearances and no doubt he did not help his own cause on occasions. His enemies in high places were too influential to allow him full rein to his self-expression. Everything in Trueman's complex nature was subordinated to the desire to be acknowledged as the greatest fast bowler who ever drew breath: even his detractors must admit that Fred made a great job of that.

Peter May & Colin Cowdrey

Peter May and Colin Cowdrey carried England's batting on their shoulders together for the best part of a decade. In the process they proved that the amateur batsman of the 1950s was as unrelenting a competitor as his professional counterpart. May and Cowdrey had enjoyed the classic public school and Oxbridge background, but the resolution of May, and Cowdrey's adaptability over a long career, placed them on a totally different plane to glamorous predecessors like Percy Chapman or Archie MacLaren. The weakness of England's batting in the fifties meant that May and Cowdrey could never really relax in Tests and give free rein to their glittering talents.

May first played for England in 1951 (appropriately enough, scoring a century on his debut) and Cowdrey made his debut three years later. For the next seven years – until May's premature retirement – they were head and shoulders above their colleagues in the batting order. Now and again an opener like Peter Richardson or Geoff Pullar would impress for a season or two; Tom Graveney, Mike Smith, Ken Barrington and Ted Dexter would all occasionally achieve great things, but invariably everything depended on May and Cowdrey. Somehow enough runs had to be chiselled out to encourage England's splendidly varied bowling attack – with Hutton, Edrich, Compton and Simpson all ageing, the major responsibility settled early on the two young amateurs.

They did not lack the necessary gifts. At Charterhouse, Peter May was the wonder of his age under the coaching of George Geary, the former England all-rounder. May shone at Cambridge amid an array of batting talent and although his early experiences with the Australians were

Cowdrey experiences the painful nature of modern Test cricket as he struggles to come to terms with Lillee and Thomson on a fast wicket at Perth in December, 1974

unnerving, he soon showed his character and class. Although a gentle and self-effacing man, May had that strain of ruthlessness which is vital to survive in the highest class. He learned a great deal about mental resolve from his county captain, Stuart Surridge and his England skipper Len Hutton, and soon he was playing with uncommon maturity for one so young. The same quality was there in the ample frame of Colin Cowdrey. He was born for cricket (the initials 'MCC'

came from his cricket-mad father) and at the age of thirteen, he became the youngest player ever to appear in a Public Schools match at Lord's. He was just twenty when he scored two fifties for the Gentlemen against Miller and Lindwall on a fiery Lord's wicket in 1953: some perceptive England selectors recalled those two innings a year later when they picked the tour party for Australia under Len Hutton. Cowdrey's inclusion was a big surprise: he had just finished his third year at Oxford and could easily shrivel in the pressure cooker atmosphere of a Test in Australia. Yet the selectors opted for class and Cowdrey did not let them down.

He was lucky to have Hutton as his mentor; Cowdrey had always greatly admired him and, like Hutton, he preferred to rely on touch and timing, rather than power of stroke. Hutton had promised Cowdrey's father that he would look after the boy on tour and when Cowdrey Senior died a few weeks later, it was the captain who comforted his young protégé. Throughout the tour, he encouraged and guided Cowdrey, and his sensitive support was handsomely rewarded on the field of play. In the second Test at Sydney, Cowdrey and May added a crucial 112 – with May taking five hours to reach his hundred – and that partnership gave Tyson and Statham something to bowl at. In the next Test, Cowdrey made 102 out of 191 all out; only three others reached double figures and he made his runs out of 158 while at the crease. Bill O'Reilly, not the most impressionable of former players, called it the greatest innings he had seen in a Test and certainly his driving, concentration and command were all faultless. He was just twenty-two, the youngest to make a hundred for England against Australia since 1912. After that innings, Colin Cowdrey was always judged by the yardstick of that Melbourne hundred – in one way an overwhelming burden but at the same time a tribute to his wonderful natural ability.

In a low-scoring series, May and Cowdrey proved the outstanding batting successes for England. They each made a century and two fifties and looked certain to dominate England's batting for as long as they wished. With Hutton, Edrich and Simpson on their last tour – and Compton struggling with knee trouble – the arrival of May and Cowdrey was indeed propitious. Then, at the age of twenty-six, May took on further responsibility when he was chosen to take over the captaincy of England after the retirement of Len Hutton. He had learned quickly and if he needed any further advice it was readily available from the new chairman of selectors, G. O. Allen, a man steeped in cricketing wisdom. That partnership between chairman and young captain was to last from 1956 to 1961, the longest of its type and one of the most successful. May was to captain England forty-one times over the next six years, and, apart from a bad tour to Australia, these were heady days for England.

In 1956, everything seemed to go right, apart from Keith Miller's great feat at Lord's. Cowdrey was pressed reluctantly into service as opener and he performed splendidly. England gambled on three batting selections – Cyril Washbrook (aged forty-one at the time), the Rev. David Sheppard (on holiday from his London curacy with just two recent innings behind him) and Denis Compton (short of match practice after a knee-cap had been removed). Washbrook made 98 at Leeds, Sheppard 113 at Old Trafford and Compton 94 at the Oval. No one could ever remember three hunches paying off so spectacularly, even if they summed up the poverty of contemporary English batting, with the exception of May and Cowdrey. In that series, May won the toss when it was most needed and watched Tony Lock and Jim Laker dominate on spinners' wickets. Laker took forty-six wickets in the series, including the remarkable figures of nineteen for 90 at Old Trafford, as most of the Australians proved hopelessly inadequate against the turning ball. Laker's feat – on a damp pitch with the sun shining on the final afternoon – was amazing, but equally astonishing was the bowling of Lock. He tried his heart out, yet finished with figures of nought for 69 off 55 overs.

Although England now possessed the

Top: Three of the best postwar amateur players gather outside church in September, 1956. Peter May (*right*) was best man for Colin Cowdrey and the Rev David Sheppard officiated in the wedding service. All three captained England

In 1954, Cowdrey looked almost as young as the boys clamouring for his autograph as he left Tilbury with the England side under Len Hutton

best bowling line-up in world cricket, the batting remained weak. When May and Cowdrey struggled, so did the rest of the team. The 1956/7 tour to South Africa was a case in point. On such excellent wickets, England should have scored comfortable runs. Yet May averaged just fifteen in the series, while Cowdrey allowed himself to get mystifyingly bogged down. He did score one century in the series, but only rarely hinted at effortless mastery against the brilliant off-spin of Hugh Tayfield. The captain, who played superbly in the State matches, was dismissed by some wonderful catches, some high-class bowling and an inordinate amount of ill-fortune, but his failure affected the team's morale. They allowed a 2/0 lead to slip and finished drawing the series. Trevor Bailey was forced to open the batting throughout the series and with England averaging just 32 runs an hour, it was clear that confidence was hardly soaring. No wonder we rarely saw a spectacular innings from May and Cowdrey in Tests; far too much depended on them.

If ever they needed to bat at their very best, it was at Edgbaston in 1957 against the West Indies. In the second innings, they forged one of the most significant partnerships in Test history. It was not just the runs involved – 411 in 511 minutes, a record for all Tests – but the impact on a great spin bowler. Sonny Ramadhin was never the same again, as May stroked him away with calm certainty and Cowdrey used his pads to frustrate him. Cowdrey kept encouraging May to hang on after the captain had reached his century and finally the little West Indian was obliterated. May scored 285 not out, Cowdrey 154. In the next Test, Cowdrey scored 152 in attractive style; the hours spent lining up Ramadhin had stood him in good stead. May averaged 97 for the series, Cowdrey 72, and England won 3/0, with Ramadhin's wickets costing 39 apiece. Cowdrey's critics point out that his innings at Edgbaston gave respectability to less talented players who used their pads to thwart the bowler. For his part Cowdrey maintains that under the existing lbw law, he could not be out by intercepting the ball just outside the off-stump, and that he saw no reason why he should make things easier for Ramadhin by attempting to play the ball with his bat. It was typical of Cowdrey that he should work out the theory so punctiliously, but there is no doubt that the overall quality of batting suffered in England after that historic Edgbaston partnership. In the same year, G. O. Allen, the chairman of selectors, had

Jim Laker saunters off the Old Trafford pitch in 1956 after returning the amazing analysis of 19 for 90. Laker's unflappability served him well in his bowling and broadcasting, and the absence of crowd histrionics at Old Trafford that day is a graphic reminder of how spectator behaviour has declined

delivered this withering broadside: 'I believe that batting is at its lowest standard of all time. Batsmen have the ability but lack the will to attack. That makes it difficult to assess the bowling.' It also underlines the responsibility felt by May and Cowdrey.

Even they could not inspire England in the next Ashes, which was disastrously lost in Australia. That England squad which left for Australia in autumn 1958 was complacently judged to be one of the strongest ever to leave these shores, on a par with the 1911/12 party, or even Percy Chapman's talented assembly in 1928/9.

Alas for fond hopes. Under the dynamic captaincy of Richie Benaud, Australia won 4/0. It has to be admitted that the bowling of Benaud, Alan Davidson and Ray Lindwall, plus the batting of Colin McDonald, Norman O'Neill and Neil Harvey, backed up by superior fielding, would have probably been decisive in any event – but the England party soon found itself embroiled in controversy. Some of the new Australian bowlers had highly suspect actions: Ian Meckiff, who headed the Test averages was subsequently 'called' for throwing, and Gordon Rorke's action was disturbingly jerky. He also dragged his back-foot so much that he usually delivered the ball from about eighteen yards! Umpiring weakness disturbed, then rattled, the English batsmen, so that a defeatist malaise settled on the team far too early. May was criticized by some newspapers for allowing his fiancee to fly out to join him and soon some sections of the press were having a field day. There were lurid stories of heavy drinking, anti-social behaviour and a lack of professional pride – the usual allegations when a much-vaunted cricket team gets thrashed abroad. The England players of the 1980s who smart at personal criticism would do well to remember that there is nothing new under the tabloid sun. Their chairman of selectors had suffered the same fate a quarter of a century earlier!

A year later, the cricket 'cognoscenti' seemed to have learned its lesson. The England team flew out to the West Indies with muted hopes. No one seemed to give them a chance. It was the new England – for various reasons there was no Laker, Evans, Lock, Graveney, Tyson, Bailey, Watson and Richardson. The West Indies still had the batting talents of Worrell and Walcott, plus newcomers of the calibre of Sobers, Kanhai, Hunte and Butcher, with Hall emerging as a great fast bowler. Only one touring side had ever won a series out there – Australia in 1954/5 – and England had only drawn two series. So much depended on the four experienced players – May, Cowdrey, Trueman and Statham. In the event, England won the series 1/0 in the unlikeliest of circumstances. Mike Smith, Ted Dexter, Ken Barrington, Raman Subba Row and Jim Parks all made Test centuries and Trueman bowled magnificently, with great support from Statham till he had to fly home. Cowdrey was a revelation: again he was persuaded to open the innings and again he played a series of wonderful innings, when his innate sense of timing picked off the fast bowlers. He also took over the captaincy for the last two Tests as the health of May broke; he had suffered internal problems for several months and the strains of captaincy were beginning to tell. The press regaled us with pictures of the new Mrs May relaxing by the poolside and made unfavourable references to the captain's poor batting performances in the series. The fact that May needed two operations and eighteen months away from first-class cricket is adequate evidence that the press campaign was monstrously unfair. Yet that West Indies tour had left its physical and psychological mark on May. Sadly, he was to play just two more full seasons.

Cowdrey took over the captaincy and despite his misgivings, played marvellously as an opener against the West Indies fast bowlers and the menace of South Africa's Neil Adcock later that year. He loved a technical challenge – against Hall and Watson, he opted for a short backlift, little movement of the feet and an obdurate refusal to get out. When the ball lost its shine and hardness, Cowdrey gradually unveiled his handsome array of shots. He worked it all out and, considering his aversion to opening, his performances in 1960 deserve the utmost credit.

Peter May did not return to the England side until the Lord's Test in 1961 against the Australians. He took over the captaincy at Leeds and then suffered a bad match at Old Trafford. It was a wonderful game of cricket, but of little consolation to Peter May, a captain who liked to win as much as anybody, despite his charming, civilized exterior. On the final day, England had two great chances to win. Firstly, David Allen spun out three Australians in the space of fifteen balls, leaving them just 154 ahead with one wicket left and the rest of the day stretching ahead. Alan Davidson, that splendid all-rounder, took a chance and plundered 20 off an over by Allen. May promptly took the off-spinner out of the attack, even though the ball was turning sharply, and May had made little effort to give Davidson a single and get the last man, McKenzie down to Allen's end.

A moment from one of the most famous partnerships in Test history – the stand of 411 by May and Cowdrey at Edgbaston in 1957. The bowler, Sonny Ramadhin, was finally mastered by astute use of the pads and May's clean strokeplay and he was never the same threat again

Against the seamers, they proceeded to add 98 precious runs. England thus needed 256 to win in 230 minutes and at one stage they were 150 for one, with Dexter playing superbly. Richie Benaud, gambling desperately, elected to bowl his leg-spin from round the wicket to pitch in the bowlers' rough, and it worked: he had Dexter caught behind for a wonderful 76. Then May was bowled second ball – playing an uncharacteristically loose sweep shot. The batting collapsed, with the lower order unsure whether to attack or defend. Australia won a famous victory by 54 runs and the demeanour of the rival captains at the end was graphic. May had let the Australians out of jail twice in a day, and he knew it.

That 1961 series was the last time Peter May graced Test cricket. Quite simply, he had had enough. Although only thirty-two, he had a family to support and a career in the City promised him security. He reasoned that he had won every honour in the game with the all-conquering Surrey team and an England side that was more often than not the best in the world during his halcyon years. His only regret was that he had not scored a hundred centuries (he finished on eighty-five), but he was never a man who coveted batting records for their own sake. By common consent, he remains England's best postwar batsman. If he was lucky in the range and talent of bowling at his disposal, he was not blessed with corresponding batting strength. If May had batted in the same side as Hobbs and Sutcliffe, or Fry and MacLaren, he would have dazzled – but when you have to open with an admirable all-rounder like Trevor Bailey, you have to cut your cloth accordingly. On that basis, Peter May's performances were even more impressive than his splendid record suggests.

While Peter May forged ahead in his business career, Colin Cowdrey still gloried in the game he loved so much. He liked nothing better than to experiment with a new grip, a fresh guard or try out some unconventional shots. His technique was so impeccable that he could answer the call from India in the winter of 1964, fly out to bolster a stricken England side and score two Test hundreds. In the Lord's Test of 1963, he walked out to bat against Wes Hall in appalling light with a plaster cast over his broken arm. It did not matter that he stood at the non-striker's end as David Allen held out for a draw: Cowdrey was ready to face Hall if necessary and he had been practising assiduously, ready to bat left-handed. The greatest tribute to his enduring skills came

one December morning in 1974, when he was asked to join the England team in Australia. For a young man, it would have been a stiff enough challenge to face Lillee and Thomson on unreliable wickets, with umpires unwilling to stamp down on blatant physical and verbal intimidation. To a man of forty-two years, it was an incredible request. Cowdrey would have been perfectly entitled to refuse, yet he answered the call. Unsurprisingly he worked out the best way to combat the fearsome fast bowlers and within five days of that phone call he was batting on the fast Perth wicket. In the second innings he even opened! He played two splendid defensive innings of 22 and 44, opting for survival because he could not get on to the front-foot to drive bowling that never seemed to offer a half-volley. Taking the circumstances into account, those two innings were among the most remarkable achievements of Colin Cowdrey's career. More than twenty years after receiving his county cap, he was still adapting, still coming to terms with the evolving modern game. Just a few months later, Cowdrey exacted full toll on those Australian bowlers, when he made 151 not out against them at Canterbury to give Kent victory by four wickets. For good measure, he was sharp enough to hook Lillee in front of square – the hallmark of the class player.

Cowdrey's career was often dogged by the vexed question of the England captaincy. In his time he lost it to Brian Close, Mike Smith, Ted Dexter and Ray Illingworth and his greatest disappointment was that he never once led an England tour to Australia. Some said he was too introverted to make a good captain, others thought him too kind and unwilling to make recalcitrant players toe the line. It must have been hard for a man so passionately involved in the game to lose the greatest honour to so many others. When necessary he certainly showed enough steel – look no further than the 1967/8 tour to the West Indies. Brian Close had lost the captaincy in controversial circumstances after alleged time-wasting at a county match at Edgbaston, and Cowdrey was given the job. He moulded the team into an efficient fighting unit, cajoled the moody John Snow into some wonderful bowling spells and when necessary, slowed down the game with all the bloody-mindedness of a Hutton. Cowdrey's strategy was to hold the middle ground against the excitable West Indians, until a chance presented itself. It came at Port of Spain, when Gary Sobers made a generous declaration, in

the hope of luring England to destruction. Cowdrey led the way with a gloriously controlled innings of 71 and the series was won. Sobers was thereafter pilloried for his declaration but perhaps he realized that England under Cowdrey would not buckle. Sobers was never the kind of captain who enjoyed a series containing five draws.

Perhaps Cowdrey would have achieved his greatest ambition if he had not snapped an Achilles' tendon early in the summer of 1969. He was the current England captain, and the post passed to Ray Illingworth, then in his first month as county captain at Leicestershire. Illingworth proved an immediate success, and took the side to Australia eighteen months later. His vice-captain was Colin Cowdrey, no doubt ruefully reflecting that the cup had been dashed from his lips yet again. Illingworth remained in charge until 1973, when – ironically – the job passed to Cowdrey's successor as Kent captain, Mike Denness.

The England captaincy apart, Colin Cowdrey can have few regrets about devoting his life to cricket. He says, 'The proudest thing in my career is that I kept surviving.' He always had enough enthusiasm to try to adapt to changing trends – even when Lillee and Thomson were making him duck at an age when carpet slippers and pipe seem infinitely preferable to batting in a Test match. He lasted for twenty-six years in the game – from the time when England's best bowlers were leg-spinners to the days of hectic limited overs cricket, where every run is vital, and he always kept abreast of the times. In another era, he would have been a classic number four for England, caressing the ball away after the openers had done the solid grafting. Sadly, this sublimely gifted batsman had to do far too much of the grafting when England's batting cupboard was depressingly empty.

May and Cowdrey. The names evoke a more romantic, chivalrous age – and that would be wrong. They came into Test cricket when it was becoming increasingly ruthless and cynical and they not only survived – they prospered. They both picked up many tips from the arch-pragmatist Len Hutton on their first Australian tour together and thereafter May and Cowdrey were never a soft touch, as Sonny Ramadhin will undoubtedly confirm. Yet they adorned cricket with charm and distinction while demonstrating that tough competitors do not need to scowl and strike theatrical poses to give of their best.

Gary Sobers

Garfield Sobers has the strongest claims to being the greatest all-round cricketer in history. For a twenty-year period, he was the complete player: dazzling batsman, deadly new ball bowler, orthodox slow left-arm spinner, unorthodox googly bowler, and a brilliant fielder in any position. Sobers could dominate any game with bat or ball; he was worth his place in a Test Match as a bowler pure and simple, or as a batsman. Towards the end of his career, he often hobbled on to the pitch, suffering from knee problems, but although many sympathized with his plight, the prevailing wisdom among the professionals was that even on one good leg he was better than the rest on two. Gary Sobers was that good. He was essentially an orthodox cricketer, a man of genius who had nevertheless mastered the basics very early. As a result, he could bat on any surface in the world and his bewildering bowling options allowed him to adopt whichever style was suited to the conditions. No cricketer has managed to combine effectiveness with style to such a high degree. Like Hammond, it was an aesthetic delight to watch Sobers stroll on to a cricket pitch – sleek, graceful with a distinctive loose-limbed walk which not even arthritic knees could ruin. His cricket was played with grace, charm and sportsmanship. Not only was he the best player, he was also the happiest in his golden years. Opponents were disarmed and spectators captivated by the effortless mastery of a genius.

Several great cricketers might dispute Sobers's claims to be the best all-rounder of all time, but detailed analysis brooks no argument. W. G. Grace was surely inferior as bowler and fielder, Sir Learie Constantine lacked consistency and Frank Woolley was probably a lesser

Sobers bowling at the Oval in 1973: even with chronic knee trouble, he still had a beautiful, flowing action

bowler, despite a harvest of wickets over a long career. Among Sobers's contemporaries, Keith Miller was as brilliant a bowler and fielder, but not as happy against pace bowling; Miller was not as safe off the back-foot, and he sometimes looked lost on English wickets, with the ball turning sharply. The Australian Alan Davidson was a wonderful new-ball bowler who shared Sobers's ability to dip the ball in late to the right-hander, and he was also a marvellous all-round fielder. Yet he was merely a good, hard-hitting batsman at the head of the tail, not from the front rank. Richie Benaud was not a good enough batsman. A generation later, Mike Procter's claims can be seriously evaluated, although he was never as fluent a mover in the field as Sobers, nor as comfortable against high pace. Ian Botham runs Sobers very close – yet he has never played as many consistent innings as Sobers, where the outcome of the game was influenced so regularly by one man. Botham's record against the West Indies also counts against him – Sobers averaged 60 against England and 43 against Australia. There is little to choose between them as fielders but the sheer variety of Sobers's bowling is relevant. Perhaps the nearest to Sobers as the complete all-rounder was Walter Hammond. Certainly the massive natural ability was there; good judges maintain that Hammond would have been a marvellous seam bowler if he had not concentrated on his batting.

Such comparisons are diverting and instructive but cannot obscure one salient fact: Garfield Sobers was immortal. Unlike many a cricketing genius, he did not dart across the firmament and disappear equally spectacularly – he was a Test player for twenty years and for at least ten of those years, he was indisputably the best player in the world. As Richie Benaud wrote: 'He gave more pleasure than any other man in the game.' Trevor Bailey, hardly a cricketer with Sobers's panache, was fulsome in his praise: 'There have been many great cricketers, but none has ever displayed such a vast range of talents before such a wide audience without ever losing his intense passion for the game.' Apart from an inevitable weariness caused by too much county cricket in the early 1970s, that sums him up perfectly.

As a batsman, he was reliable, graceful, punishing, with an impeccable technique. Frank Worrell had advised him to play in the Lancashire League to tighten up his technique and Sobers followed his beloved mentor as professional with Radcliffe. By the time he was twenty-four, everything about his batting was gloriously impressive; not only did he have the strokes, he now had the experience of English pitches. Sobers played very straight, unlike many flair players from the Caribbean. His backlift was straight and high and he had a full follow-through. A fine golfer, his strong wrists and powerful shoulders enabled him to drive the ball regularly over three hundred yards. His straight driving was in the same long category: like Ian Botham, he could mishit for 6 but invariably the shot was beautifully timed. He somehow combined murderous hitting with elegance – unlike Lloyd, Richards, Kanhai or Greenidge, he never seemed to club the ball away brutally. The Sobers's off-drive 'on the up' and that graceful cut behind point were hallmarks of his batting; he also played superbly off his legs with a natural sense of timing. Sir Learie Constantine once said, 'Sobers hits the ball as consistently hard as anyone I've ever seen' and it seems appropriate that he became the first man to hit six sixes in an over. At Swansea in 1968, Sobers ensured that the name of Malcolm Nash would always lodge in the pages of *Wisden* when he decided that Nash's experimental spinners would be plundered in the chase for quick runs. After the fourth six had disappeared out of the ground, it dawned on him that the full set was possible. As the final ball soared away, a remark from Peter Walker at slip summed up the power of Sobers's hitting: 'That's not six,' Walker said. 'It's a twelve!'

At the start of an innings, Sobers only ever needed a few minutes to sight the ball and get accustomed to the pitch. Then he was off; only Bradman of recent generations has been able to score so consistently off good-length deliveries. Although a genius, Sobers also thought about his batting. When he moved into the shot, he would aim to hit the ball hard; he knew that a fielder might drop an edge that was travelling like a shell. Unlike other batsmen of marvellous natural ability, he was a great competitor who would never cash in his chips if the going was tough. Some of his greatest innings were played with the team in desperate straits, when his dismissal would mean defeat. At Lord's in 1966, West Indies led by just 9 runs with half their second innings wickets gone. Only Sobers was left as his inexperienced cousin, David Holford, came out to join him. Sobers made an unbeaten 163, Holford 105 not out, and the game was saved. He always considered that was his most important innings, even though, by his brilliant standards, he was restrained for long periods.

It would be fascinating to see how Sobers would cope with the glut of fast bowling intimidation today. He never even bothered with a thigh pad against the fastest bowlers, and he was only hit once in his entire career – by a medium-pacer when a ball lifted sharply off a length in a county match. Otherwise, Sobers trusted to his extraordinary reflexes and innate sense of timing. As he had no discernible weakness in technique, it would be hard to imagine Sobers being dominated by incessant, short-pitched bowling. He always hooked down – with a roll of those steely wrists – so there would be no point in setting traps for him down on the deep square leg boundary.

Sobers dismisses the ball from his presence

He regularly played one particular stroke of genius against the fast bowlers – the straight six off the back-foot – so one can safely assume he would have adapted to the harsher bowling strategies of today.

As a bowler, he was remarkably versatile. He remains the only man to use three contrasting bowling styles in Test cricket, and he was successful at all of them. He began his Test career as an orthodox slow left-arm bowler, batting at number nine against England on their 1953/4 tour. He took four wickets on a perfect pitch and impressed with his lovely action, deceptive flight and sound temperament. He was just seventeen: since the war only Derek Underwood among left-arm spinners has looked as complete a bowler at such a tender age. In his early days in the Barbados team, the presence of the mighty '3 Ws' meant he could not get very far up the batting order, so he earned his corn as a spinner. Sobers developed his fast bowling in the Lancashire League in the late fifties but he did not bowl it until the 1960/1 tour of Australia. He was immediately impressive; typically, his run-up and delivery was all relaxed smoothness and from a braced right leg he released the ball at exactly the right time. He became the most dangerous new-ball bowler in the world, and a threat to the best players. His duels with Geoffrey Boycott were fascinating – Boycott watching for the one that moves away towards the slips while anticipating the famous 'in-ducker', the one that nips back and traps the batsman lbw. Sobers liked to pitch the ball up – especially in England where the ball can swing a great deal – and his essentially attacking methods are in sharp contrast to later West Indian fast bowlers who love to pitch the ball halfway down the wicket. Yet Sobers would bowl a very fast bouncer when necessary. He could be every bit as fast as Wes Hall for a short period.

The third bowling style came to Sobers in the early sixties. His positive outlook was intrigued by 'the funny stuff', the googly bowled out of the back of the hand, and he set to mastering it. With most bowlers, it can take a decade to be able to bowl googlies in a Test at will: Sobers mastered it in two years! Sporting skills came very easily to Gary Sobers – after all he played soccer, golf and basketball for Barbados – and he loved to experiment with the unorthodox. For about five years, be bowled 'chinamen' with a great deal of success, particularly in Australia where, for two seasons in succession, he performed the 'double' of 1000 runs and fifty wickets in the Sheffield Shield. In 1966, he injured his shoulder bowling the googly and he reverted to orthodox slow left-arm with continued success.

Those who doubt the effectiveness of Sobers as a bowler point out that his 235 Test wickets cost 34 runs each. Yet he was essentially an attacking bowler, who relied on changes of pace and movement with the new ball and experiments as a spinner. Googly bowling is always expensive but, as Sobers often demonstrated, it can winkle out the best batsmen. In any event, he often had to bowl on perfect wickets in Australia and the West Indies, where an analysis of five for 130 was considered superb. One thing is certain: he was worth his place in the West Indies side as a bowler, whether or not he batted.

It was not enough for Gary Sobers to bat like a genius, to bowl with multi-dimensional effectiveness. He was also one of the greatest all-round fielders. Away from the bat, his loose-limbed athleticism and whiplash throw were a salutary warning to any ambitious batsman, while he was predatory close to the wicket. He picked up shoals of catches for Lance Gibbs at short leg, or leg slip, if the ball was turning sharply. He specialized in run-outs from the leg-trap – making an instinctive stop and flicking back the ball to trap the stranded batsman. When Hall or Griffith were pounding in, he would stand at second slip and catch some snorters. A total of 110 catches in Tests puts him among the great catchers of all time.

Gary Sobers was lucky that he was born at a certain time in Barbados, otherwise his genius may not have flowered so luxuriantly. If he had been growing up in the 1920s, he would probably not have prospered, because opportunities for matchplay were then more restricted for the black boy. The white man was still the influential cricketer in the Caribbean at that time and it is a tribute to the likes of Headley and Constantine that they managed to break through the system. Yet by the 1940s, the Barbados Cricket League had been formed, giving black boys a chance of competitive cricket. Without that, Sobers would have had to get to high school to play serious cricket – and scholastic talent has never been one of Gary's outstanding qualities! At the age of sixteen, he was playing for Barbados, yet it was another two years before he showed what he could accomplish as a batsman. In the Barbados Test of 1955, Sobers opened the batting against Australia and played one of the great cameo innings: 43 out of 52 against Lind-wall and Miller striving for an early breakthrough. Even the Australians realized that day that Sobers was going to be something special. Two years later, Sobers impressed on the trip to England. It was an unhappy tour, with Ramadhin broken by May and Cowdrey, Walcott and Weekes in gradual decline and the captain, John Goddard, out of touch with his team. There were shafts of promise, though – the young tearaway fast bowler, Wes Hall, the promise of Collie Smith and Rohan Kanhai, and, above all, the precocious talent of Gary Sobers. At the Oval, with the ball turning square, Sobers played innings of 39 and 42 that would have pleased great bad-wicket players like Hutton and Hobbs. He actually looked comfortable against Lock and Laker, while the side was bowled out for 89 and 86. Yet this lad was just twenty-one, brought up on hard Barbadian wickets, with no experience of those vicious spinners' wickets which were a nightmare for a seasoned English professional. He was clearly one to watch.

The point was underlined when Sobers made 365 not out a few months later against Pakistan. Clyde Walcott was with him at the crease, guiding him past Len Hutton's record score and the cricket world prepared to greet another immortal. Sobers did not disappoint. Nor did he ever forget that cricket was meant to be a form of entertainment, one of the main criticisms of first-class cricketers at that time. In 1957, the *Times* devoted an editorial to the game's ailments. The writer railed against 'Tired Tims for whom a six-day week is business, rather than pleasure,' and the feeling of disillusionment at an over-professional approach was in sharp contrast to the joyous days of the immediate postwar period. Luckily, the West Indies players – and Gary Sobers in particular – proceeded to captivate both Australia and England over the next few years, showing what the spectators had been missing.

Arguably the two West Indies tours to Australia (1960/1) and to England (in 1963) did more good for the game than any others in history. The West Indians brought back a gaiety to Test cricket, by relying on their traditional assets of fast bowling, brilliant fielding and spectacular batting. They also showed their maturity by bolstering the batting with solid performers like Conrad Hunte, Easton McMorris and Joe Solomon; their sensible approach allowed the strokemakers freedom to attack the bowlers. Above all, West Indies had the right captain in Frank Worrell, himself a great player, revered by his team and a dominating, calming influence at excitable times. The series in Australia caught the public imagination right away, with the 'Tied Test' at Brisbane. If ever a Test Match centre deserved a great game it was Brisbane; two years earlier, England had crawled to ignominious, pusillanimous defeat, with Trevor Bailey taking seven hours to score 68. At least these West Indians would lose with flair, and if they continued to play in such cavalier style, they deserved everything that came to them. The tone of the match was set by Sobers's wonderful innings of 132 on the first day. He made his runs in 123 minutes and the new ball (available at that time after 200 runs had been scored) was taken at 2.25 on the first day! Such wanton aggression in a Test had not been seen since the days of Compton and Bradman and the Australians loved Sobers and his team for it. That tour rescued Australian cricket, at a time when other leisure pursuits were appearing more attractive. The ticker-tape farewell given to Frank Worrell's side at the end of the tour was richly deserved.

English cricket was equally grateful to Worrell in 1963. England and Australia had just played out yet another dull Ashes series, and progressive elements were now questioning the validity of the Ashes: was an urn that important, if it caused such boring cricket? The West Indies demonstrated there was more to Test cricket than attrition. Images abound from that 1963 tour: Worrell late-cutting Statham with the utmost delicacy, the stamina of Wes Hall at Lord's where Worrell's wise counsel influenced a wonderful last day, the dynamic batting of Rohan Kanhai, the wicked yorkers of the menacing Charlie Griffith and the beguiling off-spin of Lance Gibbs. The all-round contribution of Gary Sobers was crucial – a batting average of 40, eight catches and twenty wickets. All this in a wet summer, often the excuse for mundane cricket. Nobody who loved the game could begrudge the West Indies their 3/1 victory in the series. They were so popular that they were responsible for a major shake-up in the Test Match rota. As the series bubbled to a climactic end, it was revealed that the West Indies were not due back in England until 1971; it was too awful to contemplate almost a decade without these marvellous players and the authorities at Lord's acted with commendable haste. It was decreed that the West Indies would return for a full tour in 1966 and that all other Test countries (with the exception of Australia) would have to share a summer. That has

been the pattern ever since and it remains the most comprehensive tribute to Frank Worrell and his 1963 touring party.

Worrell had always been close to Sobers and he recommended him as successor to the captaincy of the West Indies. Typically Sobers took a month to reply to the invitation (he has never been a fan of paperwork), but when he finally accepted, he made an impressive start. He won the first three series, with Worrell's invaluable sound guidance and the team remained mightily strong. On the 1966 tour to England, it was a daunting prospect for the bowlers to see Sobers lope out at number six – behind players like Hunte, Kanhai, Butcher and Nurse – and he hardly failed. He averaged 103, took ten catches, picked up twenty wickets, and he won the series 3/1. He had to do a lot of bowling – Charlie Griffith was not quite the force of old, and Lance Gibbs also needed his support as second spinner – but he took on the responsibility and remained head and shoulders above anyone on either side. Typically, he would make no excuses when Brian Close led a revitalized England to a belated victory at the Oval. Sobers refused to admit that his side had coasted because they were three up in the series, and insisted on giving full credit to Close. Such chivalrous acceptance of the game's fortunes was always one of Sobers's many endearing personal qualities.

He was equally charming after losing the famous Test to England at Port of Spain two years later. Sobers declared at 92 for two, leaving England to get 215 in 2¾ hours. Thanks to Boycott and Cowdrey, they got them. Sobers was unrepentant; he pointed out that England had never scored at more than 40 runs per hour so far in the series, that he could have bowled for a draw, but kept the over-rate ticking over at 21 per hour, and that the pitch played better than expected. The press judged Sobers very harshly. That declaration lost the series and it remains one of the most costly declarations in postwar Test cricket. Yet Sobers was true to himself when he said: 'I made that declaration for cricket. If I had not done so, the game would have died.' If only other Test captains could appreciate the wider implications so altruistically.

That 1967/8 series was his first major setback as captain and there were to be many more. In his last twenty-six Tests as captain, he won just two of them – a stark contrast to his record before 1967. England proceeded to win two series, there was a convincing defeat in Australia, India won in the West Indies and even New Zealand

managed to draw two series. There were many factors involved: the decline of the fast bowlers, the lack of emerging young talent, poor catching and the inevitable turn of the tide that saw both England and Australia recover. Too much depended on Sobers. He was becoming increasingly bothered by knee trouble, a legacy of a punishing schedule that had by now taken him to English county cricket with Nottinghamshire, instead of a well-deserved rest. Despite his fatigue, he still maintained incredibly high standards – an average of 49 in Australia, of 74 against India and of 76 during his last series in England in 1973. At Lord's he hobbled to the crease and smashed 150 not out in even time; even with one good knee, he was still outstanding. A year later – after

four Tests against England – he retired from Test cricket. The knees had given way, and no wonder. In twenty years, he had hardly missed a Test, and he had also played eight seasons of Sheffield Shield and county cricket.

He had to be special when a man like Sir Don Bradman described one of his innings as, 'Probably the best ever seen in Australia. The people who saw Sobers have enjoyed one of the historic events of cricket.' This was after scoring 254 for the Rest of the World against Australia at Melbourne in 1972. Sobers was plagued

Two great players from West Indian cricket in the Sobers Age. Rohan Kanhai (*below*), masterful batsman of immense flair, and Lance Gibbs, the only spinner to take 300 Test wickets

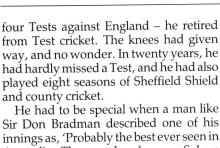

by marital problems at that time and Dennis Lillee had dismissed him first ball in the first innings. As captain of the Rest of the World, Sobers felt a keen responsibility to the polyglot elements in the team. He tore into Lillee with a rare destructiveness and effectively won the match. Only one other batsman got to 50, but Australia lost by 96 runs, after being bowled out for 317. Sobers had won the game, with a style and daring no one could match. His hundred at Sabina Park against England in 1968 was equally amazing. Again he had made nought in the first innings and West Indies had to follow on with the pitch opening up, and John Snow aiming for the cracks, bowling shooters. He made 113 with astonishing certainty and when England batted, they finished on 68 for six, in deep trouble with the ball playing all sorts of tricks. For good

Above: Three avid horse-racing fans gather round the TV set to await developments – Denis Compton (*left*), Ted Dexter (*centre*) and Gary Sobers. Has the camera ever captured a trio of retired cricketers that gave so much pleasure over so many years?

Left: Arise, Sir Gary. The Queen bestows the accolade on a great sportsman

measure Sobers took three of those six wickets after his wondrous batting.

As a cricketer, he was intelligent; he was not lucky, he did not take outrageous risks like Ian Botham, and he knew that on his day, he would give best to nobody.

As a human being, he had faults like anyone else. He was politically naive – his visit to Rhodesia to play in a double wicket competition in 1970 caused a furore in the Caribbean and he eventually apologized to the West Indies Board of Control, as the politicians began pulling the strings. Sobers's openness of character might have proved an embarrassment in later years, when trips to South Africa caused endless reverberations in world cricket. Sometimes Sobers drank too heavily and his fondness for gambling worried his wife and his many friends. This apart, he

is above criticism. He gave wonderful entertainment for two decades, in the process enriching the game by his personality and sportsmanship. If Gary Sobers had never scored a hundred, he would still be remembered with affection by all cricketers of his acquaintance. He had the rare ability to play the game better than anyone else on earth, while treating it with the same unspoilt joy as any club cricketer. When the Queen knighted him in 1975, she was merely confirming what the cricket world already knew – that Gary Sobers was of the rarest breed.

Geoffrey Boycott

Geoffrey Boycott's career has coincided with the most fundamental changes in the game so far this century. It is a tribute to Boycott's enduring skill and professionalism that he lasted at the top for more than a quarter of a century, at a time when cricket placed greater emphasis than ever on athleticism and physical fitness. He has never won any popularity contests but even Boycott's most trenchant critics admit that no one prepared himself better for his job of work, no one made better use of whatever talent he possessed.

Since Boycott's debut for Yorkshire, the game has been radically reshaped. In his first season (1962), the outmoded distinction between amateur and professional was finally eroded. It had been an anachronism for several decades, with many amateurs being paid by their clubs as either secretaries or captains. The well of talent from Oxbridge was drying up, as examiners demanded higher academic standards for entry, at the expense of sporting excellence. The glut of talented Oxbridge players in the immediate postwar years reflected the best from a whole generation; they could not disport themselves on the cricket field until the serious business of war had been completed. After that initial influx of high talent after the war, cricket at Oxford and Cambridge became something of a backwater – despite an occasional Cowdrey, Smith or Dexter – and very few of them enriched the county game for any length of time. From 1962 onwards, a cricketer was free to negotiate honestly and openly with his county employer and the majority of cricket-lovers saw it as a victory for realism.

A year later, another radical innovation: one-day cricket. English cricket had been atrophying for the past decade. Despite

Boycott meets a young admirer in the West Indies, 1981

great success in the Test arena, the standard of English first-class cricket had been depressingly low. Yorkshire and Surrey in particular were way ahead of other counties every season in the championship race, and many county sides carried mediocre performers. Wickets lacked pace, batsmen were generally short of flair and many bowlers garnered flattering analyses as the elements turned pitches into severe tests of character and technique. Above all, there was a lassitude about English cricket after that first fine careless rapture of the postwar years. When Denis Compton retired in 1957, it seemed as if a light had gone out of the game for good. His departure symbolized the feeling that first-class cricket was becoming a technical exercise for twenty-

two players, with the spectator an irrelevance. Far too many games were being left drawn, as captains became bogged down in grudge matches or long hauls in search of batting bonus points. The lawmakers at Lord's did their best, as they tinkered around with the bonus points system and even brought the boundary rope further in, to encourage more six-hitting – but a lack of will among captains and players was more important. By the start of the 1960s, first-class cricket in England was winding down stultifyingly.

In 1963, it was decided to try a national experiment that had been successful with local counties. 'Knock out', or limited overs cricket proved an immediate boost to the flagging image of the game. Gillette, the sponsors of the first national competition, were equally delighted with the publicity it achieved at a cheap cost. The first final at Lord's – between Worcestershire and Sussex – was an exciting contest, and almost immediately the one-day game was firmly established in the public consciousness. Since 1963, different competitions have proliferated – National Westminster now sponsor the longer, 60 overs brand, while Benson and Hedges favour the 55-over game and on Sundays, the 40-over John Player Special League has remained very popular. Arguments about the merits of the one-day game have raged for two decades: the traditionalists say that a whole generation of players have emerged who cannot defend, who play outrageous strokes which have no place in the coaching manual, and lack the mental discipline to build an innings in a Test. The progressive elements maintain that the presence of hordes of batsmen who could play a highly professional, technically correct innings helped to empty grounds before the dawn of limited

Brian Close – great captain of Yorkshire, controversial leader of England. Under Close's captaincy, Yorkshire cricket regained its self-respect after a decade of near-misses. If he had not been sacked from the job in 1970, Boycott might have avoided some of the blood-letting and gained valuable time before he took over the Yorkshire captaincy

overs cricket made them take chances. They point to the undeniable leap in fielding standards and overall fitness; certainly it was an invigorating sight to watch players of advancing years throw themselves at the ball when one-day cricket started. Normally a specialist batsman or bowler would not work unduly at his fielding, if the natural ability was not there. The limited overs game caused everyone to think harder about fielding, and as a result the game appeared more stimulating.

The harmful effects on spin bowling are more important when considering the impact of one-day cricket. The need to bowl flat and tight has spawned a mass of medium-pacers who can bowl accurately to a field and wait for a mistake. If the wicket is properly prepared, one-day cricket is definitely a game for the batsman: the bowler is restricted to a certain amount of overs and there is

hardly an attacking gesture in field placing. The spinner – essentially an attacker – is deemed something of a luxury, despite statistical evidence which suggests that good bowlers of whatever pace will influence cricket matches of whatever duration. The same applies to batsmen: invariably the player with a good championship or Test record fares well in the frenetic one-day game. Good cricketers will always influence cricket matches, whatever the playing regulations. Yet captains still do not trust the spinner.

In 1968, the English game underwent another radical overhaul. In an attempt to stimulate further interest, it was decreed that overseas players could turn out in county cricket. The rule was one per county, although that has been honoured more in the breach than the observance in later years. Immediately English cricket enjoyed a heartening boost as Gary Sobers, Rohan Kanhai, Barry Richards, Mike Procter and Clive Lloyd revealed world-class skills every day. There had been nothing like it before – merely a trickle of overseas players who had to serve a two-year qualification period. English cricket was fundamentally for the

English. Now young English players could learn at first-hand from the greatest cricketers in the world. Over the next two decades, almost every world-class player has appeared in county cricket and the trend has been mutually beneficial: the player has acquired valuable experience of English conditions, while the county has had a prospect of success that was denied to all but Surrey and Yorkshire in the 1950s. The standards around the counties have evened out, with only three counties yet to win the championship, while one of the four available trophies has been won at least once by every county. It is true that some overseas players have given less than full value and it is arguable that their presence has hindered the development of young English batsmen – but it is undeniable that the influx of overseas players was good for English cricket in 1968.

In the last two decades, English cricket has truly mirrored the society in which it has existed. It has become a more racialist society – the D'Oliveira Affair of 1968 and the abortive South African tour of 1970 has reflected that in cricket. Violence has become more commonplace: the crowd invasions and boorish behaviour of many

The on-drive to the boundary off Greg Chappell that brought Boycott into the ranks of the immortals. At Leeds in 1977, he became the first batsman to score his hundredth century in a Test

spectators at cricket grounds are distressingly symptomatic of that trend. The exhibitionism of the sixties has been mirrored in the 'streaker' and spectators who feel that they are entitled to do more than just sit quietly and watch cricket. Increased materialism and the lure of the advertising agencies have led top cricketers into areas where vast sums of money are earned. As a result media exposure on the 'personality cult' in cricket has risen to a floodtide. Wage demands have thrown successive governments off course in the past twenty years and the professional cricketer has

become equally aware of his bargaining power. To aid them in an understandable desire to earn more money for the same amount of work, they now have their own union, the Cricketers' Association. Formed in 1967, it has been an admirably sane influence on the contemporary cricket scene, but their very existence only underlines the fact that the game is simply an ingredient of a society that has become increasingly institutionalized.

Greed has become as much a part of cricket as any other walk of life. Kerry Packer proved that in 1977, when he revolutionized world cricket because he could not win exclusive coverage of the Ashes Tests for his television station. Just like any other entrepeneur faced with a similar problem, Packer went for the jugular vein

and snapped up most of the world's best cricketers to play for him. It was a classic industrial relations ploy: aided by the restlessness of the workers, he gave them more money to be employed by him, thereby kicking the chair from under the backside of the traditional, paternalist employer who thought loyalty would be enough to guarantee full employment. The sequels were straight out of the usual labour disputes scenario: threats of strike action, 'divide and rule' tactics whereby non-Packer players argued with the rebels, wheeler-dealing in smoke-filled rooms and finally a squalid compromise.

Packer's success in cocking a snook at the established form of international cricket encouraged other entrepreneurs to meddle in cricket. A series of 'pirate' tours to South Africa led to bans, and the inevitable interest of politicians on the make. The naive view was that 'politics should not be a part of sport' – a cosy shibboleth that acknowledged the unpopularity of opportunist politicians and a craving for the retention of the status quo. It was an unrealistic posture, however; politics had been part of sport for a long time before South Africa cast its long shadow over world cricket. The fulminations of Adolf Hitler when the black Jesse Owens mastered the German athletes at the Berlin Olympics in 1936; the 'Black Power' salute of two American athletes at the Mexico Olympics; the appalling massacre of Israeli athletes at the Munich Games in 1972 – all of these confirmed that sport could not claim immunity from reality. Cricketers rail at such interference by the politicians, while conveniently forgetting that large sums of money are freely available to players who will sign for tours to South Africa that inevitably court controversy. The money would not be available without the controversy. The 'cake and eat it' philosophy is as deeply ingrained in cricket as in any other stratum of society.

Kerry Packer. Coloured clothing. Floodlit cricket. Tests on a Sunday. Political machinations. Massive cash rewards. Limited overs cricket. A decline in behaviour on and off the field. The demise of the 'shamateur'. Geoffrey Boycott has seen all this, and much more in his remarkable career. His Yorkshire club remains the only one to stick out against employing overseas cricketers, or indeed anyone born outside the Broad Acres – a stance that tells us much about Boycott and the quirky, opinionated county club which has employed him for so long, through so many schisms and palace revolutions. Perhaps the highest

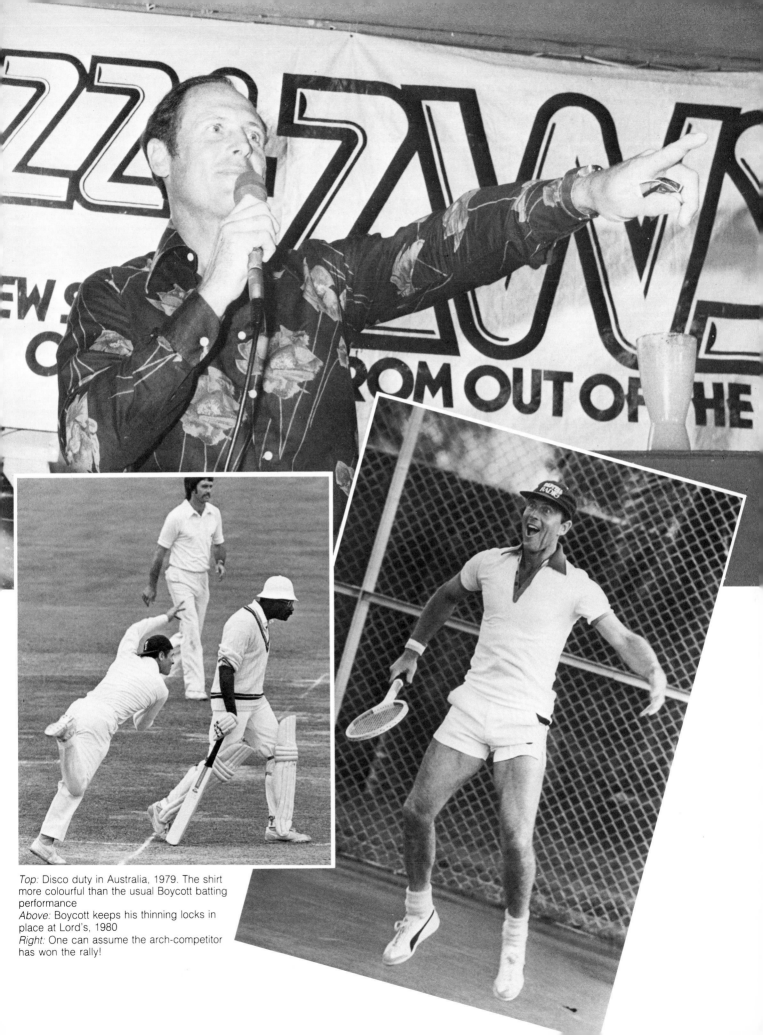

Top: Disco duty in Australia, 1979. The shirt more colourful than the usual Boycott batting performance
Above: Boycott keeps his thinning locks in place at Lord's, 1980
Right: One can assume the arch-competitor has won the rally!

praise one can mete out is that he has kept going. He has survived the brutalizing dominance of modern fast bowlers, and at an age when many former players are waddling around Test grounds with the rose-coloured spectacles firmly donned, Boycott is still fit and technically brilliant enough to keep coming back for more. It is a measure of his professional standards that he was the only English cricketer to practise every day for a month on the ill-fated tour to the West Indies in 1986 – yet Boycott was only there as a newspaper columnist! Even more remarkably, it was seriously suggested in some influential quarters that Boycott should have been drafted into the team, as they continued collapsing ignominiously. At the age of forty-five, that would have been his greatest achievement.

The young bespectacled Boycott who encountered the gentle medium pace of Grahame Corling on his Test debut in 1964 faced much sterner examinations of his courage and technique over the next eighteen years in England colours. He has always been a marvellous player of spin bowling, with the defensive technique to survive on bad wickets and the patience to pick off the runs from bad deliveries, but the real tests came from fast bowling. Regrettably, spinners like Bedi, Chandra, Gibbs, Sobers, Gleeson and Intikhab faded away during Boycott's first decade as an England batsman, and they were never adequately replaced. Fast bowlers got fitter and stronger, the wickets throughout the world became more unreliable and umpires generally failed to clamp down on intimidation that would have been deemed unacceptable in other eras. Yet Boycott remained very impressive against the barrage – even in his forty-first year, at a time when the reflexes and nerve are slowly drifting. In 1981, his last full year as England opener, Boycott weathered the cynical assaults of the West Indian fast bowlers in the Caribbean, then came back to combat the wiles of Dennis Lillee and the pace and cut of Terry Alderman, his impressive new partner. His hundred at the Oval, after a fascinating duel with Lillee, was a masterpiece of controlled, resourceful batting. His performances in that last year convincingly rebutted the slur by Tony Greig that Boycott did not fancy quick bowlers, a reference to Boycott's non-availability for that traumatic tour to Australia in 1974/5, when Lillee and Thomson were lethally hostile. Many faults can be laid at the door of Geoffrey

Boycott, but physical cowardice is not one of them. As Viv Richards was heard to comment to Clive Lloyd during the 1981 series, 'You've got to hand it to this guy, he never gives it away.' Mike Brearley, the England captain who enjoyed a wary yet respectful relationship with Boycott, admired the way he pulled himself together on the 1979/80 tour to Australia. The previous year Boycott had a nightmare tour in Australia: distracted by another Yorkshire captaincy saga, grieving over the death of his mother, he was never in the proper frame of mind to do himself justice. On the next tour, he reverted to his usual orthodox stance, the footwork improved and he played superbly in the Tests and the one-day internationals. Brearley particularly admired the way Boycott went up several gears in the one-day games: 'He was a revelation – playing the West Indies quickies off the back-foot through the covers and going down the wicket to hit people like Max Walker over the top. All this plus his immense skill at placing the ball, and getting twos instead of ones.'

In case the pro-Boycott prose gets too fulsome, it has to be admitted that his definition of a perfect day's cricket has usually featured a century by one G. Boycott, preferably unbeaten – nothing wrong with looking at the averages, especially if you are at the top of them. No cricketer of comparable status has encapsulated more vividly the agonizing dichotomy between the aims of the individual and the needs of his side. Boycott saw his mission clearly: if he made a stack of runs, the team would not lose, with any luck. The altruism of a Trumper or a Compton never appealed to a man for whom gargantuan averages were a passport to a better social status and presumed professional acceptability. Boycott clearly felt his blinkered approach to crease occupation was justified by the inferiority of his batting partners; certainly his time with Yorkshire and England were hardly periods of batting cornucopia. Yet too often run-rates became irrelevant to Boycott, as lesser players sacrificed themselves at the other end. The prevailing 'star system' that had been gleefully fostered by the media brought Boycott the status of a demi-god among his fanatical, vociferous supporters – in turn this cult of the superstar alienated many who genuinely admired him. The civil war in Yorkshire cricket over the past decade has largely centred around the ambitions of Geoffrey Boycott: disastrously, the wider

interests of the team became subordinated to the influence of one player. As a result, Yorkshire cricket remains a laughing stock to those who resented their superiority in the halcyon period of regular championship victories, while those of a more charitable nature wish better days for a county of such great cricketing tradition.

To call Geoffrey Boycott a complex character is rather like suggesting that Eric Morecambe was occasionally good for a muffled titter. He has thrived on the adulation while complaining about press intrusions into his private life; he has claimed a naiveté that leads him into straight talking, while showing sophisticated qualities of in-fighting that would not disgrace a political heavyweight from Tammany Hall. The media must shoulder its fair share of blame – building a batsman up so much that in the end, he and his disciples began to believe they were more important than the team. In a less assertive age, the media would have kept Boycott's deeds firmly on the sports pages and treated matters like his claims for the England captaincy with the proportion they warranted. Yet Fleet Street has remained fascinated in an idiosyncratic cricketer who may be approaching middle age but still bats exceptionally well. Geoffrey Boycott has probably never heard of Tom Wolfe, but when he wrote that the sixties were 'The Me Generation' he could have chosen no better model for the slogan than a man who likes nothing better than standing at a crease, playing back and across, back and across, with the left elbow jutting towards the sky for the defensive stroke.

Yet give the man credit. His record, for those who cherish such matters, is truly remarkable. A cricketer cannot achieve such statistical greatness without genuine talent, no matter what his detractors allege. Boycott's approach towards practice and fitness is irreproachable and those lucky enough to be taken into his confidence confirm that his knowledge of the game is immense. Certainly his public pronouncements on the intricacies and subtleties of cricket are marvellously illuminating. He has seen off all his early English contemporaries – Dexter, Edrich, Cowdrey, D'Oliveira, Graveney and Barrington – and he is durable enough to be still around when later colleagues like Gooch, Gower and Botham are publishing their memoirs. The game may have altered dramatically during Geoffrey Boycott's career, but its most lasting institution has not.

Tony Greig & Basil D'Oliveira

Tony Greig and Basil D'Oliveira were two South African cricketers whose impact on the game extended far beyond the confines of the playing area. They were from different backgrounds: D'Oliveira, the Cape Coloured who had to come halfway round the world to play Test cricket, Greig the white South African who qualified to play for England because his parents were Scottish. D'Oliveira had to battle through racial prejudice and advancing years to earn the right to play for England while Greig breezed through his cricket career, only troubled by epileptic attacks that cleared up after prolonged rest.

Unwittingly Basil D'Oliveira was responsible for the cessation of Test links with South Africa. No doubt a flashpoint would have occurred at some later stage, but it was the inclusion of D'Oliveira in the England tour party to South Africa in 1968 that led to historic repercussions. The South African Government refused to allow D'Oliveira to return to his homeland in England colours. They suspected the influence of the politicians and the anti-apartheid movement, especially as he was a late inclusion, having been left out of the original squad. That tour was called off and the sands of time started to run out for South Africa's Test players. In 1970, the Labour Government exercised enormous pressure on the Cricket Council to call off the proposed visit by the South Africans. The Home Secretary feared public disorder if the tour went ahead and eventually the Government won. That was the end of South Africa in Test cricket for the forseeable future. A whole generation of Test players – including Mike Procter, Barry Richards, Clive Rice, Peter and Graeme Pollock – were consigned to limbo, relying on English county cricket

Tony Greig revealing a theatrical streak which appalled the traditionalists but delighted television producers

and pirate tours for their further professional satisfaction. Basil D'Oliveira remained a dignified figure Through it all. He refused to become embroiled in the saga, and continued to play with distinction for England until 1972 and for Worcestershire till 1979. He remains a well-loved institution on the English cricketing stage – unlike his fellow-South African, Tony Greig.

The fame of Tony Greig rests less on his accomplished all-round skills and rather more on a series of persuasive phone calls he made to a host of world-class cricketers in the spring of 1977. For Tony Greig was

the chief recruiting agent for the most cataclysmic revolution to shake the game: World Series Cricket (WSC). A decade after Greig joined forces with Kerry Packer, the effects of their partnership are still reverberating throughout world cricket. Although cricket, like life, is evolutionary there is no doubt that the game has altered more dramatically since Packer than at any comparable stage in its history. Some of the drastic changes have been worthy, others more deleterious – but it is undeniable that at the top level, cricket is now a harder and less enjoyable game to play. For good or ill, money has become a major consideration in the minds of the best players. Tony Greig and Kerry Packer were responsible for that, by bringing cricket into the market-place.

For some time, international cricketers had been niggling about the poor financial rewards from Test cricket. The long tours, separation from families, the uncertainty about job prospects, the insecurity stemming from a distrust of selectors – all these factors made some players believe they deserved more money. Test cricket was getting harder and harder – especially against the West Indian fast bowlers and their Australian counterparts, Lillee and Thomson – and more players were coming to understand the way of the business world. The commodity was very sound: consider the great success of the first World Cup in 1975, the crowd-pulling appeal of the Australians and the West Indies and the tremendous impact of the Centenary Test at Melbourne in 1977. It seemed obvious to many top players that it was time they shared in the rich pickings. It became a common complaint from the Australian Packer players that they received less from the Centenary Test than the refuse collectors who tidied up

Basil D'Oliveira spreads the gospel of cricket in Durban. The year was 1966 and D'Oliveira had just been capped by England. Two years later, he was to be plunged into a political whirlpool that would have wrecked a lesser man

the ground every night. If that is the case, the refuse men were being paid very well indeed, since the Australians stood to make 725 dollars for each Test in the 1976/7 season, an increase of almost a third over the past two years. In addition, they received 30 per cent of the sponsorship money that had been ploughed into the Australian game since 1974. It was not enough; this new breed of player knew more about the mores of the commercial world, he was at ease with a briefcase in his hand and a pocket calculator to punch. Traditional cricket was about to come a cropper.

Tony Greig was in a unique position to influence events at this time. He was the captain of England, a charismatic figure who handled the media and his players with equal facility. He lacked the tactical sagacity of Mike Brearley, but his positive attitude inspired his players and they would go through the proverbial brick wall for him. He had just led England on a very successful tour of India, where the series was won by 3/1 and Greig proved a great success with crowds and players alike. When the Centenary Test came along in March 1977 he played his full part in the ritual homage of obeisance to the traditions of Test cricket, even though he was then plotting a rival brand.

Ironically, Greig did not desperately need the money that would accrue from joining World Series Cricket; he was earning a comfortable living from commercial endorsements, apart from his cricket wages. The advertising agencies loved Tony Greig – he was charming, plausible, dominating and thoroughly professional in his approach, just the qualities that endeared him to the players he captained. Greig had spent the winter of 1975/6 in Sydney captaining Waverley in Grade cricket and he had fallen in love with the Australian way of life. As a South African, he did not have a sheepish attitude to making money or changing cricket horses in mid-stream. The English traditions did not restrain him; the England captaincy was all very well but the Establishment would get him in the end. He came close to being dropped during the 1976 season against the West Indies and he always walked a delicate tightrope between his desire for free speech and the restraint expected of an England captain. He once wrote, 'If you talk to me long enough, I will say something controversial,' a trait that did not appeal to the Establishment. So Greig took a hard-headed view of Kerry Packer's blandishments. He was due a benefit with Sussex, and that would no doubt be

successful, yet Packer was offering to set him up for life, with a regular job after his cricket days were over. It was never really a contest and Greig threw his considerable resources into the task of recruiting the best players in the world over a few short weeks.

He was very successful. Even more impressively, absolute secrecy was maintained almost until Kerry Packer was ready to unveil his devastating coup. When the news finally broke, six weeks after the Centenary Test, the roll call of names indicated this was no ordinary splinter group. No less than thirty-five had been signed up on three-year contracts (the total eventually swelled to fifty-one). Alan Knott, Derek Underwood and John Snow were lined up alongside Tony Greig – they were later joined by Bob Woolmer and Dennis Amiss. Almost every West Indian and Australian star was on the list, and to the South Africans it was a godsend, starved as they were of representative cricket since 1970.

Cricket's Establishment reacted with unconcealed fury and soon the lawyers and the accountants were locked in conclave with cricketers, as the full implications of Kerry Packer's coup beganmto sink in. A flurry of activity from Lord's in the summer of 1977 led to Greig losing the England captaincy, a ban on all WSC players from Tests and desperate attempts to prevent others signing for Packer. In the autumn, Packer won a High Court injunction that prevented the International Cricket Conference (ICC) banning Packer players from Tests, and it also meant the Test and County Cricket Board (TCCB) could not keep Packer players out of county cricket. This set up more divisions in world cricket: the West Indies continued to select those who had stayed loyal to traditional cricket. As a result, cricketer was set against cricketer and feelings ran high for two years. In addition, the High Court action cost the ICC and the TCCB a matter of £250 000.

The split lasted for two years and then WSC ended as dramatically as it had begun. There were several reasons. Crowd figures for the two seasons of WSC matches were not impressive and it was rumoured that Packer was losing a good deal of money. Australia seemed the only country where he could play his games, apart from the West Indies, and a WSC tour there in the spring of 1979 was disastrous. With the bellicose Ian Chappell captaining the Australian side, the Caribbean trip was a public relations disaster (with Chappell on board, that was hardly a shock), and riots by spectators and indifference among players did the image of WSC no good at all. All the hype attached to WSC did not impress the average Australian fan, because his team was regularly rolled over by the West Indian speed juggernaut and the combined talents of the World Eleven. Few Australians can stomach the sight of the national side losing regularly – a fact known to the Australian Board of Control as well. Attendances for the official brand of cricket in Australia were also poor during WSC's history. For the first time ever, England's visit in 1978/9 made a loss – partly because Australia was thrashed 5/1 and also because Packer's version took away some cricket supporters. The Australian Board of Control expected to lose around £450 000 for the past two seasons, and such a financial haemorrhage could not continue. The World Cup was due to be played in England within a few months and there was a very real danger that the competition would be an unmitigated disaster if some of the best players were not picked.

Peace broke out at the end of April 1979. Kerry Packer got what he had wanted all along – exclusive rights for television coverage of the major games in Australia for the next three years. Back in 1976, Packer could not accept that the Board was tied to a contract until 1979 with the Australian Broadcasting Corporation; he ignored the fact that he would no doubt get exclusive rights when the contract went out to tender, if only because he would offer more money. He achieved his aim three years later, after devaluing Test cricket and souring many friendships. Packer saw the project in strictly business terms: he wanted something sooner, rather than later, and the only way he could get that was by the common business practice of capitalizing on a weakness of his opponents. That weakness was the declining loyalty of the top players towards traditional cricket. He said that cricket was the easiest game in the world to take over, because nobody bothered to pay the players their true worth. In essence the dispute was about television rights, rather than improving the lot of the players; Tony Greig may have thought he was leading a crusade but Packer kept his eye firmly on the ball of exclusivity. He was perfectly happy to wind up WSC when he got what he wanted in the spring of 1979 – a minimum of 360 hours of exclusive cricket coverage. To the mogul of a commercial television station, exclusivity is the lifeblood, and on balance Packer did not have to pay all that much for it. He also managed to annex sole rights for marketing Australian cricket for the next ten years, and this has proved a disastrous capitulation by the Australian Board of Control. Over the previous two years, the Board had been more hawkish about Packer than any of the other countries in the ICC, yet they then proceeded to lie down alongside him. Money caused the volte-face: Packer had it in abundance and the Board was broke. So Packer insisted that England and the West Indies had to come to Australia at the end of 1979, to launch a round-robin of Test and one-day matches involving the three most glamorous Test sides. Poor India, who were due on tour, were told to wait their turn because Channel 9 needed to get their ten-year coverage off to a rousing start. England reluctantly agreed, although they insisted that the Ashes should not be at stake for a series of just three Tests. England won that particular battle but since then all Test sides have been shuttled in and out of Australia on a bewildering whistle-stop tour of cricket centres, playing innumerable one-day internationals and far too many Tests. Kerry Packer has ushered in new concepts like floodlit cricket, coloured clothing, a white ball, and 30-

Kerry Packer and Tony Greig go to law in October, 1977

yard circles in limited overs games – and cricket's Establishment has acceded. All because of the insatiable demands of television.

Now that all international cricketers have been made aware of their financial worth, it is inevitable that money influences them far more than before Packer. They now know how important it is to stay in the Test Match limelight, because their commercial potential is enhanced by succeeding in front of a wide audience that is influenced by television. The top cricketers are now on a financial roller-coaster, playing far too many representative games but worried about stepping off for a rest in case their incomes suffer. Test cricket since Packer has occasionally appeared meaningless because of its quantity. In the winter of 1983/4, no less than twenty-eight Tests were played throughout the world, while at one stage, India's Sunil Gavaskar played fifty-two Tests in the space of five years. The first 500 Tests took eighty-five

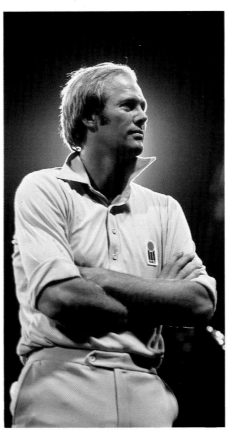

Tony Greig, the Golden Boy of Packer's version of cricket. He was more successful subsequently (*below*) talking to the camera during the Ashes series of 1982/3 in Australia. Soon he was a natural television linkman

years to be played – yet the last twenty-three years have crammed in nearly 550 Tests. There were 250 Tests between 1974 and 1984, and England have toured every winter since 1975. Kerry Packer may be happy, as his television station churns out endless one-day matches, but the purist knows that such a glut of representative cricket conjures up a vision of a certain goose and a certain golden egg.

Of course there are plus factors from WSC. The players can now earn vast sums if they are talented or charismatic enough, and even if they are not, professional cricket is now a reasonably well-paid existence. Almost immediately after Packer's incursions, the fees for English players went up from £210 to £1000 per Test and two years later, umpires in English Tests were getting the same amount. On the first England tour after Packer, the fee per player went up from £3000 to £5000. This stemmed from the sponsorship of Cornhill Insurance, who ploughed a million pounds into English cricket over five years from 1978 onwards, and then at recurring stages ever since. The greater awareness of players' financial needs also helped the English county cricketer – the counties agreed to a minimum wage of

£4500 for a capped player in 1979 and that figure has been increased in subsequent years. At last cricketers of promise need not disappear from the game because the could not earn enough money: the incentive to play Test cricket was now a financial as well as professional one.

The extra money available has undoubtedly made the game more competitive, and given the players a clear justification to train harder to prolong their careers. As a result, fielding standards continue to improve. Yet the game is more ruthless now and the greater financial rewards must be partly responsible. Tony Greig suggested as much when, during the second year of WSC, he wrote, 'The competition is so intense, that teams can no longer afford to allow the opposition tail-enders to hang around. Consequently the pace bowlers are dishing out an unprecedented amount of bouncers to the rabbits.' Greig was under the impression that such a macho attitude to the game was admirable, that the sight of a great batsman like Barry Richards fending off systematic intimidation brought greater glory to the game. In the first season of WSC, twenty-five batsmen were hit on the head and immediately the helmet became a vital piece of equipment. No longer could a tail-ender rely on the opposition's sense of fairness; he had to wear a helmet and expect to duck and dive. It is hard to imagine chivalrous cricketers like Bob Woolmer, Dennis Amiss and Derek Underwood appreciating such ruthlessness, but they had to buckle down to the task and don the helmet.

When WSC ended, the more unpleasant aspects filtered through to the traditional game. Winning became the Holy Grail, not just for the money, but also for the media-manipulated glory, and the means justified the end. That meant fast bowling, lots of it, and it was now directed at the head, rather than the stumps. The great fast bowlers of the past used the bouncer sparingly, as a threat, but their successors in the 1980s employed it as their stock-in-trade. The standard of umpiring throughout the world remained depressingly weak against this barrage of intimidation and any efforts at meting out justice were invariably met by histrionic self-righteousness. In 1980, the West Indian fast bowler Michael Holding kicked over the stumps because the New Zealand umpire had turned down an appeal for a catch at the wicket off Holding's bowling. In the next Test, umpire Fred Goodall was barged over by Colin Croft after the West Indies expressed displeasure at one of his decisions. Then

Holding bowled four successive bouncers at the New Zealand captain, Geoff Howarth, and they took the field ten minutes late after the tea interval. When New Zealand won that series, to the unconfined joy of the home supporters, the behaviour of the West Indies was outrageously boorish and unsporting. Yet just a year earlier, Kerry Packer had been encouraging them to behave in this fashion. He decreed that his viewers wanted to see snarling teeth and foul-mouthed imprecations in close-up; the ratings demanded that cricket should get into bed with rollerball, rather than the game adorned by Keith Miller and Denis Compton. A decade after WSC, there seems little sign of a worldwide improvement. On the rare occasions when England have been involved in a chivalrous series (at home to New Zealand in 1983 and Australia two years later), the contrast has been gratifying, a reminder that the game can still be played hard but fairly.

Tony Greig would not be unduly abashed by cricket's decent into meretriciousness, by the quest for the fast buck. He always said that cricket had to move with the times, and in the outside world, that meant a greater materialism. Greig never took a sentimental view of cricket, nor bewailed its tarnished standards of recent years. For him, it was meant to be a tough, relentless exercise, just like the world of business. He relished taking on Lillee and Thomson in that traumatic 1974/5 series, signalling boundaries with calculated disdain. When he said that he intended to make the West Indians 'grovel' in the summer of 1976, he accepted all the bouncers and flak that came his way from their fast bowlers; he even enraged them into bowling badly at Leeds, when he told each one he was a chucker! As a result, Greig scored 116 and 76 not out off wayward bowling and kept his place. In the Centenary Test, he cheerfully admitted that he tried to talk David Hookes out of his concentration, as he fielded just a few yards away from the young debutant. Just because a few old buffers were droning on about the glorious traditions of Ashes contests did not mean that Greig had to drop his usual practice of 'sledging' an opponent; the Australians did it to him, so why should he change the habits of a lifetime?

Greig took most of the media opprobrium in the summer of 1977, and it did not seem to bother him a jot. He was his usual disarming self in countless interviews and when he was booed by some traditionalists during the Test series, he

enjoyed the notoriety. One had to admire his boundless self-confidence and respect the undoubted popularity he enjoyed with his England colleagues, including those who turned down Packer. He may not have been the most talented all-rounder England have had, but his record was tremendous. A batting average of 40, eight centuries, 141 wickets and 87 catches puts him just behind Sobers and Botham in the all-time list of Test all-rounders. He was weak outside the off-stump, he was vulnerable to the yorker and he did not use his great height sufficiently when he was bowling – but he was a wonderful fighter, who communicated defiance when all around him was falling apart. On the 1973/4 West Indies tour, he helped drag England back from the abyss, along with Geoffrey Boycott and Dennis Amiss, and Greig's thirteen wickets at Port of Spain brought England an unexpected win and an undeserved share of the series. In 1977, he effectively won the Calcutta Test with a hundred, batting more than seven hours with a fever. He was always the man for the big occasions, a fact underlined by the disparity between his Test batting average and his overall first-class average – 40 compared with 31. As an all-round fielder, he was also in the Botham and Sobers class.

It would be wrong to judge Tony Greig too harshly. When one newspaper wrote at the height of the Packer furore that 'after all, he is not English through and through', it was easier to side with Greig in the face of such ridiculous jingoism. Yet his own feeling that he was an outsider must have been relevant. He could have played a hundred Tests for England, if Packer had not influenced him – but equally he might have talked his way out of the England side before very long. Tony Greig got what he wanted: a luxurious lifestyle in Sydney and a job for life with Kerry Packer. When his form slumped disastrously during WSC, he swiftly diversified. He became managing director of an insurance brokers, part of the Packer empire, and soon he was thriving under the new challenges. England did not miss him all that much: Mike Brearley successfully took over the captaincy and Ian Botham took the all-rounder's place in the side, with spectacular results. Tony Greig did not feel the slightest twinge of envy for the new young lion of English cricket. The game of cricket was only ever a signpost along the road of Tony Greig's life, it was never going to consume him. It was precisely that unsentimental detachment which made him such an important man in cricket history.

Dennis Lillee

Dennis Lillee was undeniably one of the greatest fast bowlers of all time, if not *the* greatest. He won more Test series than Harold Larwood, even if he lacked his blistering pace. His arm was higher than Ray Lindwall's, so that he could achieve bounce even with an old ball and the batsman well set. He dominated Test cricket longer than Fred Trueman and surmounted a series of severe injuries that would have beaten all but the most courageous.

Lillee was inextricably linked with Kerry Packer, and gloried in the required extravagances, but he was nevertheless a wonderful cricketer both before and after WSC. He made his Test debut against England in the 1970/1 series, along with Greg Chappell and Rodney Marsh. This trio formed the backbone of the Australian team for the next decade and a half, and significantly they all retired from Test cricket at the same time, in 1984. Over that period, they had invested a new meaning to the phrase 'tough Aussie', but even the temperamental excesses could not obscure their quality as cricketers.

Lillee was the one who stood out, both for his brilliance and his reluctance to yield the spotlight to anyone on the field. Like many young Australians of Test class, he spent an instructive season in the Lancashire League, coming to terms with the vagaries of English wickets, and he subsequently bowled superbly in this country. On his first Australian tour, he took thirty-one Test wickets. At the age of twenty-three, he was a young tearaway with a long, surging run-up, a thrilling final leap and a gloriously uninhibited follow-through. He and Bob Massie were an effective pair that series – Massie the freakish swing bowler, Lillee the shock force. Already he had shown his high

Lillee popularised the spectacular appeal and positively dared the umpire to demur

pain threshold by battling through a painful back injury, to finish the series. A few months later, he broke down in the West Indies and a stress fracture of the vertabrae was diagnosed. It would have finished many players, but Lillee's dedication dragged him through the long months of rehabilitation. He emerged a stronger individual and the enforced inactivity had also made him think about his bowling. Slowly he began to put together the technical weaponry that was to be so impressive. Before he became a complete bowler, he enjoyed two more series of high pace and dramatic results.

In two successive seasons, Lillee and Jeff Thomson put the English and West Indians to the sword as Australia won nine of the twelve Tests. There is perhaps less excuse for the West Indies because they knew what to expect after the lacerating experience of England in the previous year. In any case, one would have expected batsmen such as Clive Lloyd, Alvin Kallicharran, Viv Richards, Roy Fredericks, Lawrence Rowe and Gordon Greenidge to fare rather well against pace bowling – but their mental approach was shattered all too easily. Lillee and Thomson took fifty-six wickets between them, to add to the fifty-eight against England a year earlier. They were a frightening sight: it was not just a matter of speed, it was also a case of fast, short-pitched bowling on wickets that were under-prepared and dangerous. Every English batsman who played in that 1974/5 series lost his nerve at some stage, and there is no dishonour in saying that. John Edrich and Dennis Amiss suffered broken bones, David Lloyd was distressingly struck in the groin area, and it was simply a question of either hanging on grimly to take a battering, or following the example

The Lillee action. Only deteriorating knees prevented him bowling in Tests at the age of forty

of Tony Greig and throwing the bat at anything within reasonable distance. There was rarely a delivery to drive off the front-foot, as lax umpires allowed the fast bowlers to dig the ball in short. England could not reply in kind, with Bob Willis troubled by knee injuries and the others strictly fast-medium. It looked a different game as Derek Underwood and Fred Titmus bowled spin, while Lillee and Thomson steamed in, all malevolence and fire. The carefully orchestrated theatricals of Lillee hardly added to the gaiety of the occasion, as he foul-mouthed his way through the series. Behind the batsman, Rod Marsh and his captain Ian Chappell would vie with each other in profanity. Chappell, the grandson of Victor Richardson, had no doubt been weaned on tales of the Bodyline series by his grandfather, one of the few Australian batsmen to fight it out against Larwood and his support bowlers. Forty years later, and it was time to pay back the Poms. When Keith Fletcher deflected a ball on to his cap and crumpled in a heap as it dropped just short of a diving cover-point, Ian Chappell probably thought his grandfather would approve if he had been alive to witness the carnage. One can only hope that the reaction of Vic Richardson – a combative but essentially a cheerful, sporting cricketer – would have surprised Chappell. This comment by the editor of *Wisden* was particularly telling: 'Never in the 98 years of Test cricket have batsmen been so grievously bruised and battered by ferocious, hostile, short-pitched balls.'

That series was the forerunner of many more over the next decade and the hype that accompanied the excesses was particularly distasteful. Jeff Thomson played up to the hairy-chested image, boasting about 'blood on the pitch', but he never really believed all that nonsense. Until he retired in 1986, Thomson remained a doughty opponent, but he rarely troubled umpires by straying beyond the confines of justifiable aggression. His famous partner was somewhat different.

It became clear that Lillee needed to be pumped up to give of his best on the field. He genuinely appeared to hate batsmen and he developed a vicious streak that demeaned a man of modest charm when he was not playing cricket. When Kerry Packer's publicity machine whirred into action, Dennis Lillee was the principal agent for all the ballyhoo. Packer liked to see his star players act like larger-than-life creations, in the same way expected of movie legends in Hollywood in the 1930s. This taste for high drama affected play. It

The unique, javelin-thrower's action of Jeff Thomson, Lillee's partner in carnage for several exhilarating years

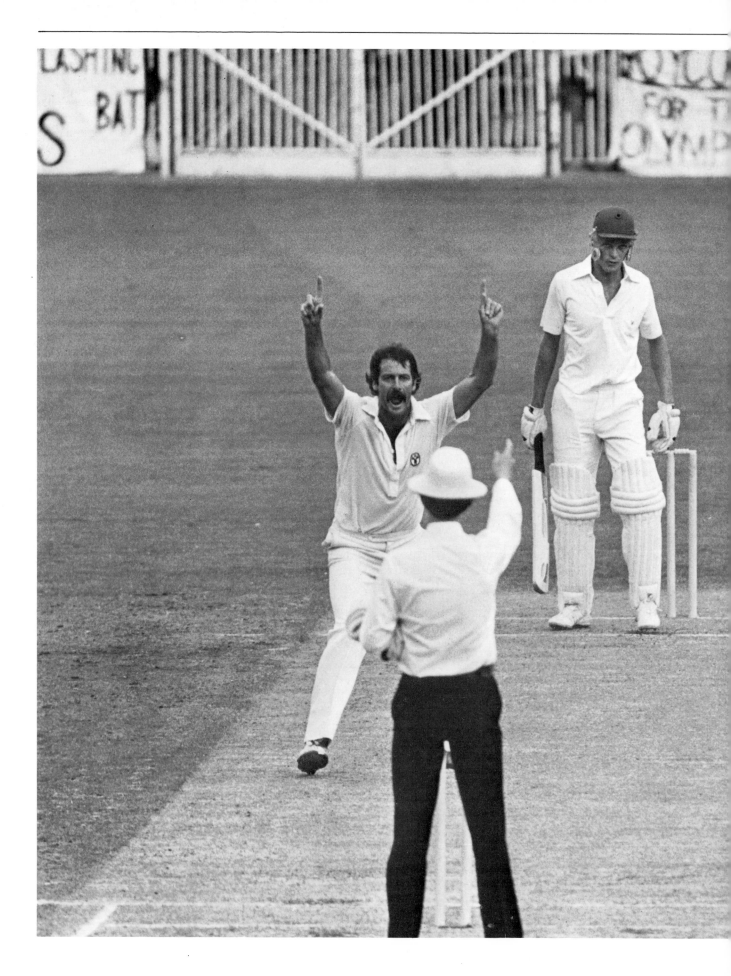

Always the extrovert. Lillee was the darling of the masses

Left: Lillee and Rod Marsh were the most successful bowler/wicket-keeper combination in Test history. Their appeals never lacked conviction. David Gower did not survive this one

was deemed good television to see Lillee endorse a certain product on screen between overs – then cut back to the play to see if he could knock someone's head off. The swaggering, beer-swilling yobs cultivated by Lillee loved it; in turn he seemed to need mindless adulation to give of his best. These were not the histrionics of a Fred Trueman – a fast bowler of bristling bravado, raucous appealing and theatrical stares at the unfortunate batsmen. This was more sinister. As Lillee ran in, bulging-eyed, with thigh muscles pumping, the more moronic sections of the crowd would chant 'Kill! Kill! Kill!' Without the helmet, that might have been the case.

When WSC ended, the captaincy of Australia passed between Greg Chappell and Kim Hughes for several years. Lillee always seemed happier under Chappell's command; Hughes had not been signed by Kerry Packer, and Lillee and the rest seemed to resent Hughes's sound relationship with the Australian Board of Control. The rebel needed a cause at all times, and if that involved a longing for the old days under Ian Chappell, so much the better. Chappell's brother was the nearest he would get to those blissful days of bouncers and broken bones. To be fair to Lillee, he had so much pride in his own

performance that he would surmount physical obstacles that would have daunted most cricketers. On the 1981 tour to England, he took thirty-nine wickets, even though he began the tour with viral pneumonia and struggled with a degenerative knee condition. He was still a marvellous sight – running in like a thoroughbred racehorse, a final leap and a controlled delivery of power and beauty. He had become a master of swing and deviation off the pitch – in both cases, at speed. He seemed to have mellowed somewhat, indulging in banter with umpire 'Dickie' Bird, commending Ian Botham for his batting exploits, and even signing a few Pommie autograph books. Was this the new Lillee?

A few months later, a sharp kick up the backside of Pakistan's captain swiftly reasserted the recidivist in Dennis Lillee. Javed Miandad's outraged reaction and Lillee's raised fists only increased the horror that Test cricket had descended to such depths. As an 'agent provocateur' Javed Miandad had been in a class of his own in recent years, but whatever the provocation, Lillee's actions were appalling. Yet his captain, Greg Chappell, said it was the Pakistani's fault, that he had been trying to bait Lillee! While Chappell settled easily into the role of cricket's

Nero, fiddling while the last citadel of sportsmanship burned, the Australian Board took a leaf out of Pontius Pilate's book. They banned Lillee for two of the one-day international games, thereby ensuring that their best bowler would be available for the next Test. Once again, the Board had been given a golden opportunity to curb Lillee's excesses, and again they had flunked it. *Autres temps, autres moeurs* . . . In 1965, England had dropped Ken Barrington for a Test because he had compiled a hundred too slowly. Barrington had been out of form, but in his usual determined way, he battled through to make 137 against the New Zealanders. England won the match by nine wickets. Barrington accepted his punishment like a true professional and he came back better than ever. Yet Dennis Lillee sparks off a fight on the field and the admonishment is handed out by a feather duster.

The Australian Board's effete response to Lillee was not unexpected. Since the capitulation to Kerry Packer's demands in 1979, the Board had shown that the velvet glove had concealed a fist of wimpish fatalism. In hock to Packer, the Board knew that the show had to go on, even if it meant tacitly condoning bad behaviour. In December 1979, Lillee was allowed to hold up an Ashes Test for ten minutes while advertising an aluminium bat. He simulated rage when the umpires told him he could not play with it, gratified the Ocker instincts by haranguing the England captain, Mike Brearley, and remonstrated with Greg Chappell when he was told to revert to an orthodox willow. He knew exactly what he was doing and the more cynical observer wondered when he would apply for an Equity card. Once again Lillee was reprieved; his presence was too important to Kerry Packer and, by implication, the Board of Control. So Lillee continued to make Mike Brearley's life a misery on the field in that series, with the result that the more objectionable members of Lillee's fan club taunted the England captain in every match. Stones were thrown at the English team during a floodlit match at Sydney, and the anti-English behaviour at Melbourne was so bad that the Australian team manager John Edwards apologized to Brearley and remarked that he felt ashamed to be an Australian. The Board, acting on the principle that the messenger should be shot if he bears bad news, have not asked Edwards to manage an Australian side since.

Even after Test cricket settled down to its hectic post-Packer flurry of activity, the

The Chappell brothers, Greg and Ian – backbone of the Australian batting for a decade and captains who could always get the best out of Lillee

Dennis Lillee gives Tony Greig yet another final warning

malign side of Dennis Lillee kept pace with his wonderful bowling. In the season of the aluminium bat, he turned in a magnificent spell of bowling at Melbourne, where he took eleven English wickets on a lifeless pitch to win the Test. It was the kind of effort that no other fast bowler on earth could have accomplished with such brilliance. In 1981, while Lillee was impressing so many with his stamina and resource, he bet against his own side in the famous Leeds Test. His defence that the odds of 500/1 were too tempting to turn down would have struck a responsive chord in the breast of Tony Greig. It was not that anyone doubted Lillee's commitment to the cause – he took seven wickets in the match and almost won it on the final afternoon with some sensible

hitting. The bet was just typical of Lillee and anyone who thought he was wrong would automatically be branded a woolly reactionary.

When Trevor Chappell bowled an underarm delivery to deny New Zealand victory in a one-day match, he was summing up the Lillee era. It was February 1981 and the score was one-all in the four match series. New Zealand needed 6 to win off the final ball and then Chappell – instructed by his brother – bowled his grubber, Australia won the match and went on to take the series, and that remained the prime justification in the eyes of Greg Chappell and his henchmen. It mattered little that the New Zealand Prime Minister fired off a telegram, accusing them of 'an act of cowardice', nor the subsequent admonishment of Greg Chappell by his own Board of Control. Australia had carried

off the Benson and Hedges World Series Cup for that year – and with it, the money. Nothing could be left to the spirit of the law any more; sharp minds were primed for any lucrative loophole. The 'grubber' was soon banned in Australia, but the damage was done. Expediency had again triumphed.

Dennis Lillee was, like John McEnroe, a symbol of our sporting times. A fundamental malaise merged with a streak of exhibitionism and found a positive response from many who could never approach the great ability of either Lillee or McEnroe. It was deemed socially acceptable to join in the umpire-baiting by creating a cacophony of abuse. Like McEnroe, Lillee needed a real or imagined grievance to function at his magnificent best and if the crowd wished to graft the atmosphere of a bull fight on to a beautiful game, that was their privilege. They had

Not every Australian player in the 1980s pulled in the same direction as their beleaguered captains – Kim Hughes (*left*) and his successor Allan Border

paid their money – that ubiquitous word – and they should not be expected to show enough self-discipline to sit and appreciate the finer points. How could the players criticize the exhibitionism of spectators when they greeted the fall of every wicket with hysterical embraces on the field? Whenever Dennis Lillee reacted to the dismissal of Mike Brearley with his usual braggadocio, he was simply sanctioning equally unpleasant behaviour on the boundary edge.

It is hard to believe that Lillee would have been a lesser bowler if he had possessed the behavioural standards of a Willis or a Statham. He had everything the ideal performer would need. Within a year of his Test debut he had shown his capabilities with a superb exhibition against the Rest of the World side. On the fast Perth wicket, Lillee tore the heart out of a batting line-up that included

Gavaskar, Kanhai, Zaheer, Lloyd, Greig and Sobers. He took eight for 29 and the Rest of the World were bowled out for 59. Lillee took twenty-four wickets in that series, against great batsmen with proper professional pride, who did not take kindly to humiliation from a 22-year-old rookie. After that series, no batsman was ever immune to Lillee as he continued learning his craft, streamlining his action, adding subtleties to his blinding pace. He became the star attraction of a very fine Australian side that dominated the world from 1972 to 1977. Ian Chappell's ruthless captaincy got the very best out of his bowlers, the fielding was brilliant (particularly in the slip and gully areas), and Rod Marsh became a most accomplished wicket-keeper/batsman. The batting – the two Chappells, Walters, Redpath, Edwards, Stackpole and McCosker – was deep and experienced in all conditions. Their bristling hostility made them hard to love, but easy to respect. The fact that the Packer negotiations were conducted in such secrecy confirms their

alienation from the Board of Control. Such a tight-knit relationship among the players helped make them such a powerful unit, even if their public relations smacked of Attila the Hun with a migraine. If they had not signed up 'en masse' with Packer, the Australians would have continued to dominate world cricket. By the time they reassembled in the established version, the West Indies were about to sally forth and mow down all opposition with their 'scorched-earth' policy of concentrated fast bowling.

None of those West Indian fast bowlers could compare however with Dennis Lillee. No one in modern Test history has worked so hard to keep fit for so many years and no one managed to adapt so successfully to all wickets throughout the world. More than any other fast bowler, he meant the difference between the two sides, because he had the priceless quality of a big heart to set alongside his matchless ability. That was a winning combination, as Lillee never failed to remind anyone while he was on the cricket field.

Viv Richards

Viv Richards has been the world's outstanding batsman for the past decade and the jewel in the crown of one of the most powerful Test sides in history. Without Richards, the West Indies would still have been pre-eminent because of their production line of fast bowlers – but Richards has humanized the side's ruthless image by his easy grace, and nobility of batting.

Comparisons between Don Bradman and Viv Richards are inevitable. Both dominated their generation by sheer weight of runs and power of personality. When Richards first toured England in 1976, the purists said he would struggle on pitches where the ball turns and seams around; he played across the line too much, he could not keep playing the pull shot to a ball of good length and survive, he could not get away with whipping a ball on the off-stump through the leg-side field, and his defence was non-existent. Richards replied by scoring 829 runs in four Tests, and Bradman's series record of 974 in 1930 might easily have been toppled if Richards had been fit for the Lord's Test. In the calendar year of 1976, Viv Richards scored no less than 1710 Test runs. At the age of twenty-four, he was positively Bradmanesque. Like the great Australian, he became a symbol of his people. Bradman lifted morale for thousands of jobless Australians during the Depression days: Richards has done the same for the black man. His fierce pride in his colour, and his espousal of the Rastafarian philosophy have inspired many who react to racial prejudice with militancy. Richards would never advocate extreme measures to assert black power, not least of all because he has too much respect for the customs of England, but he is not the kind of brilliant West Indian

A contemplative return to the pavilion for Richards

cricketer who used to be indulged and patronized by the white man on the plantations. By his deeds and demeanour he has indirectly contributed to a growing black consciousness in the Caribbean. Significantly, it is now more than a decade since a white man played for the West Indies, and few of them make the grade

at Shell Shield level. The days when white men like John Goddard and Karl Nunes captained a team of varied colours have gone, surely for ever.

A true conception of Richards's dominance of world cricket can only be appreciated by listing his colleagues in succeeding West Indian sides. They have been magnificent cricketers. Among batsmen – Fredericks, Greenidge, Haynes, Kallicharran, Lloyd, Gomes and Dujon. The bowlers have included the versatile Roberts, the lissom Holding, the intimidating Croft, the unique Garner, the destructive Marshall and Patterson, the latest of a frightening breed. With such an array of fast bowlers, the wicket-keeper has only needed to be an athletic long-stop wearing gloves, but the two Murrays and Dujon have done all that was necessary. That adds up to an awesome concentration of talent over just a decade – but Richards has symbolized the hegemony. The best all-round fielder in a team of athletes, he has also been the man to rally the fortunes if the side occasionally faltered. More than any other current batsman, he has made runs when they were desperately needed. The vital innings he has played at Lord's for Somerset and the West Indies have confirmed that he is a man at his best when the stakes are high and he is required to turn in the big score. At the World Cup Final in 1983, the delighted reaction of the Indians at Richards's dismissal underlined how important he is: only after Richards was out could the Indians conceive the chance of victory. Richard seems to be able to make runs more or less at will, when he decides that the occasion is sufficiently important. He lacks Bradman's killer instinct, but seems to have a pre-determined appointment with a big

Clive Lloyd receives the first World Cup from the Duke of Edinburgh at Lord's in 1975 after a thrilling victory by the West Indies over Australia. The late, greatly missed Ken Barrington looks on

Top: The unacceptable side of West Indies cricket: Michael Holding reacts to a failed appeal by kicking down the stumps at Dunedin, 1980. The fact that it was out of character for Holding to behave in such a manner did nothing to ease the mind

score. When Antigua staged its inaugural Test in 1981, it seemed only appropriate that Richards would score a hundred. He did not let his adoring friends down. Nor did he, five years later, with the fastest hundred in Test history.

A big innings from Richards transcends partisanship. Like Sobers and Hammond, he is a rare sight to behold as he makes his stately, serene progress to the wicket. He seems to have two shots for each delivery when the fires of inspiration are lit–the peerless leg-side play, the crashing shot through the covers after making room for himself, or when he hits the ball 'on the up', and the lofted on-drive that soars away after little apparent effort. For more than ten years, Richards has reduced Test bowlers to chopping blocks; he induces a weary fatalism when a delivery good enough to get a batsman caught in the slips is cracked past midwicket's left hand. Cricket devotees all over the world are no doubt bored with West Indian supremacy, with the monotonous use of deadly fast bowlers, but they would be devastated if a shift in the balance of power meant the eclipse of Viv Richards.

Right: Viv Richards – when the muse of inspiration is with him, no bowler is safe

However there seems little prospect of a decline in the fortunes of Viv Richards and his juggernaut of a team. Modern Test cricket is simply a case of West Indies' dominance and the rest nowhere. They now play a totally different game to the other countries and, sporting and aesthetic considerations apart, they are probably the most effective unit of all time. With various personnel changes, they have led the way for a decade and show no signs of muting their relentless surge through the record books. Since the start of the 1976 series in England, the West Indies have played seventy-nine Tests, and lost just six of them: two of those occurred during the years when their best players were turning out for Kerry Packer and just a couple of those six defeats came when they were operating with their full hand of four fast bowlers. The stability of the side has been a vital ingredient in the West Indies' success–in those seventy-nine Tests, the West Indies have used forty-six players, while in the

same period England's total is seventy-six. Without being a particularly special captain, Clive Lloyd ended up with a remarkable record – most Tests as captain (seventy-four), most victories (thirty-six), most successive victories (eleven), most consecutive matches without defeat (twenty-six). He lost just twelve Tests and seven of those came in his first thirteen Tests, when he was coming to grips with the job. Impressively, he batted supremely well as captain – an average of 51 compared with 38 when not in charge. Although captaincy of the West Indies invariably consisted of nothing other than perming two from four fast bowlers, it has to be admitted that Lloyd knitted together the potentially disparate elements in the side. A West Indies team will always be prone to petty jealousies and outside influences because of the various selections from different islands; Lloyd's greatest achievement was to make them play as a team, rather than as a collection of highly talented individuals.

Lloyd was the man who launched West Indies on their astonishing run of success, by taking an historic decision in 1976. In April of that year, India won remarkably at Port of Spain, when they got the highest fourth innings target in history: chasing 406, the largest total in the match, they strolled home by six wickets. Lloyd had gone into the game with two fast bowlers – the young Michael Holding and the fast-medium Bernard Julien. He even had to bowl 6 overs of seam himself, and then rely on his spinners to winkle out the Indians. They failed lamentably – Padmore, Imtiaz Ali and Jumadeen bowled 105 overs in the second innings and did not take one wicket. Imtiaz, a leg-spinner never played again for his country while Padmore's off-spin was used once more, and Jumadeen's slow left-arm was seen five times more in Tests. For the next Test a fortnight later, Lloyd brought in four fast bowlers – Holding, Daniel, Julien and Holder. On a fiery Sabina Park pitch, they were blatantly intimidatory and, with little support from the umpires, the Indians had five men injured. Bishen Bedi, their captain, declared the second innings closed at 97, with just five wickets down. A cricketer who epitomized the game's grace and sportsmanship gave the match on a plate to the West Indies, leaving them just thirteen for victory. Bedi was sickened by the brutality of the bowling and wanted an end to it, before someone was killed. Lloyd had just suffered a stunning 5/1 defeat in Australia at the hands of Lillee and Thomson and his tactics at Sabina Park a few months later indicated the way he would now be conducting affairs.

In the summer of 1976, England's batsmen were blitzed by sustained pressure from Holding, Roberts, Daniel and Holder. A few perfunctory overs of spin from Jumadeen, Richards and Fredericks did not obscure the game plan. If the pitch was fast, at least two of the quartet was sharp enough; when the Oval wicket was slow, Mike Holding's speed through the air was decisive; when the Old Trafford pitch was badly prepared, they were lethal. Just one hour's batting at Old Trafford gave the cricket world a foretaste of Test cricket's decline as a varied, attractive force. John Edrich and Brian Close were subjected to a vicious barrage of bouncers on a dangerous wicket, and yet the umpires merely indulged in finger-wagging. After Old Trafford, Edrich, one of the game's great fighters, decided to retire from Test cricket and his words have a chilling prescience:

I just couldn't see the point in standing out there for hours, waiting to get my head knocked off and wondering if I'd ever get a chance to score. I calculated that the amount of short-pitched bowling allowed me about six deliveries an hour to have a chance of runs. I was fed up of being a target man, with no hope of taking the fight to the bowlers.

Many a Test batsman will echo the thoughts of John Edrich, uttered in the year when Clive Lloyd and a collection of weak umpires allowed the game to enter a disturbingly unpleasant phase. When Old Trafford finished the careers of brave men like Brian Close and John Edrich, there had to be concern at the sinister trends. Yet it has simply got worse.

After the peace with Packer in 1979, the West Indies strengthened their hold on Test cricket. Holder and Daniel were replaced by two fast bowlers of remorselessly awkward style. Joel Garner's massive height allowed him to achieve bounce on the flattest of wickets, his yorker proved the deadliest in world cricket and it was usually impossible to score consistent runs off his bowling. Colin Croft bowled round the wicket from the very extremity of the crease – sometimes illegally so – and slanted the ball in at the batsman's body. Invariably, Croft's line of attack had little to do with the position of the stumps: the target was the batsman. In many ways he was the most physically dangerous of all the West Indian fast bowlers and figures of 125 wickets in just 27 Tests indicate both his success and the lack of umpiring mettle.

When Croft joined a 'pirate' tour to South Africa, Malcolm Marshall was already installed as a devastating shock force. A smallish man of immense fitness, his bouncer can be terrifyingly fast and his skilful variations are a tribute to his intelligence and the experience afforded him by English county cricket. Unlike many fast bowlers, Marshall always wants to bowl; he has so much talent and sheer speed that no batsman can expect to withstand his assaults for a whole session.

We now almost take this concentration of fast bowling for granted. Nothing like it has been seen over a long period in Test history. The assaults of Gregory and McDonald were at least tempered by the extravagant leg-spin of Arthur Mailey and the more accurate version from Warwick Armstrong; Larwood and Voce were complemented by Hammond's medium-pace, Verity's left-arm spin and Allen's off-side fast bowling in the Bodyline series; Lindwall and Miller were supported by Johnston's left-arm cut and swing, the leg-spin of Benaud, the left-arm medium pace of Toshack and the off-spin of Ian Johnson; Tyson and Statham were backed up by Wardle and Appleyard's spin and the talented fast-medium pace of Bailey. Even the West Indies attack of the 1960s had some variety after the initial pace onslaught of Hall and Griffith: Sobers and Gibbs would bowl many overs of spin and the attack was very successful because it was so balanced, with Sobers's versatility crucial. Such a roll-call is a necessary reply to the defensiveness of the West Indies when they say, 'What are you complaining about? The Aussies were just the same with Lindwall and Miller, and what about Bodyline?' It is not the same at all: the West Indies bowling strategy in the 1980s has centred on sheer pace, blatant physical intimidation and a criminally slow over-rate. On the rare occasions when their attack has been mastered, the West Indies have bowled their overs so slowly that no batting side could run away with the match and leave themselves enough time to bowl out the West Indians twice. The West Indies say that if they did bowl their overs faster, the game would end that much quicker: that would be all to their credit and surely no one would cavil at that.

Even if umpires successfully stamped down on intimidation, the West Indies would remain the best team in the world by a huge margin. They are great athletes, with a hunger for success that contrasts admirably with the world-weary attitude of some Australian and English players. A place in the West Indies team is a

Joy unconfined: the West Indies retain the World Cup at Lord's in 1979, as England are comfortably beaten

passport to riches, prestige and social status in islands that still contain much poverty. The streets and bars in the Caribbean are teeming with young, strong teenagers who just love to bowl fast. The climate, the physical advantages enjoyed by a man of Afro-West Indian stock, and the burning ambition to succeed all combine to ensure that this dominance will not be broken. Competition for a place in the national side is now intense: that is why the established players train so hard, that is why their fast bowlers have lasted so long. Their training sessions before a day's play are impressively professional; no one, not even the great Richards, is excused, and Richards remains the hardest trainer of all. Their fast bowlers are fully limbered up before they come on

to the field; sweating, supple and fully extended, they are ready to fire in at full pace from the first ball. In contrast, opening bowlers from other countries often have to strive for length and line in their early overs. When you bat against the West Indies, you are mentally and physically on the back-foot from the start.

Provided the captain can instil the necessary professionalism into the players, the job of leading a modern West Indian side could be accomplished by any competent first-class cricketer. All that Lloyd and Richards have needed to do in recent years is rotate the bowlers, secure in the knowledge that the cordon of brilliant close catchers would gobble up any snicks, and that the all-round athleticism of the fielders would ensure that quick

singles would never consistently disrupt the bowlers' rhythm. A daily diet of more than two hundred bouncers or deliveries rising towards the chest means the batsmen never get a chance to establish any mastery, and the risk of physical injury increases as long as umpires continue to abdicate responsibility. In the last three years, twelve batsmen have been seriously injured in internationals against the West Indies – three broken fingers, two broken arms and a smashed nose are part of the grisly tally. There seems every prospect of further injuries, as groundsmen in the Caribbean continue

Viv and Ian Botham take a break from the 1986 hostilities in the Caribbean. Here they are, majestically sunning themselves, two great cricketers in a mirror image pose

to offer pitches that are under-prepared, grassy and of uneven bounce. In the first Test against England at Kingston in 1986, the quality and physical threat represented by the West Indian fast bowlers made even hardened Test veterans shudder. The pitch was criminally slanted in favour of the fast bowler and the half-centuries scored by Graham Gooch and Peter Willey were worth 150 in less exacting Test matches. Batsmen were hit every over and the West Indies speed attack established a psychological hold over the batsmen that lasted the entire series. After Kingston, they did not need to bowl so many bouncers because it was clear that the collective nerve of the English batting had gone, that far too many were not getting in line. Some of the former Test players who holidayed in the Caribbean during that series may well have felt they would have coped more satisfactorily in their pomp, but they

would have been deluding themselves. At no stage in Test history has a batsman had to face such unrestricted intimidation on unreliable wickets for so long. The West Indies are now playing a game that is foreign to the experience of everyone over the age of fifteen.

It seems that legislation will only be introduced to curb such unfair intimidation when someone is killed at the crease. The interpretation of unfair short-pitched fast bowling is inexact and umpires are too lax in their attitudes to the law. The West Indians say it is up to the individual umpire – yet indulge in petulance on the rare occasion when an umpire calls 'enough', as Harold Bird experienced at the hands of Clive Lloyd at Edgbaston in 1984. Whenever there is talk about curbing the excesses of fast bowling, the West Indians bridle, suspecting dark plots to rob them of their strike force. Yet their bowlers are so versatile, so fast and so tactically intelligent that they would still be the world's best side if just one short-pitched delivery was allowed per over. No other country can choose from such a reservoir of fast

bowling talent and nothing the legislators do can alter that. Even the West Indian batsmen are suffering from this fast bowling dominance – in the 1985/6 Shell Shield season, there were only seven totals of more than 300 in sixty innings. Young Caribbean batsmen are suffering the same fate as the other Test countries and there is no sign of a new Kanhai, a Sobers or a Richards. The fact that Richards averages just 25 against the all-conquering Barbados attack prompts the thought: how would the West Indies batsmen face against their own fast bowlers in a Test?

There has to be something disturbing about a sport where raw courage is more crucial than skill. Cricket has always managed to marry the attributes of natural talent, bravery and mental steel into a coherent unit and when the vast majority of the Test match countries play each other, those qualities are still to the fore. When the West Indies get involved, the picture changes dramatically – and there seems little hope that they are willing to continue their deserved dominance by more acceptable means.

Ian Botham

Ian Botham's name is often on the front, rather than the back page of a newspaper in these days of the sporting superstar. His presence in gossip columns and lurid exposés is as much a comment on media mores as Botham's apparent reluctance to regard himself purely as a cricketer who has played the game better and more excitingly than most.

Botham is a mass of contradictions. The greatest English entertainer since Denis Compton, he sometimes seems to have little respect for a game that has brought him so much glamour. The supreme individualist, yet a supportive team-man to less talented players. A bitter critic of the prurient curiosity of the press, yet he is a well-paid columnist for a tabloid newspaper that is a byword for the sensational and the sleazy. No stranger to the pugilistic arts, yet a sentimental lover of children. A political reactionary, a staunch supporter of the monarchy, yet a man who cultivates an iconoclastic image, embracing the world of the rock star and picking up a drugs conviction along the way. Apparently self-indulgent, but he walked the length of Britain to raise a vast sum of money for leukaemia research. A man who still wants to captain England, even though his brief tenure coincided with an alarming loss of form. Above all, Ian Botham polarizes opinion. You either love him or hate him, and how Fleet Street will cope with his eventual retirement is a matter that must give news editors sleepless nights.

Even Botham's sternest critics have to acknowledge his record, not least of all because he has never set out to achieve statistical monuments. From first to last, he has been an entertainer and if he had a fraction of Boycott's yearning for personal records, he would have set even greater

Ian Botham takes another wicket in typically subdued manner

targets. A man of Botham's colossal natural ability does not need to worry about missing out on a good pitch and tired bowlers – like Keith Miller, Gary Sobers and his great friend Viv Richards, he thrives on the big occasion. Unfortunately, such inspiration has rarely fired against the West Indies. By the time he lined up against them, they were the best team in the world and have remained so during Botham's tribulations as England captain, his reasonable all-round performances in 1984 and his traumas against hopeless odds in 1986. Botham's

comparative mediocrity against the West Indies will always tarnish some of the gloss, but it would have been interesting to see how the other great all-rounders would have fared, bowling at Greenidge, Haynes, Richards, Lloyd and the others, and then marching in at number six, with the early batting devastated by fearsome speed.

One of Botham's most endearing characteristics remains his positive attitude to the game. He plays the same way in a Test as in a Sunday League game, and his attacking inclinations have led to some towering achievements. No cricketer has turned in three successive performances of the type he managed in the 1981 Tests against Australia. He had reached his lowest ebb, resigning the captaincy minutes before he was due to be sacked, and his form was sadly awry. At Leeds, he gave England hope with a joyfully uninhibited innings of 149 not out and Bob Willis then bowled England to sensational victory. At Old Trafford, his hundred was a masterpiece of textbook aggression – the *Times* devoted a front-page article to it, with the headline, 'Was Botham's innings the greatest ever?' At Edgbaston, Botham took five for 1 in a spell of 28 balls for a 29-run victory. With due respect to Willis's marvellously sustained bowling, and to the imaginative captaincy of Mike Brearley, it was Botham who revitalized the series and England's fortunes. With crowds flocking to the Tests, and money flowing into the English game, there were several county cricketers grateful to Botham's flair; without the boost of generous Test Match receipts, some counties would have been forced to offload players. Botham has always been big at the box-office.

As a batsman, his yearning to dominate

and to hit massive sixes has perhaps obscured the basic orthodoxy of his technique. No one plays straighter in defence, and his driving off front- and back-foot is right out of the textbook. He hooks in the air, a tendency that gets him out, but also a vast amount of sixes. When Botham takes on a fast bowler – relishing the square cut, launching into massive pulls and hooks – it is one of cricket's most invigorating sights. His batting in the 1985 season, when he set a new record of eighty sixes in the first-class game, was consistently stirring. No one but Botham would have the self-confidence and certainty to begin a Test innings with sixes off his first and third balls, as he did to McDermott at Edgbaston. They were both magnificent long drives – straight and over long-on into the pavilion – and the crowd's ecstatic reaction was a fitting salute to a great entertainer.

Botham's bowling has attracted more criticism. It is part of his restless nature that he loves to experiment and he would be the first to admit that he does bowl rubbish at times. Yet he has the happy knack of picking up wickets with bad deliveries, partly because he imposes himself on some batsmen and unnerves them. You cannot take more than 350 Test wickets by a consistent diet of long-hops and half-volleys, even though some former Test bowlers who criticize Botham seem to have been paragons of line and length, who never bowled a bad spell or got a chance to clean up the tail. Botham irritates so many cricketers-turned-critics because he somehow bounces back with wickets as soon as his bowling obituary is published. He is undoubtedly a lucky bowler, but he often bowls the kind of full length that gets wickets – or concedes runs.

As a fielder, Botham is outstanding anywhere. He defies convention in the slips, standing there with his hands on knees, yet he manages to see the ball quicker than most and picks up outstanding catches with regularity. Away from the slips, he is surprisingly agile and fast, with an impressive record of run-outs. His fielding off his own bowling is outstandingly supple for a man of his bulk, who is often off-balance. Definitely in the class of Sobers and Richards as an all-round fielder.

Whatever his detractors say, he must be judged England's greatest all-rounder since W. G. Grace. With bat and ball, he has won more Test Matches single-handedly than any other Englishman, and only Gary Sobers can rival him for influence. When he first bowled for England, he was fortunate to have at the other end seam bowlers of the calibre of

Mike Brearley, the captain who seemed to get more out of Botham than anyone else

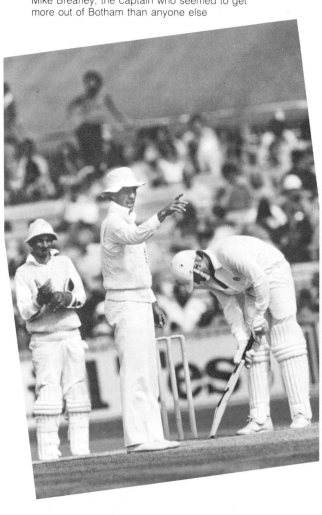

England were fortunate to have two great wicket-keepers on hand during Ian Botham's prolific years as a bowler. Bob Taylor and Alan Knott remained friends despite a healthy rivalry that lasted more than a decade

Bob Willis, Mike Hendrick, John Lever and Chris Old; Botham would pick up wickets from batsmen fretting at tight accuracy from the other end. Yet Botham was also a marvellously versatile bowler; he could make the outswinger dip very late, slip in a prodigious inswinger, and bowl a wickedly fast bouncer when necessary. He may have lost that nip, and the ability to swing the ball late may have waned, but he can still bowl for long periods. He would be an even better bowler if some of the flights of fancy were curbed, yet Botham without his fondness for improvisation would be less of an attraction. He would not have performed such wonders if conformity had been part of his cricketing make-up: you might as well ask Keith Miller to bowl every delivery from exactly the same run-up.

Botham has never been particularly strong on self-criticism and it is difficult to believe he has many regrets about the way he has played cricket. Nor should he – only a colossus like Bradman could marry monumental dedication with supernatural ability. Botham has approached cricket in character: expansively, outrageously and bravely. Unlike

many fine players, he has not been frightened to try things, to risk making a fool of himself. Who dares, wins. The darker side of an essentially generous, naive nature shows itself in his brushes with the law – either of the land, or the law of cricket's headquarters, at Lord's. Botham has long believed that 'they' were out to get him and at various times, the generic term 'they' has encompassed police, cricket's hierarchy and the press. Without apportioning any blame, such incidents are the natural corollary of the desire to turn a marvellous cricketer into a superstar.

Left: An expensive bowler, and a lucky one – but Ian Botham has never lost the knack of taking wickets

Below: Botham remains the delight of Fleet Street picture editors, whatever the opinions of their journalistic colleagues

In the post-Packer years, a player of Botham's gifts and undoubted charisma was bound to make a very comfortable living. The rewards from endorsing cricket equipment, publishing books and ghosted newspaper articles were as much as playing for England – and at around £1500 a Test that was munificent enough anyway. Yet Botham's restless nature encompassed a wider world than the stereotyped one of cricket and its profitable offshoots. He engaged a manager whose brief was to sell Ian Botham to a wider audience. Now Botham has always been a man for the nine-day wonder, rather than the global complexities of life, and he genially co-operated with ambitious projects like a career in Hollywood, posing as 'Rambotham' in a newspaper and launching a new range of leisurewear. The fun and the excitement

At the tensest moments in a Test Match, Botham invariably sees the funny side of life – except when an appeal goes against him.
Here David Hookes gets the benefit of the doubt during a dramatic stage in the famous Melbourne Test of 1982, which England won by 3 runs when all seemed lost

from the new interests relaxed him and his splendid form throughout the 1985 season reflected his serenity. Unfortunately his new manager, Tim Hudson, proved an ephemeral influence. His habit of talking in exclamation marks hardly endeared him to the business world and a gift for hyperbole that would have shamed even Phineas T. Barnum did not impress Hollywood, that citadel of hype. The superstar and his manager parted company amid the latest drugs rumours and yet another colourful chapter in Ian Botham's life was closed. It was simply a harmless enough interlude for Botham and the next challenge would soon present itself. He may not be the most cerebral of cricketers, but his sang-froid in the face of intense media pressure is remarkable.

The press maintain that Botham was fair game for the investigative journalists once he and Hudson had decided to use the media for publicizing their business exploits. The name of Harry Truman and a certain hot kitchen was regularly invoked by grizzled hacks who did not know their Capitol Hill from their Fifth Amendment.

It was bound to end in tears, with innocents like Botham's family suffering from the glare of exposure. Botham himself has always seemed capable of fielding the flak but harassment of his friends and family has been distasteful. The whole sorry saga of 'Botham's Image' has been a parable of our times, with two factions diametrically opposed. Botham repeatedly invokes the classic sportsman's paranoia about 'the press building you up, then knocking you down again', while Fleet Street pompously deals out the old canard about 'the Freedom of the Press', while ignoring the equally relevant jounalistic watchword: 'Comment is free, but facts are sacred.' The bitter circulation war between Fleet

Left: Botham batting in his usual expansive manner

Below: Bob Willis after bowling England to an historic victory at Leeds, 1981

Street newspapers has revived memories of the iniquities of 'the Yellow Press' in Chicago during the 1920s and men like Botham have remained in the firing line, as managing editors gaze up at graphs on their office walls. For his part, Botham should not demean himself with a ghosted column for a tabloid firmly in the vanguard of Fleet Street's brutalizing tendencies.

All of this would be irrelevant, apart from the way it affects Botham's great gifts as a cricketer and as an example of the way the game is now big business. After England did not capitalize on the World Cup victory in 1966, soccer failed to hold the public's affection for many reasons. Cricket became more and more popular through the one-day game, the good offices of sponsorship, skilled coverage by television and radio, the influx of great overseas players and a

succession of marvellous Test Matches. The influence of Kerry Packer has helped foster a star system in cricket, and with so much booty available, the media perceives its duty as giving the public a run for the players' money. Newspaper coverage has been trivialized into spurious controversies, a quest for 'quotes', and a dearth of forensic analysis on the game. Cricket is now far too near the 'pop' end of the sporting market, with showbiz clichés at the ready. The press will say that is the price for being paid handsomely, while the players privately admit that almost every man has his price, even though he can also publicly bemoan the trivialization of a subtle game. Such a circle can never be squared and it falls to Ian Botham to be in the firing line. It may be disturbing to many but, apart from the Royal Family, he is probably the best-known Englishman around today: in such a sophisticated

Above: A droll suggestion to Ian Botham that he should lose some weight – Brisbane, December 1982. Botham was as amused as anyone at the stunt, and ignored such subtle hints. His form suffered while he maintained he was perfectly fit

Left: Jimmy Greaves attempts to conduct an interview with Ian Botham on the historic leukaemia walk from John O'Groats to Land's End. For almost a month Botham enjoyed the rare luxury of an almost exclusively favourable press coverage

electronic age, he reaches far more homes than W. G. Grace ever managed, even if the Queen does not inquire after his health in the same solicitous manner as Queen Victoria did for the good doctor.

Just as Grace epitomized late-Victorian complacency, as the rewards accrued from hard work and a missionary zeal, so Ian Botham symbolizes an unruly, aggressive age. Like the society he inhabits, he is anarchic, yet imbued with a genuine commitment to charitable causes. Above all, he is cricket's very own Militant Tendency. Somehow it needs a vivid imagination to picture Botham in the commentary box, lambasting the current crop of cricketers, and lapsing into rambling anecdotes about the summer of 1981. He has always been his own man, to the relief of cricket-lovers.

David Gower

David Gower has been a consistent source of aesthetic pleasure in an era of Test cricket that has seen far too much brutalism. While helmets and protective clothing render a batsman increasingly anonymous, Gower remains apart – a player of elegant charm, deft touch and unimpeachable sportsmanship. Those who remember the great Frank Woolley discern many similarities – both tall, willowy left-handers from Kent with a natural sense of timing that gloried in a wide range of strokes. Yet Woolley hit the ball harder and further, while Gower teases bowlers by subtle placement rather than raw power. 'Hard enough for four is hard enough,' could be Gower's cricketing maxim, but he has so many shots, so much time to spare in playing them that he scores faster than many batsmen who trade in sixes and belligerent intentions.

When David Gower first played for England at the age of twenty-one in 1978, the press gratefully latched on to the 'golden boy' tag: the stylish batting, his boyish, blond good looks and his relaxed attitude to life all contributed to the image. One could imagine Gower transported back in a time machine and relishing the convivial elegance of country house cricket. P. G. Wodehouse would surely have found a role for him in Bertie Wooster's escapades – and Gower would have fared better with the fair sex than the egregious Bertie. Most things seem to have come easily to Gower, without undue exertion. He lasted one term as a law undergraduate at University College, London, and decided a cricket career would be less tedious. When Kent failed to show much interest in the Canterbury-born teenager, Leicestershire gratefully signed him. Kent's administrative myopia

Gower's languid charm at the Oval, during his 157 against Australia in 1985

must rank alongside the rejection by Essex of Jack Hobbs as one of the great Cricketing Cock-Ups. Gower was lucky to enjoy the invaluable advice of Ray Illingworth and Jack Birkenshaw at Leicester and he proceeded to breeze into the England team. He hooked his first ball in Test cricket to the boundary and settled into the side as if to the manner born. One wonders if he would have played that early without the poaching talents of Kerry Packer, but no matter, Gower has

invariably been in the right place at the right time. He became an England player just as vast sums of money were beginning to flood into the game, and he has prospered since. Gower is an agent's dream: articulate, charming and professional when there is a public relations job to do. With colonial service in the family, and a prep and public school education, Gower is well-equipped with the necessary equanimity to cope with life's tribulations. He is a man of quiet, steely determination when necessary, rather than the 'up and at 'em' leader like Tony Greig or Mike Gatting. Those who bewail Gower's alleged lack of drive should remember that by temperament and upbringing, he has never been a stormer of ramparts; he would prefer to negotiate quietly with the man who has the castle keys.

Gower has known some troughs as well as many peaks. He was dropped by England in 1980 and again the following year and his batting form fluctuated when he captained England, but his class and pedigree invariably see him through. It may be galling to a player with greater application and powers of concentration, but someone with Gower's rare gifts does not need to bat for hour after hour in the nets. His attitude to net practice has always been fairly relaxed, for various reasons. Usually the standard of nets are low on overseas tours and Gower reasonably points out that confidence can suffer if a batsman gets worked over on uncertain surfaces. As a touch player, Gower relies a great deal on timing and he does not need to hit too many balls to decide if he is in good enough form. More culpably, Gower does cleave towards a fairly relaxed view of the world. He takes the view that cricket should not be the all-consuming passion of a civilized adult and that a certain amount of perspective is necessary to give of one's best on the field. Such a stance is infinitely preferable to the self-absorption of a Boycott or the melodramatics of a Lillee, yet it brings Gower the brickbats when he is playing badly or his side has struggled. Trying to graft a careworn professionalism on to such a gifted sportsman is self-defeating, however; he has not exactly failed while remaining true to himself.

Typically Gower did not strive to attain the England captaincy. Typically it dropped into his lap in March 1984 when Bob Willis handed over the job on his sick-bed in Pakistan. Although Gower had hardly seemed captaincy material while number two to Willis, there were few rivals for the post; Ian Botham had ruffled too many Establishment dovecotes, Mike Gatting was still trying to establish himself as an England regular, experienced crick-eters like Gooch, Emburey and Boycott were banned for their South African venture and none of the impressive county captains were good enough players to get into the England side. Gower made all the right noises and proceeded to do what comes naturally; he led by example, scored two big hundreds against Pakistan and stopped the rot. A sensible, low-key approach steadied the ship and England recovered some self-respect. That was soon dissipated when the West Indies handed England a 5/0 thrashing, and soon the knives were being sharpened for the man Fleet Street had just welcomed with open arms. Gower's style of captaincy was never assertive enough to stem the tide of Carib-bean invincibility, but a combination of Mike Brearley, Ray Illingworth and Richie Benaud would not have done that. Perhaps a couple of Tests might have been saved, but that 1984 West Indian side was one of the greatest touring teams in Test history and England could never get free of them. Gower's form with the bat slumped alarmingly and the rumour machine clanked into action, suggesting that here was yet another England captain not up to a job which had also emasculated him as a player.

It was against this background of disil-lusionment that David Gower entered his most rewarding phase of captaincy. His revival began in India on a tour which posed immense diplomatic and playing problems. The assassination of Mrs Ghandi and the British Ambassador, Mr Percy Norris, were great tests for Gower and his manager, Tony Brown, as they tried to get the players' minds back to the

Above: Sunil Gavaskar, the Indian captain who lost the 1984/5 series to Gower in India. Gavaskar has dominated Test cricket for almost two decades by dint of a perfect technique, relentless concentration and a hunger for runs
Right: Mike Gatting reveals the type of injury that will always be possible against the conveyor belt of West Indian fast bowling

David Gower has always ensured that cricket does not dominate his leisure time. Whether playing tennis in Adelaide or wind-surfing in the Caribbean, he looks as relaxed as he invariably does at the batting crease

Right: David Gower with his loyal vice-captain Mike Gatting in happier times on the tour to India. Within eighteen months, Gatting had taken over in the hot seat from his friend

cricket and away from the risk of physical danger. England also lost the First Test at Bombay by eight wickets, and for Gower (with scores of 13 and 2) it was his sixth successive Test defeat in just five months. He was at his most impressive at this stage, doggedly insisting that the series could still be won and refusing to be negative about the umpiring, the wickets and all the other aggravations of a tour. Gower admirably placed his faith in slow bowling – almost a heresy for a modern Test captain – and Phil Edmonds and Pat Pocock responded magnificently. England won the series 2/1 and their excellent team spirit was decisive. Gower only managed one half-century, but that hardly seemed to matter amid the euphoria. Not many Test captains manage to come from behind to win a modern series and Gower seemed to have established himself as captain. This was underlined when England beat Australia 3/1 in a series illuminated by Gower's majestic batting.

After a disastrous May, when he hardly made a run, Gower failed in the first two internationals. He even uttered the opinion to the press that he might have

to bat at number seven in the final one-day match at Lord's. After being jeered at Edgbaston for several fielding errors – surely a first for Gower – he was now being pilloried by some sections of the press. One eminent former player said Gower should be dropped and the guessing game about his successor was starting in earnest. Gower sensibly elected to play at Lord's and bat in his usual position: he scored a hundred and England won the match handsomely. You could see the anxiety oozing out of him as he played his usual exquisite drives and cuts that had been previously landing in fielders' hands. That Lord's century was the turning point – he often talks about 'the wheel of fortune' and he was certain that it would again be swinging his way. In the Test series, he made two beautiful hundreds and a double century of the highest class. It is true that the Australian bowlers seemed to run out of steam and penetration midway through the tour – but Gower made them pay for earlier nightmares in the most handsome fashion. Everything started to go his way as captain as well: the selections proved inspired and the tourists wilted visibly.

Gower had triumphed in his usual style, without resort to crashing cymbals and clenched-fisted aggression. He and Allan Border established such a rapport as opposing captains that the series was a delightful reminder of a brand of sportsmanship that used to imbue every Ashes series. To the Englishman who likes his sporting heroes to be rather laconic, modest and under-stated, David Gower was a paragon.

It was no great surprise to those who knew Gower – and his next reverse at the hands of the West Indies was equally in character. As England stumbled from humiliation to humiliation in the Caribbean, the captain's head was regularly demanded on the tabloid platter. No England captain has ever surpassed Gower's grisly record of ten successive defeats by a Test side and it appeared that Gower had settled for a weary fatalism rather early. It was not his fault that the Sabina Park pitch was terrifyingly under-prepared for the First Test, that Mike Gatting suffered two bad injuries, that Ian Botham's form slumped amid Fleet Street's prurient curiosity into his private life, or that the practice wickets were so

Bishen Bedi: like Gower, a left-handed genius. He played against Gower towards the end of his career and the Indian remains one of the most graceful and effective of all slow bowlers. Like Gower, he played the game with aplomb and chivalry

resort to calculated effervescence. The 'froideur' that served Gower so well against India and Australia would usually be adequate enough, but the West Indies are not a typical team.

Perhaps the England captaincy was never all that vital to David Gower. Unlike Geoffrey Boycott or Colin Cowdrey, he never coveted the job, he eased into it by default. His agent found it easier to market the England captain, rather than just a glamorous England batsman, but in the end that only meant an extra nought or two in the bank account. Gower was sensible enough to keep the role of England captain in perspective; he has been in the game long enough to know that success comes in cycles and that a lucky captain is one who is around to capitalize on that success. In the case of Mike Brearley, that also involved winning a lot of Tests at a time when Packer's incursions had diluted the overall standard – and getting out of the job before the West Indies returned in all their awesome majesty. Like Ian Botham, Gower was unfortunate to captain the side a good deal against the West Indies, but unlike Botham, he would never allow himself to be deluded by facts. He was realistic enough to know that a lack of alternatives had not harmed his captaincy ambitions and mature enough to carry on playing with distinction for England, whoever gets to toss the coin.

He will always infuriate some influential former players, who question his attitude when the runs are scarce. They will rightly point to his static footwork, his carelessness outside the off-stump and his apparent indifference to technical proficiency. Gower will smile at such railings, and quietly work out how to play it his own way. Perhaps the generation gap is one of the problems. Giants of the past who did their national service and were paid peanuts for playing for England find it hard to warm to a cricketer of flawed brilliance who likes to travel on the Orient Express, to take a bobsleigh down the Cresta Run and foster an interest in fine wines and gourmet food. When Gower slips from his high standards, it is all too easy to blame it on his lifestyle, his bulging bank balance, his supposed lack of professionalism. Yet he does not need to don a hair shirt to appease his critics. Lovers of classic style, timeless elegance and sinuous beauty will hope that David Gower carries on viewing cricket in the same rational manner. Few current players of such quality possess his serene detachment, his ability to 'treat those twin impostors just the same'.

poor. If Gower had been able to unleash the West Indian fast bowlers against Viv Richards and the rest, then Gower would have won the series. It was as simple as that. Of the hundred English wickets to fall in the series, ninety-four of them went to the fast men. The England captain was criticized for his apparent lack of drive, his reluctance to crack a few heads together or decree compulsory net practice every day – yet Gower was simply being his usual self. It has never been his style to give the Agincourt speech in the dressing-room, like a cricketing Henry V; Gower is a man for the quiet, consoling word, rather than raised decibels behind locked dressing-room doors.

The influential members of the cricket media who urged Gower's appointment on Peter May in the spring of 1984 were well aware of his foibles of temperament – most of them had been touring with Gower since 1978, and he has always been an accessible character, with no pretensions towards a complex approach to a game that he plays effortlessly well. It is hard to praise Gower for his common sense, his refusal to get ruffled when the tactical wheels fall off – and then chastise him for a lack of vim and vigour. A man who learned the captaincy trade under the likes of Ray Illingworth, Mike Brearley and Keith Fletcher has a sound enough grasp of the basics without needing to

Cricket Around the World

Test combat at Queen's Park Oval, Port of Spain, Trinidad

As the world gets smaller, cricket grows in influence. Governments may try to use Test Match cricket as a political pawn, but the enduring appeal of the game survives despite such interventions. Official tours get shorter, due to the wonders of air travel; as a result international cricketers are now almost blasé about their global experience. They can talk with personal knowledge of floodlit cricket in Australia, of the exchange rates in India, of martial law in Pakistan, or the dichotomy between idyllic beach life and fast bowling traumas in the West Indies. Within a week of spending Christmas around the fireside the England player invariably finds himself dehydrated in exotic places like Fiji or Sri Lanka en route to the serious business of Test cricket. That is the nature of the modern game. Gone for ever the leisurely boat trip to a part of the world that is fresh and exciting. These days you can bump into a cricketing acquaintance at a Test match thousands of miles from home and be surprised merely at his choice of shorts, rather than his presence on the scene.

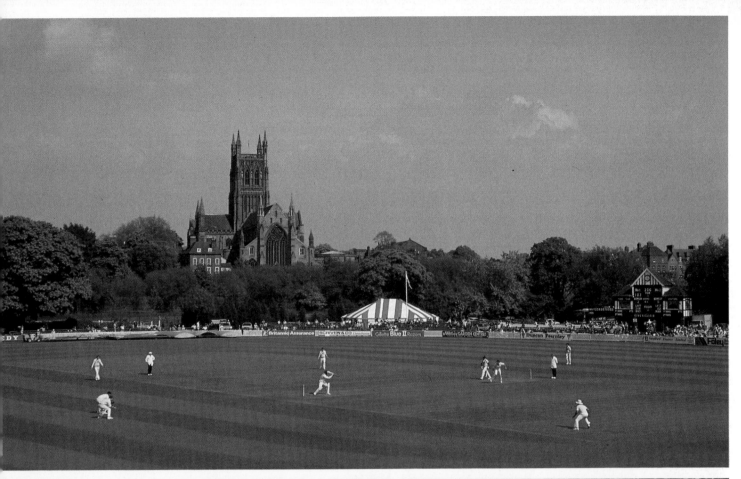

Left: Barbados – and the world's most fertile cricketing island stages yet another impromptu game

Top: The county ground at Worcester – a delight for spectators and cathedral lovers and a graveyard for bowlers over the years

Bottom: Andover, Hampshire. The game still flourishes at grass roots level in the county that popularized cricket towards the end of the eighteenth century

Above: Cricket in India. The pre-innings ritual for one batsman after a hurried tea in the Bombay gymkhana

Top left: Umpire Swarup Kishen finds his duties a trifle tedious as yet another placid batting surface emasculates the bowlers

Top right: Some Indian supporters are less lethargic than the umpires. Their fanaticism can take dangerous forms

Right: Yet invariably the passion for cricket in India is channelled into more constructive areas – here Bombay is the setting

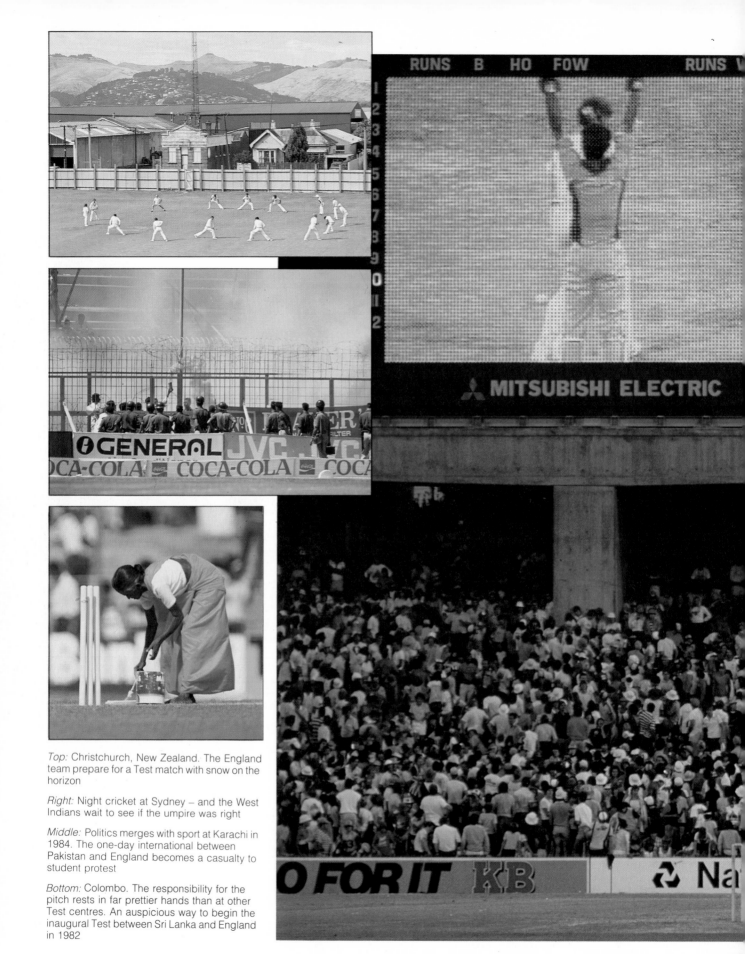

Top: Christchurch, New Zealand. The England team prepare for a Test match with snow on the horizon

Right: Night cricket at Sydney – and the West Indians wait to see if the umpire was right

Middle: Politics merges with sport at Karachi in 1984. The one-day international between Pakistan and England becomes a casualty to student protest

Bottom: Colombo. The responsibility for the pitch rests in far prettier hands than at other Test centres. An auspicious way to begin the inaugural Test between Sri Lanka and England in 1982

Two facets of English cricket in all its unpredictability. A hailstorm
increases the popularity of the beer tent at Arundel while a combination
of perfect weather and the historic Ashes packs out the Oval ground

Statistical Appendix

BY ROBERT BROOKE

All figures are up to the start of the 1986
English season.

CAREER RECORDS OF FEATURED PLAYERS

William Gilbert Grace

Born: Downend, Bristol 18.7.1848
Died: Mottingham, Kent 23.10. 1915

CAREER RECORDS

First-class cricket: 1865 to 1908

Batting:

Matches	Inns	n.o.	Runs	H.S.	Av'ge	100s
872	1483	104	54518	344	39.53	126

Bowling:

Runs Conceded	Wickets	Av'ge	Best	5 in inns	Ct/st
51238	2823	18.15	10–49	241	879/5

Test cricket: 1880 to 1899

Batting:

Matches	Inns	n.o.	Runs	H.S.	Av'ge	100s
22	36	2	1098	170	32.29	2

Bowling:

Runs Conceded	Wickets	Av'ge	Best	5 in inns	Ct/st
236	9	26.22	2–12	–	19/-

Highest Score: First-class cricket
344 MCC *v.* Kent, Canterbury 1876

Highest Score: Test cricket
170 England *v.* Australia, The Oval 1886

Best Bowling Analysis: First-class cricket
10–49 MCC *v.* Oxford University, Oxford 1886

Best Bowling Analysis: Test cricket
2–12 England *v.* Australia, Lord's 1890

Some Batting Feats:

First-class cricket

The first batsman to reach career totals of 10,000 runs (1873); 20,000 runs (1879); 30,000 runs (1887); 40,000 runs (1894); 50,000 runs (1900)

The first batsman to score 2000 runs in a season; 2739 (av. 78.26) in 1871. This remained a record until 1896 (see K. S. Ranjitsinhji).

Altogether scored 1000 runs in a season in England on 28 occasions. A record until equalled by F. E. Woolley in 1938, and remains unbeaten.

Batting average of 78.25 in 1871 was first of more than 70 in a season. Record until beaten by A. Shrewsbury (78.71) in 1887.

1000 runs in May 1895 – first such feat. Reached on 30 May, a record until 1927 (see W. R. Hammond). 1024 runs in August 1871 – first instance of 1000 runs in a month. 1278 runs in August 1876 – best for any month until 1936 (see W. R. Hammond).

Best score 344, MCC *v.* Kent, Canterbury 1876. The first triple century scored in first-class cricket, remained record until 1895 when beaten by A. C. MacLaren. Still highest score in any Kent match, for MCC, and at Canterbury. Two triple centuries in 1876 – still unequalled in English season. 318* *v.* Yorks at Cheltenham 1876 remains best score for Gloucs and in Gloucs, and against Yorkshire. 301 for Gloucs *v.* Sussex, Bristol 1896 aged 48 years, 17 days. Oldest Triple century scorer.

First batsman to score one hundred centuries; 100th hundred 288, Gloucs *v.* Somerset, Bristol 1893. Only player to complete feat until 1913 (T. W. Hayward). Career record of 126 centuries best until 1925 (see J. B. Hobbs).

130 & 102* South *v.* North (of Thames), Canterbury 1868. First to score two hundreds in match since W. Lambert (1817). First recorded hundred before lunch on first day of match – 116* MCC *v.* Kent, Canterbury 1869.

Test Cricket

Scored first Test century for England – 152 *v.* Australia, The Oval 1880. Also first Test century in England and first for England on Test debut. Remained best score by England opener until his 170 *v.* Australia at The Oval in 1886. This remained best score by England opener until J. B. Hobbs' 187 *v.* South Africa, Cape Town 1909–10, best in England until Hobbs' 211 *v.* South Africa, Lord's 1924, best *v.* Australia until L. Hutton's 364 at The Oval 1938.

Some Bowling Feats

First bowler to take 2000 wickets (1886). Career total of 2823 wickets a record until overtaken by J. T. Hearne (1912).

All-round Cricket

In 1874 became first player to perform 1000 run/100 wicket 'double' and in 1876 became first to perform 2000 run/100 wicket 'double'. Performed 100 run/10 wickets match 'double' a record 14 times; for MCC *v.* Oxford U (Oxford) 1886 performed unique 'double' of century and 10 wickets.

John Berry Hobbs

Born: Cambridge 16.12.1882
Died: Hove, Sussex 21.12. 1963

CAREER RECORDS

First-class cricket: 1905 to 1934

Batting:

Matches	Inns.	n.o.	Runs	H.S.	Av'ge	100s
825	1313	106	61167	316*	50.67	197

Bowling:

Runs Conceded	Wickets	Av'ge	Best	5 in inns		Ct
2666	107	24.91	7–56	3		334

Test cricket: 1907–8 to 1930

Battling:

Matches	Inns	n.o.	Runs	H.S.	Av'ge	100s
61	102	7	5410	211	56.94	15

Bowling:

Runs Conceded	Wickets	Av'ge	Best	5 in inns		Ct
165	1	–	–	–		17

Highest Score: First-class cricket

316* Surrey *v.* Middlesex, Lord's 1926

Highest Score: Test cricket

211 England *v.* South Africa, Lord's 1924

Best Bowling Analysis: First-class cricket

7–56 Surrey *v.* Oxford University, Oxford 1911.

Some Batting Feats:

In 1930 overtook W. G. Grace's career total of 54,518 runs to become heaviest scoring batsman of all time; retains his top position to this day. His 43,554 runs (av. 49.72) and 144 centuries are both records for Surrey. In 1925 became the first Surrey batsman to score a century against every other county.

In 1925 he became the leading century scorer in first-class cricket, overtaking the previous record of 126 held by W. G. Grace. His final total of centuries – 197 – remains a record, and his total of centuries in England – 175 – is also a record. In 1925 scored 16 centuries in the season, beating the previous record of 13 by C. B. Fry in 1901. Hobbs' record lasted until 1947 (*see* D. C. S. Compton).

He scored one hundred runs or more before lunch on the first day of a match on thirteen occasions. This is a record, as is his overall total of 20 centuries before lunch.

Hobbs obtained 2000 runs in an English season 17 times – a record. He became the first batsman to score more than 1000 runs in a South African season in 1909–10 and his total of 1489 runs (av. 74.45) in South Africa in 1913–14 was a record until 1948–49 (see D. C. S. Compton). Hobbs scored 26,441 runs (av. 58.63) after his 40th birthday. This beat the 22,141 scored by W. G. Grace and is still a record.

Test cricket

Hobbs was the first batsman to score 4000 runs (1926) and 5000 runs in Test cricket.

Hobbs's best Test score – 211 *v.* South Africa in 1924 was the highest by an England opening bat until 1938 (see L. Hutton). It remains the best score by an opening batsman against South Africa in all Test cricket.

When scoring 142 *v.* Australia at Melbourne Hobbs became the oldest ever Test century scorer at the age of 46 years, 82 days. This remains a record.

Hobbs' 3636 runs against Australia is the highest total for any country against Australia.

2000 runs in an English season:

Year	Inns	n.o.	Runs	H.S.	Av'ge	100s
1907	63	6	2135	166*	37.45	4
1909	54	2	2114	205	40.65	6
1911	60	3	2376	154*	41.68	4
1912	60	6	2042	111	37.81	3
1913	57	5	2605	184	50.09	9
1914	48	2	2697	226	58.63	11
1919	49	6	2594	205*	60.32	8
1920	50	2	2827	215	58.89	11
1922	46	5	2552	168	62.24	10
1923	59	4	2087	136	37.94	5
1924	43	7	2094	211	58.16	6
1925	48	5	3024	266*	70.32	16
1926	41	3	2949	316*	77.60	10
1928	38	7	2542	200*	82.00	12
1929	39	5	2263	204	66.55	10
1930	43	2	2103	146*	51.29	5
1931	49	6	2418	153	56.23	10

1000 runs in a South African Season:

Year	Inns	n.o.	Runs	H.S.	Av'ge	100s
1901–10	20	1	1194	187	62.84	3
1913–14	22	2	1489	170	74.45	5

Victor Thomas Trumper

Born: Darlinghurst, Sydney, New South Wales 2.11.1877
Died: Darlinghurst 28.6.1915

CAREER RECORDS

First-class cricket: 1894–95 to 1913–14

Batting:

Matches	Inns	n.o.	Runs	H.S.	Av'ge	100s
255	401	21	16939	300*	44.57	42

Bowling:

Runs Conceded	Wickets	Av'ge	Best	5 in inns	Ct
2031	64	31.73	5–19	2	171

Test cricket: 1899 to 1911–12

Batting:

Matches	Inns	n.o.	Runs	H.S.	Av'ge	100s
48	89	8	3163	214*	39.04	8

Bowling:

Runs Conceded	Wickets	Av'ge	Best	5 in inns	Ct
317	8	39.62	3–60	–	31

Highest Score: First-class cricket
300* Australians *v.* Sussex, Hove 1899

Highest Score: Test cricket
214* Australia *v.* South Africa, Adelaide 1910–11

Best Bowling Analysis: First-class cricket
5–19 Australians *v.* Cambridge University 1902

Best Bowling Analysis: Test cricket
3–60 Australia *v.* South Africa, Johannesburg 1902–03

Some Batting Feats:

First-class cricket

In 1899 scored 300* for The Australians *v.* Sussex at Hove; this was to remain the highest score of his career and at the time was the best score for an Australian Tourist, beating W. L. Murdoch's 286*, also against Sussex at Hove, in 1882. It was to remain a record only until 1905, when W. W. Armstrong scored 303* against Somerset at Bath. Trumper at the time was only the seventh batsman to score a triple century in English first-class cricket, and only four Australian tourists have subsequently exceeded his score.

Trumper's last major innings was 293 for A. Sims' Touring team *v.* Canterbury at Christchurch in 1913–14, a few months before his final illness. This remains the highest score in first-class cricket by a no. 9 batsman. During this innings Trumper added 433 for the 8th wicket with A. Sims. This established a new record for this wicket, beating the previous record – by R. Peel and Lord Hawke for Yorkshire against Warwickshire at Edgbaston in 1896 – by 141 runs, and it remains the record for this wicket by this amount of runs. Trumper also shared a stand of 270 for this wicket with E. P. Barbour for New South Wales *v.* Victoria at Sydney in 1912–13 and this remains third on the all-time list.

In 1902 Trumper scored 2570 runs (average 48.49) for the Australian tourists in England. This remained a record for a touring team until D. G. Bradman's 2960 runs in 1930 and is still the second best for an Australian team. Trumper's 11 centuries in 1902 constituted a record for a tourist which was unbeaten until 1938, when D. G. Bradman obtained 13, and Trumper remains second on the list.

In 1910–11 Trumper scored 1246 runs (av. 69.22); this was the highest total by a non-tourist in an Australian season and remained so until beaten by D. G. Bradman in 1928–29.

Four of Trumper's 11 hundreds in 1902 were scored before lunch. This is one short of the season's record – 5 by L. C. H. Palairet in 1901 – but remains a record for any tourist.

When Trumper scored 292* for New South Wales *v.* Tasmania at Sydney this established a new record as the highest maiden century in first-class cricket. This remained a record until beaten by Pervez Akhtar (337* for Pakistan Railways *v.* Dera Ismail Khan at Lahore in 1964–65), and is still second on the list.

Test Cricket

Trumper's 104 *v.* England at Old Trafford in 1902 included a century before lunch, the first pre-lunch hundred scored on a first day in Test cricket.

2000 runs in English season:

Year	Inns	n.o.	Runs	H.S.	Av'ge	100s
1902	53	0	2570	128	48.49	11

1000 runs in an overseas season:

Year	Inns	n.o.	Runs	H.S.	Av'ge	100s
1910–11	20	2	1246	214*	69.22	3

Charles Burgess Fry

Born: East Croydon, Surrey 25.4.1872
Died: Hampstead, Surrey 7.9.1956

CAREER RECORDS

First-class cricket 1892 to 1921

Batting:

Matches	Inns	n.o.	Runs	H.S.	Av'ge	100s
394	658	43	30886	258*	50.22	94

Bowling:

Runs Conceded	Wickets	Av'ge	Best	5 in inns	Ct/st
4872	166	29.34	6–78	9	240

Test cricket: 1895 to 1912

Batting:

Matches	Inns	n.o.	Runs	H.S.	Av'ge	100s
26	41	3	1223	144	32.18	2

Bowling:

Runs Conceded	Wickets	Av'ge	Best	5 in inns	Ct
3	0	–	–	–	17

Highest Score: First-class cricket
258* Hampshire *v.* Gloucs., Southampton 1911

Highest Score: Test cricket
144 England *v.* Australia, The Oval 1905

Best Bowling Analysis: First-class cricket
6–78 Oxford University *v.* Cambridge University, Lord's 1895

Some Batting Feats:

First-class cricket

In 1901 Fry obtained the following scores in consecutive innings. 106, Sussex *v.* Hants, Portsmouth; 209, Sussex *v.* Yorks, Hove; 149, Sussex *v.* Middlesex, Hove; 105, Sussex *v.* Surrey, The Oval; 140, Sussex *v.* Kent, Hove; 105 Rest of England *v.* Yorkshire, Lord's. No batsman had previously scored more than three consecutive hundreds. Fry's record was equalled by D. G. Bradman (1938–39) and M. J. Procter (1970–71). Fry's record of five consecutive County Championship hundreds during the above run remains a record.

Fry obtained his 14th double century when scoring 214 for Sussex *v.* Worcs at Hove in 1908, beating the previous record held by Dr W. G. Grace. Fry eventually scored 16 double centuries, and this remained a record until beaten by E. H. Hendren in 1929–30.

Fry's total of 13 double centuries for Sussex is second to K. S. Ranjitsinhji (14) for the county but his eight at Hove constitutes a record for the ground. It was a record for any ground until 1936, when E. H. Hendren scored his 9th double century at Lord's. D. G. Bradman subsequently scored 9 double centuries at both Sydney (1946–47) and Adelaide (1947–48).

Fry obtained a century in each innings of a match on five occasions; this remained a record until beaten by J. B. Hobbs in 1932.

During 1901 Fry obtained scores of 241, for Sussex *v.* Cambridge University and 219* for Sussex v Oxford University in consecutive matches in the same week.

Fry's 13 centuries during the 1901 season beat the previous record of 12 established by R. Abel in 1900. Fry's record stood until 1925, when beaten by J. B. Hobbs.

Bowling Feats:

Fry achieved the hat-trick when dismissing T. C. O'Brien, C. W. Wright and A. H. Heath, Oxford University *v.* MCC, Lord's 1894. On various occasions in 1898 and 1900 Fry was no-balled for illegal delivery and ceased serious bowling.

All-round feats:

For Sussex *v.* Nottinghamshire at Trent Bridge in 1896 Fry scored 89 and 65 and had bowling figures of 5–81 and 5–66. Thus Fry achieved the 'Match Double' of 100 runs and 10 wickets but also became the first player ever to perform the much rarer feat of fifty in each innings and 5 wickets in each innings.

2000 runs in an English season

Year	Inns	n.o.	Runs	H.S.	Av'ge	100s
1899	55	1	2366	181	43.81	5
1900	41	3	2325	229	61.18	9
1901	43	3	3147	244	78.67	13
1903	40	7	2683	234	81.30	9
1904	42	2	2824	229	70.60	10
1905	44	4	2801	233	70.02	10

Kumar Shri Ranjitsinhji

Born: Sarodar, India 10.9.1872
Died: Jamnagar, India 2.4.1933

CAREER RECORDS

First-class cricket: 1893 to 1920
Batting:

Matches	Inns	n.o.	Runs	H.S.	Av'ge	100s
307	500	62	24692	285*	56.37	72

Bowling:

Runs Conceded	Wickets	Av'ge	Best	5 in inns	Ct/st
4601	133	34.59	6–53	4	233

Test cricket: 1896 to 1902
Batting:

Matches	Inns	n.o.	Runs	H.S.	Av'ge	100s
15	26	4	989	175	44.95	2

Bowling:

Runs Conceded	Wickets	Av'ge	Best	5 in inns	Ct/st
39	1	39.00	–	–	13

Highest Score: First-class cricket
285* Sussex *v.* Somerset, Taunton 1901

Highest Score: Test cricket
175 England *v.* Australia, Sydney 1897–98

Best Bowling Analysis: First-class cricket
6–53 London County *v.* Cambridge University, Crystal Palace 1901

Some Batting Feats

On his debut for Sussex, against MCC at Lord's in 1895, Ranjitsinhji scored 77 and 150 – an unprecedented county debut.

Ranji obtained 14 double centuries for Sussex, a record for the county. During the 1900 season he obtained five double centuries for Sussex. This established a record for one county in a season which still stands. The only player to have scored six double centuries in a season was D. G. Bradman in 1930.

The following double centuries were scored in consecutive innings; 222 Sussex *v.* Somerset, Hove; 215* Sussex *v.* Cambridge U., Cambridge, both 1900; 285* Sussex *v.* Somerset, Taunton; 204 Sussex *v.* Lancs, Hove, both 1901.

For Sussex *v.* Yorkshire at Hove, 1896, Ranji scored 100 and 125*, the only time he obtained a century in each innings of the match. A unique facet of the feat is that all the runs were scored on the third day.

On three occasions Ranji obtained centuries in three successive innings. In 1896 for Sussex he scored 165 *v.* Lancashire and 100 & 125* *v.* Yorkshire, all at Hove.
In 1900 he performed the feat twice; 127 *v.* Gloucs, 222 *v.* Somerset, both at Hove, 215* *v.* Cambridge at Cambridge. Later he scored 103 *v.* Surrey, and 202 *v.* Middlesex, both at Hove, then 109 *v.* Gloucs at Bristol. All these innings were for Sussex.

Ranji obtained 1037 runs (av. 79.76) in June 1899, 1059 runs (av. 96.27) in July 1900 and 1011 runs (av. 77.76) in August 1899. He is the only batsman ever to score 1000 runs in three different months. Ranji was also the first batsman to exceed 1000 runs in two separate months of the same season, 1899. It has subsequently been equalled only by C. B. Fry (June & August 1901) H. Sutcliffe (June & August 1932) and L. Hutton (June & August 1949).

In 1899 Ranji became the first batsman to score 3000 runs in an English season, making 3159 (av. 63.18). He repeated the feat in 1900 and in 1901 R. Abel beat his record 1899 aggregate, and C. B. Fry and J. T Tyldesley also exceeded 3000 runs.

Test Cricket

In 1896 Ranji became the first batsman to score a century in the second innings of his Test debut, and the second to score a century on debut for England. The score was 154*, against Australia at Old Trafford.

During his innings of 154* above, Ranji moved from 41* to 154* in the third morning. This was the first instance of a batsman scoring 100 runs before lunch in a Test match.

2000 runs in an English season

Year	Inns	n.o.	Runs	H.S.	Av'ge	100s
1896	55	7	2780	171*	57.91	10
1899	58	8	3159	197	63.18	8
1900	40	5	3065	275	87.57	11
1901	40	5	2468	285*	70.51	8
1904	34	6	2077	207*	74.17	8

Frank Edward Woolley

Born: Tonbridge, Kent 27.5.1887
Died: Halifax, Nova Scotia, 18.10. 1978

CAREER RECORDS

First-class cricket: 1906 to 1938

Batting:

Matches	Inns	n.o.	Runs	H.S.	Av'ge	100s
978	1530	84	58959	305*	40.77	145

Bowling:

Runs Conceded	Wickets	Av'ge	Best	5 in inns	Ct/st
41058	2066	19.87	8–22	132	1018

Test Cricket: 1909 to 1938

Batting:

Matches	Inns	n.o.	Runs	H.S.	Av'ge	100s
64	98	7	3283	154	36.07	5

Bowling:

Runs Conceded	Wickets	Av'ge	Best	5 in inns	Ct/st
2815	83	33.91	7–76	4	64

Highest Score: First-class cricket
305* MCC *v.* Tasmania, Hobart 1911–12

Highest Score: Test cricket
154 England *v.* South Africa, Old Trafford 1929

Best Bowling Analysis: First-class cricket
8–22 Kent *v.* Gloucs, Maidstone 1921

Best Bowling Analysis: Test cricket
7–76 England *v.* New Zealand, Wellington 1929–30

Some Batting Feats:

When obtaining the highest score, 305* above, he reached 300* in 205 minutes, the fastest triple century until D. C. S. Compton's 300 in 181 minutes in 1948–49. It is still the highest first-class score in Tasmania and was the highest against Tasmania until W. H. Ponsford's 429 for Victoria at Melbourne in 1922–23. It was the first triple century for any tourist in Australia.

Woolley scored 1000 runs in a season 28 times in succession – a record. Total of 28 times equals record of W. G. Grace.

Career total of 47,868 runs (av. 41.77) and 122 centuries, both records for Kent. Season's total of 2894 (av. 59.06) in 1928 also a Kent record.

First Kent batsman to score centuries against every other county. Scored 26,273 runs after the age of 40; second to J. B. Hobbs. Holds English 10th wicket record of 235 with A. Fielder – Kent *v.* Worcs, Stourbridge 1909.

In 1929 Woolley scored four centuries in successive innings; they were 155, Kent *v.* Derbys at Chesterfield; 108, Kent *v.* Somerset at Tonbridge; 131 Kent *v.* Yorks at Tonbridge; 117 Kent *v.* Hants at Folkestone.

Some Bowling Feats:

Woolley achieved the hat-trick for Kent *v.* Surrey at Blackheath in 1919. His victims were C. T. A. Wilkinson, A. E. R. Gilligan and E. C. Kirk.

Test Cricket

Woolley's match figures of 10–49 for England *v.* Australia at The Oval, 1912 are statistically the best for ten wickets in all Test cricket.

Some All-round Feats:

First-class cricket

Woolley performed the 2000 runs, 100 wickets double on a record four occasions, and his eight 'ordinary' doubles are a record for such a prolific run scorer.

Woolley achieved the 'match double' of 100 runs and 10 wickets on six occasions, a record beaten only by W. G. Grace and G. Giffen.

2000 runs in an English season

Year	Inns	n.o.	Runs	H.S.	Av'ge	100s
1914	52	2	2272	160*	45.44	6
1921	50	1	2101	174	42.87	6
1922	47	3	2022	188	45.95	5
1923	56	5	2091	270	41.00	5
1924	49	2	2344	202	49.87	8
1925	43	4	2190	215	56.15	5
1926	50	3	2183	217	46.44	6
1928	59	4	3352	198	60.94	12
1929	55	5	2804	176	56.08	11
1930	50	5	2023	120	44.95	5
1931	51	4	2301	234	48.95	5
1934	56	1	2643	176	48.05	10
1935	56	0	2339	229	41.76	6

150 wickets in an English season

Year	Runs Conceded	Wickets	Av'ge
1920	2633	185	14.23
1921	2697	167	16.14
1922	2995	163	18.37

Maurice William Tate

Born: Brighton, Sussex 30.5.1895
Died: Wadhurst, Sussex 18.5.1956

CAREER RECORDS

First-class cricket: 1912 to 1937

Batting:

Matches	Inns	n.o.	Runs	H.S.	Av'ge	100s
679	970	102	21717	203	25.01	23

Bowling:

Runs Conceded	Wickets	Av'ge	Best	5 in inns		Ct/st
50571	2784	18.16	9–71	195		284

Test cricket: 1924 to 1935

Batting:

Matches	Inns	n.o.	Runs	H.S.	Av'ge	100s
39	52	5	1198	100*	25.48	1

Bowling:

Runs Conceded	Wickets	Av'ge	Best	5 in inns	Ct/st
4055	155	26.16	6–42	7	11

Highest Score: First-class cricket
203 Sussex *v.* Northants, Hove 1921

Highest Score: Test cricket
100* England *v.* South Africa, Lord's 1929

Best Bowling Analysis: First-class cricket
9–71 Sussex *v.* Middlesex, Lord's 1926

Best Bowling Analysis: Test cricket
6–42 England *v.* South Africa, Headingley 1924

Some Batting Feats:

First-class cricket

Of Tate's 23 centuries, three were scored before lunch, as follows:
121 Sussex *v.* Northants, Hastings 1925 (Day 2)
133 MCC *v.* Parsees & Europeans, Bombay 1926–27 (Day 1)
101 Sussex *v.* Hants, Portsmouth 1927 (Day 1)
The last century above came in 68 minutes on the first morning.

Tate shares the Sussex partnership records for the second and sixth wickets:
2nd E. H. Bowley & Tate; 385; *v.* Northants, Hove 1921
6th K. S. Duleepsinhji & Tate; 255; *v.* Northants, Hove 1930.

Some Bowling Feats:

First-class cricket

When achieving his best first-class innings bowling figures, 9–71 for Sussex *v.* Middlesex at Lord's in 1926 he hit the stumps five times and won three lbw verdicts, so only needed the help of the field on one occasion. During the innings he dismissed C. N. Bruce, G. O. Allen and N. E. Haig with successive balls to achieve the 'hat-trick'. Later in the same season Tate achieved another hat-trick, for The Rest *v.* England at The Oval, and he achieved the third hat-trick of his career for Sussex *v.* Northants at Peterborough in 1934.

When achieving his best ever match figures of 14–58 for Sussex *v.* Glamorgan at Hove in 1925 Tate bowled unchanged throughout the match with A. F. Wensley. This is the first and only time two Sussex bowlers have bowled unchanged throughout a County Championship match.

Test cricket

When Tate took 38 wickets (av. 23.18) for England *v.* Australia in the 1924–25 series this was the highest total of wickets in any series between the two countries. It remained a record for England *v.* Australia until beaten by J. C. Laker (46 in 1956) and is still the record for England *v.* Australia in Australia.

Tate bowled 712 balls for England *v.* Australia at Sydney in 1924–25, a new record for Test cricket which was beaten by J. C. White (England *v.* Australia) who bowled 749 balls at Adelaide in 1928–29.

Some All-round Feats:

Tate achieved the 'match double' of 100 runs and 10 wickets twice. He scored 90 and 35 and took 11–90 for Sussex *v.* Oxford at Hove in 1920 and in 1927 scored 101 and took 10–95 for Sussex *v.* Hants at Portsmouth.

Tate achieved the 'double' of 1000 runs and 200 wickets three times, in 1923, 1924 and 1925, which remains a record. Tate achieved the 1000 runs/100 wickets 'double' eight times, in every season from 1922 to 1929 inclusive, and uniquely in India for MCC in 1926–27.

150 wickets in a season

Year	Runs Conceded	Wickets	Av'ge
1923	3061	219	13.97
1924	2818	205	13.74
1925	3415	228	14.97
1928	3184	165	19.29
1929	2903	156	18.60
1932	2494	160	15.58

Walter Reginald Hammond

Born: Dover, Kent 10.6.1903
Died: Durban, South Africa 1.7.1965

CAREER RECORDS

First-class cricket: 1920 to 1951

Batting:

Matches	Inns	n.o.	Runs	H.S.	Av'ge	100s
634	1005	104	50551	336*	56.10	167

Bowling:

Runs Conceded	Wickets	Av'ge	Best	5 in inns	Ct/st
22391	732	30.58	9–23	22	819/3

Test cricket: 1927–28 to 1946–47

Batting:

Matches	Inns	n.o.	Runs	H.S.	Av'ge	100s
85	140	16	7249	336*	58.45	22

Bowling:

Runs Conceded	Wickets	Av'ge	Best	5 in inns	Ct/st
3138	83	37.80	5–36	2	110

Highest Score: First-class cricket and Test cricket
336* England *v.* New Zealand, Auckland 1932–33

Best Bowling Analysis: First-class cricket
9–23 Gloucs v. Worcs, Cheltenham 1928

Best Bowling Analysis: Test cricket
5–36 England *v.* South Africa, Johannesburg 1927–28

Some Batting Feats:

First-class cricket

His highest score, 336* above was at the time the highest score in Test cricket, the record lasting until 1938 (see L. Hutton). It remains the highest score by an English Tourist.

Hammond scored four triple centuries, a total only exceeded by D. G. Bradman who obtained six. Hammond's three triple centuries in the County Championship is a record total; his 317 *v.* Notts at Gloucester in 1936 is a Championship record for Gloucs. Hammond scored two triple centuries *v.* Glamorgan, the only instance in the Championship of one player scoring more than one against one county, and the only triple centuries against Glamorgan in all first-class cricket.

In 1946–47 scored his 36th double century to overtake D. G. Bradman; Bradman reclaimed the record in 1947–48.

Hammond scored a century in each innings on seven occasions, a record until beaten by Zaheer Abbas in 1982–83.

Hammond reached 1000 runs for season 1927 on 28 May, a record until beaten by Bradman (27 May 1938). Hammond's completing 3000 runs for the season on 20 August 1937 equalled the record held by T. W. Hayward since 1906, and remains the joint best. Hammond's 1042 runs (av. 74.42) in May 1927 remains the record for that month, while his 1281 runs (av. 98.53) in August 1936 is a record for *that* month. Both previous records were held by W. G. Grace.

During 1945 and 1946 Hammond scored six hundreds in seven consecutive innings; 121, 102, 132, 134, 59*, 143, 104; this feat has only been equalled three times – by E. Tyldesley (1926), V. Merchant (1940–41, 1941–42) and P. N. Kirsten (1976–77).

Hammond holds the Gloucestershire records for runs in a season (2860 in 1933), runs in a career (33,664) and centuries in a career (113).

Hammond's 31,165 first-class runs in the 1930s is the record for any decade.

Hammond scored centuries for Gloucestershire against every other county.

Test cricket

Hammond's 905 runs (av. 113.12) for England *v.* Australia in 1928–29 was a record at the time for one series, and has only been beaten by D. G. Bradman (974) in 1930.

Hammond was the first batsman to score 6000 runs (1938) and 7000 runs (1946) in Tests. His 22 centuries have been equalled for England only by M. C. Cowdrey and G. Boycott.

Other feats:

Hammond's 78 catches in 1928 and 10 catches in the match for Gloucs *v.* Surrey at Cheltenham in the same season both remain as records for non-wicketkeepers.

2000 runs in a season

Year	Inns	n.o.	Runs	H.S.	Av'ge	100s
1927	47	4	2969	197	69.04	12
1928	48	5	2825	244	65.69	9
1929	47	9	2456	238*	64.63	10
1930	44	6	2032	211*	53.47	5
1932	49	4	2528	264	56.17	8
1933	54	5	3323	264	67.81	13
1934	35	4	2366	302*	76.32	8
1935	58	5	2616	252	49.35	7
1936	42	5	2107	317	56.94	5
1937	55	5	3252	217	65.04	13
1938	42	2	3011	271	75.27	15
1939	46	7	2479	302	63.56	7

Donald George Bradman

Born: Cootamundra, New South Wales 27.8.1908

CAREER RECORDS

First-class cricket: 1927–28 to 1948–49

Batting:

Matches	Inns	n.o.	Runs	H.S.	Av'ge	100s
234	338	43	28067	452*	95.14	117

Bowling:

Runs Conceded	Wickets	Av'ge	Best	5 in inns	Ct/st
1367	36	37.97	3–35	–	131/1

Test Cricket: 1928–29 to 1948

Batting:

Matches	Inns	n.o.	Runs	H.S.	Av'ge	100s
52	80	10	6996	334	99.94	29

Bowling:

Runs Conceded	Wickets	Av'ge	Best	5 in inns	Ct/st
72	2	36.00	1–8	–	32

Highest score: First-class cricket
452* New South Wales *v.* Queensland, Sydney 1929–30

Highest Score: Test cricket
334 Australia *v.* England, Headingley 1930

Best Bowling Analysis: First-class cricket
3–35 Australians *v.* Cambridge U., Cambridge 1930

Some Batting Feats:

Bradman's 452* above remained the highest score in first-class cricket until beaten by Hanif Mohammed (499, Karachi *v.* Bahawalpur 1958–59). It is still the second highest, the highest not out innings and the highest second innings score.

Bradman's career average of 95.14 is by far the highest for anyone with any sort of career. Similarly his Test average of 99.94 is easily the best.

Bradman's 334 for Australia *v.* England at Headingley in 1930 was the best Test score at the time, and remains Australia's best.

Bradman's six double centuries in 1930 beat the previous record of five held by K. S. Ranjitsinhji since 1900, and remains the record for a season. Bradman scored consecutive double centuries on four occasions; this too is a record.

Bradman held the record for number of double centuries until overtaken by W. R. Hammond in 1946/47 but in 1947/48 he regained the record and his total of 37 remains the best.

In 1938 Bradman achieved an average of 115.66; this was the first time a batsman had averaged more than 100 in an English season and remains the highest average. W. A. Johnston (1953) and G. Boycott (1971 and 1979) have also achieved a season's average of 100.

During 1938–39 Bradman became the second batsman after C. B. Fry to score six consecutive centuries. The record has subsequently been equalled by M. J. Procter but remains unbeaten. During the same period Bradman went on to score 8 centuries in 11 innings. Twice, in 1931–32 and in 1948–49, Bradman scored four consecutive centuries and seven times scored three centuries consecutively. In 1947–48 Bradman equalled E. Tyldesley's record of 10 consecutive fifties.

In 1930 during his innings of 334 against England at Leeds, Bradman scored 309 in a day's play, a record still for Test cricket. His 334 remains the best at Headingley. During the innings Bradman scored 105* before lunch. Bradman's 254 in the 1930 Lord's Test and his 299* against South Africa at Adelaide in 1930–31 remain the best Test scores at these grounds.

Bradman's 5028 runs and 19 centuries are both records in Tests against England, while his 29 Test centuries remained a record until beaten by S. M. Gavaskar.

Bradman shares the Test partnership records for the 2nd wicket – 451 with W. H. Ponsford *v.* England at The Oval 1934; 5th wicket – 405 with S. G. Barnes *v.* England at Sydney 1946–47; 6th wicket – 346 with J. H. Fingleton *v.* England at Melbourne 1936–37.

Bradman scored his 1000th run of 1938 on 27 May – the earliest ever date for reaching 1000 runs. Bradman also scored 1000 runs before the end of May 1930 and is the only batsman to have achieved this feat on two occasions.

2000 runs in English season

Years	Inns	n.o.	Runs	H.S.	Av'ge	100s
1930	36	6	2960	334	98.66	10
1934	27	3	2020	304	84.16	7
1938	26	5	2429	278	115.66	13
1948	31	4	2428	187	89.92	11

Douglas Robert Jardine

Born: Malabar Hill, Bombay 23.10.1900
Died: Montreux, Switzerland 18.6.1958

CAREER RECORDS

First-class cricket: 1920 to 1948
Batting:

Matches	Inns	n.o.	Runs	H.S.	Av'ge	100s
262	378	61	14848	214	46.84	35

Bowling:

Runs Conceded	Wickets	Av'ge	Best	5 in inns	Ct/st
1493	48	31.10	6–28	1	188

Test cricket: 1928 to 1933–34
Batting:

Matches	Inns	n.o.	Runs	H.S.	Av'ge	100s
22	33	6	1296	127	48.00	1

Bowling:

Runs Conceded	Wickets	Av'ge	Best	5 in inns	Ct/st
10	0	–	–	–	26

Highest Score: First-class cricket
214 MCC *v.* Tasmania, Launceston 1928–29

Highest Score: Test cricket
127 England *v.* West Indies, Old Trafford 1933

Best Bowling Analysis; First-class cricket
6–28 Oxford University *v.* Essex, Oxford 1920.

Some Batting Feats:
First-class cricket

Despite a restricted first-class career, Jardine achieved 1000 runs in a season 8 times in England plus once in Australia, in 1928–29. His best season was 1926, when he scored 1473 runs (av. 46.03).

Jardine achieved extremely high averages in two English seasons:

Years	Inns	n.o.	Runs	H.S.	Av'ge	100s
1927	14	3	1002	147	91.09	5
1928	17	4	1133	193	87.15	3

Only G. Boycott (102.53 in 1979 and 100.12 in 1971), H. Sutcliffe (96.96 in 1931) and R. M. Poore (91.23 in 1899) have beaten Jardine's 1927 average for an English season among English players.

Test cricket

Jardine's only Test century – 127 v. West Indies at Old Trafford in 1933 – was the best score by an England captain against West Indies until W. R. Hammond's 138 at The Oval in 1939.

Although having little record as a bowler Jardine achieved outstanding figures for Oxford University *v.* Essex at Oxford in 1920. His complete analysis was 12.3 overs, 4 maidens, 28 runs, 6 wickets, and in one spell of 7 overs and 3 balls he had figures of 6 for 6. The batsmen dismissed were A. C. Russell, J. R. Freeman, P. A. Perrin, N. H. Saint, F. L. Fane, F. J. Scoulding – at least four outstanding specialist batsmen. Jardine took another wicket – that of J. G. Dixon – in the second innnings, recording an analysis of 6 overs, 3 maidens, one wicket for eight runs.

An analysis of the seasons when Jardine scored 1000 runs is of interest for the generally high batting averages he achieved.

Year	Inns	n.o.	Runs	H.S.	Av'ge	100s
1921	28	2	1015	145	39.03	2
1924	38	7	1249	122	40.29	2
1925	36	3	1020	87	30.90	–
1926	36	4	1473	176	46.03	3
1927	14	3	1002	147	91.09	5
1928	17	4	1133	193	87.15	3
1928–29	19	1	1168	214	64.88	6
1931	30	13	1104	106*	64.94	2
1932	39	11	1464	164	52.28	3

Harold Larwood

Born: Nuncargate, Notts 14.11.1904

CAREER RECORDS

First-class cricket: 1924 to 1938
Batting:

Matches	Inns	n.o.	Runs	H.S.	Av'ge	100s
361	438	72	7290	102*	19.91	3

Bowling:

Runs Conceded	Wickets	Av'ge	Best	5 in inns	Ct
24994	1427	17.51	9–41	98	234

Test cricket: 1926 to 1932–33
Batting:

Matches	Inns	n.o.	Runs	H.S.	Av'ge	100s
21	28	3	485	98	19.40	–

Bowling:

Runs Conceded	Wickets	Av'ge	Best	5 in inns	Ct
2212	78	28.35	6–32	4	15

Highest Score: First-class cricket
102* Notts *v.* Sussex, Trent Bridge 1931

Highest Score: Test cricket
98 England *v.* Australia, Sydney 1932–33

Best Bowling Analysis: First-class cricket
9–41 Notts *v,* Kent, Trent Bridge 1931

Best Bowling Analysis: Test cricket
6–32 England *v.* Australia, Brisbane 1928–29

Some Batting Feats:
First class cricket

Larwood's best score – 102* *v.* Sussex at Trent Bridge in 1931 saw him add 136 for the 10th wicket with W. Voce. This is the third best Notts last wicket stand, after the 152 added by E. B. Alletson and W. Riley *v.* Sussex at Hove in 1911 and the 140 put on by S. J. Staples and T. L. Richmond *v.* Derbyshire at Worksop in 1922.

Test cricket

Larwood's best Test score – 98 at Sydney in 1932–33 – remained the highest score by a 'nightwatchman' until Nasim-ul-Ghani's 102 for Pakistan at Lord's in 1962.

Some Bowling Feats:
First-class cricket

Larwood's best innings analysis was 9–41 against Kent at Trent Bridge in 1931, a match winning effort which saw one spell of 5–10.

Larwood achieved two first-class hat-tricks in his career. The first was for Notts *v.* Cambridge University at Cambridge 1926. His victims were W. K. Harbinson, R. S. Machin and L. G. Irvine. His second hat-trick came against Glamorgan at Trent Bridge in 1931. His hat-trick was part of an innings analysis of 8–54 and a match winning analysis of 11–70.

In 1932 Larwood took more than 150 wickets for the first and only time.

Season	Runs	Wkts	Av'ge
1932	2084	162	12.86

In two other seasons though taking less than 150 wickets he averaged below 13 runs per wicket

1931	1553	129	12.03
1936	1544	119	12.97

Test cricket

In the 1932–33 series with Australia, Larwood obtained 33 wickets (av. 19.51). This is the second best tally for a series in Australia by an England bowler, beaten only by M. W. Tate (38 in 1924–25). It is the best series aggregate by any genuine English fast bowler.

William Voce

Born: Annesley Woodhouse, Notts 8.8.1909
Died: Nottingham 6.6.1984

CAREER RECORDS

First-class cricket: 1927 to 1952

Batting:

Matches	Inns	n.o.	Runs	H.S.	Av'ge	100s
426	525	130	7583	129	19.19	4

Bowling:

Runs Conceded	Wickets	Av'ge	Best	5 in inns	Ct
35961	1558	23.08	8–30	84	286

Test cricket: 1929–30 to 1946–47

Batting:

Match	Inns	n.o.	Runs	H.S.	Av'ge	100s
27	38	15	308	66	13.39	–

Bowling:

Runs Conceded	Wickets	Av'ge	Best	5 in inns	Ct
2733	98	27.89	7–70	3	15

Highest Score: First-class cricket
129 Notts *v.* Glamorgan, Trent Bridge 1931

Highest Score: Test cricket
66 England *v.* New Zealand, Christchurch 1932–33

Best Bowling Analysis: First-class cricket
8–30 Notts *v.* Somerset, Weston-super-Mare 1939

Best Bowling Analysis: Test cricket
7-70 England *v.* West Indies, Port-of-Spain 1929–30

Some Batting Feats:

First class cricket

During Voce's highest first-class score *v.* Glamorgan in 1931 he completed his century in 45 minutes. This remains the fastest century for Notts and the 10th fastest of all time.

Some bowling feats:

First-class cricket

Voce's best innings analysis was obtained on a drying turf and played a major part in a Notts victory over Somerset in 1939 of 97 runs.

Voce's best figures against an Australian team were his 8–66 for Notts at Trent Bridge in 1934.

Test cricket

Voce's best Test series was against Australia in 1936–37, when he took 26 wickets. This was the best return for an English left arm bowler since F. R. Foster's 32 wickets in Australia in 1911–12.

In the match in which Voce achieved his best Test innings analysis, against West Indies at Port-of-Spain 1929–30, his match figures were 11–149, which were the best match figures in any West Indian Test to that time. They remained the best for England in the West Indies until A. W. Greig's 13–156 in 1973–74.

Denis Charles Scott Compton

Born: Hendon, Middlesex 23.5.1918

CAREER RECORDS

First-class cricket: 1936–58

Batting:

Matches	Inns	n.o.	Runs	H.S.	Av'ge	100s
515	839	88	38942	300	51.85	123

Bowling:

Runs Conceded	Wickets	Av'ge	Best	5 in inns	Ct/st
20074	622	32.27	7–36	19	415

Test cricket: 1937 to 1956–57

Batting:

Matches	Inns	n.o.	Runs	H.S.	Av'ge	100s
78	131	15	5807	278	50.06	17

Bowling:

Runs Conceded	Wickets	Av'ge	Best	5 in inns	Ct/st
1410	25	56.40	5–70	1	49

Highest Score: First-class cricket

300 MCC *v.* North East Transvaal, Benoni 1948–49

Highest score: Test cricket

278 England *v.* Pakistan, Trent Bridge 1954

Best Bowling Analysis: First-class cricket

7–36 MCC *v.* Auckland, Auckland 1946–47

Best Bowling Analysis: Test cricket

5–70 England *v.* South Africa, Cape Town 1948–49

Some Batting Feats

Compton scored 3816 runs (av. 90.85) in the 1947 season, beating the previous record of 3518 set by T. W. Hayward in 1906. Compton's total remains the best.

Compton's 300 for MCC *v.* North East Transvaal in 1948–49 is the highest score by any tourist in South Africa and was obtained in 181 minutes. It is therefore the fastest ever triple century. Compton's 1781 runs (av. 84.81) in South Africa during this season was a record for a season's total in that country until J. R. Reid (New Zealanders) scored 1915 in 1961–62. Compton's 8 centuries in 1948–49 remains a South African record, though it was equalled in 1949–50 by R. N. Harvey and A. R. Morris for the Australians.

Compton's 18 centuries in 1947 beat the previous record of 16 by J. B. Hobbs in 1925 and is still the record.

During the 1947 season Compton scored 1187 against the South African tourists – a record against one team in a season.

Compton scored 1004 (av. 34.62) in his debut season and is the youngest player to exceed 1000 runs in his debut season.

Compton shares with W. J. Edrich the English 3rd wicket record partnership of 424 unbeaten for Middlesex *v.* Somerset, Lord's in 1948. It is the largest ever unbroken 3rd wicket partnership and the highest stand at Lord's.

Test cricket

Compton scored 102 for England *v.* Australia at Trent Bridge in 1938 aged 20 years, 19 days and remains England's youngest century maker in Tests. Compton's best Test score – 278 – was at the time the highest score against Pakistan and it remains the highest for England against Pakistan and the highest in any Trent Bridge Test match.

With W. J. Edrich, Compton established the Test record for the 3rd wicket, adding 370 against South Africa at Lord's in 1947. This was beaten in 1982–83 by Mudassar Nazar and Javed Miandad, who put on 451 for Pakistan *v.* India at Hyderabad.

Compton scored 2205 runs in Test *v.* South Africa, more than any other batsman.

All-round feats

Compton achieved a 'match double' for Middlesex *v.* Surrey at The Oval 1947. He scored 137* in his only innings and took 12 wickets for 174 runs.

2000 runs in a season

Year	Inns	n.o.	Runs	H.S.	Av'ge	100s
1939	50	6	2468	214*	56.09	8
1946	45	6	2403	235	61.61	10
1947	50	8	3816	246*	90.85	18
1948	47	7	2451	252*	61.27	9
1949	56	4	2530	182	48.65	9
1951	40	6	2193	172	64.50	8

Leonard Hutton

Born: Fulneck, Pudsey, Yorks 23.6.1916

CAREER RECORDS

First-class cricket: 1934 to 1960

Batting:

Matches	Inns	n.o.	Runs	H.S.	Av'ge	100s
513	814	91	40140	364	55.51	129

Bowling:

Runs Conceded	Wickets	Av'ge	Best	5 in inns	Ct/st
5090	173	29.42	6–76	4	400

Test cricket: 1937 to 1954–55

Batting:

Matches	Inns	n.o.	Runs	H.S.	Av'ge	100s
79	138	15	6971	364	56.67	19

Bowling:

Runs Conceded	Wickets	Av'ge	Best	Ct/st
232	3	77.33	1–2	57

Highest score: First-class cricket

364 England *v.* Australia, The Oval 1938.

Highest score: Test cricket

364 as above.

Best Bowling Analysis: First-class cricket

6–76 Yorks *v.* Leics, Leicester 1937

Some Batting Feats:

First-class cricket

Hutton's best score – 364 for England in 1938 – remained a record for all Test cricket until G. S. Sobers' 365* for West Indies *v.* Pakistan at Kingston in 1957–58. It beat the previous record for The Oval – 357* by R. Abel, Surrey *v.* Somerset, The Oval 1899, and remains the Oval record. Lasting 797 minutes it became the longest innings in first-class cricket, beating the 630 minutes taken by H. Moses (297*), New South Wales *v.* Victoria, Sydney 1887–88. Hutton's time was exceeded by Hanif Mohammed, whose 337 for Pakistan *v.* West Indies at Bridgetown in 1957–58 occupied 970 minutes, and remains the record. During

Hutton's innings 770 runs were scored; this is still a record for a Test.

Hutton scored centuries for Yorkshire against every other county. Hutton scored 1294 runs (av. 92.43) in June 1949, the highest for one month by one batsman. Hutton also scored 1050 runs (av. 75.00) in August 1949, becoming the fourth batsman after K. S. Ranjitsinhji, C. B. Fry and H. Sutcliffe to perform this feat.

Hutton reached 100 centuries in 1951 in 619 innings, the third fastest ever and an English record until D. C. S. Compton completed his 100 centuries in 552 innings in 1952.

Test cricket

Apart from those records mentioned above, Hutton's 364 is still the best for a Test no. 1. During the innings Hutton added 382 for 2nd wicket with M. Leyland and 215 for 6th wicket with J. Hardstaff. This is the only instance of one batsman sharing two double century stands in the same Test innings.

Hutton added 359 for 1st wicket with C. Washbrook, England *v.* South Africa at Johannesburg 1948–49. This remains the England 1st wicket record and was the record for all Test cricket until beaten by V. Mankad and P. Roy, 413, India *v.* New Zealand at Madras 1955–56.

Hutton carried his bat for 202 out of 344 *v.* West Indies, The Oval 1950 and for 156* out of 272 *v.* Australia, Adelaide 1950–51. He is the only batsman to achieve the feat twice for England.

2000 runs in a season

Year	Inns	n.o.	Runs	H.S.	Av'ge	100s
1937	58	7	2888	271*	56.62	10
1939	52	6	2883	280*	62.67	12
1947	44	4	2585	270*	64.62	11
1948	48	7	2654	176*	64.73	10
1949	56	6	3429	269*	68.58	12
1950	40	3	2128	202*	57.51	6
1951	47	8	2145	194*	55.00	7
1952	45	3	2567	189	61.11	11
1953	44	5	2458	241	63.02	8

Keith Ross Miller

Born: Sunshine, Australia 18.11.1919

CAREER RECORDS

First-class cricket: 1937–38 to 1959

Batting:

Matches	Inns	n.o.	Runs	H.S.	Av'ge	100s
226	326	36	14183	281*	48.90	41

Bowling:

Runs Conceded	Wickets	Av'ge	Best	5 in inns	Ct/st
11087	497	22.30	7–12	16	136

Test cricket: 1945–46 to 1956–57

Batting:

Matches	Inns	n.o.	Runs	H.S.	Av'ge	100s
55	87	7	2958	147	36.97	7

Bowling:

Runs Conceded	Wickets	Av'ge	Best	5 in inns	Ct/st
3906	170	22.97	7–60	7	38

Highest Score: First-class cricket

281* Australians v. Leicestershire, Leicester 1956

Highest Score: Test cricket

147 Australia v. West Indies, Kingston 1954–55

Best Bowling Analysis: First-class cricket

7–12 New South Wales v. South Australia, Sydney 1955–56

Best Bowling Analysis: Test cricket

7–60 Australia v. England, Brisbane 1946–47

Some Batting Feats:

First-class cricket

Miller scored 181 on his first-class debut, Victoria v. Tasmania, Melbourne 1937–38 and scored 102* for Notts v. Cambridge University at Trent Bridge in 1959 on his Notts debut, and in his final first-class match.

Miller scored 1000 runs on two full tours of England and twice scored more than 1000 runs in an Australian season.

The details of his Australian seasons are as follows:

Season	Inns	n.o.	Runs	H.S.	Av'ge	100s
1946–47	19	3	1202	206*	75.12	4
1950–51	20	3	1332	214	78.35	5

Miller obtained centuries on his first appearances in both England (105 for Australian Services v. England XI, Lord's 1945) and New Zealand (139 for Australians v. Auckland, Auckland 1945–46).

Miller added 377 for the 4th wicket with J. H. De Courcy, Australians v. Services, Kingston on Thames in 1953. This is the best 4th wicket stand outside Test matches for any touring team in England.

Test cricket

Miller established a record 3rd wicket stand for Australia v. West Indies when he added 224 with R. N. Harvey at Kingston in 1954–55. This was beaten later in the same series when C. C. McDonald and Harvey added 295.

Miller established a 4th wicket record for Australia v. West Indies when adding 235 with A. L. Hassett at Sydney in 1951–52; this record lasted until 1968–69, when W. M. Lawry and K. D. Walters added 336 at Sydney.

In 1954–55 Miller and R. G. Archer added 220 for the 5th wicket at Kingston against West Indies, and this record still stands; in the same series at Bridgetown, Miller and Archer added 206–6th wicket, and this also still stands.

Some Bowling Feats:

First-class cricket

Miller's innings figures of 7–12 for New South Wales v. South Australia at Sydney in 1955–56 remains, statistically, the best ever innings analysis in The Sheffield Shield, beating 7–13 by H. Ironmonger, Victoria v. Queensland, Melbourne 1932–33.

Test cricket

Miller's match analysis of 10–152 against England at Lord's in 1956 was the best match analysis for an Australian at Lord's since C. T. B. Turner's 10–63 in 1888.

Raymond Russell Lindwall

Born: Mascot, New South Wales 3.10.1921

CAREER RECORDS

First-class cricket: 1941–42 to 1961–62

Batting:

Matches	Inns	n.o.	Runs	H.S.	Av'ge	100s
228	270	39	5042	134*	21.82	5

Bowling:

Runs Conceded	Wickets	Av'ge	Best	5 in inns	Ct/st
16956	794	21.35	7–20	34	123

Test cricket: 1945–46 to 1959–60

Batting:

Matches	Inns	n.o.	Runs	H.S.	Av'ge	100s
61	84	13	1502	118	21.15	2

Bowling:

Runs Conceded	Wickets	Av'ge	Best	5 in inns	Ct/st
5251	228	23.03	7–38	12	26

Highest Score: First-class cricket
134* New South Wales *v.* Queensland, Sydney 1945–46

Highest Score: Test cricket
118 Australia *v.* West Indies, Bridgetown 1954–55

Best Bowling Analysis: First-class cricket
7–20 Australians *v.* Minor Counties, Stoke-on-Trent 1953

Best Bowling Analysis: Test cricket
7–38 Australia *v.* India, Adelaide 1947–48

Some Batting Feats:
First-class cricket

Lindwall's highest score, 134* above, was made from no. 9 in the batting order, a very low position for so high a score.

Test cricket

Lindwall's first Test century – 100 *v.* England at Melbourne 1946–47 came in 113 minutes, with the second fifty taking 37 minutes. Lindwall and D. Tallon added 154 for the 8th wicket in 88 minutes.

When obtaining his best Test score – 118 *v.* West Indies in 1954–55 – he added 79 for the 8th wicket with I. W. Johnson and 61 for the 9th wicket with G. R. A. Langley.

Lindwall added 107 for the 8th wicket with A. L. Hassett *v.* England at Trent Bridge in 1948. This was the best 8th wicket stand against England in England and remains the best for Australia in England.

Some Bowling Feats:
First-class cricket

Lindwall's best bowling analysis – 7–20 for The Australians v Minor Counties at Stoke-on-Trent in 1953 – was gained without help from the field, 6 being clean bowled and one 1bw.

Lindwall's bowling in England was extremely economical on all his tours. Tour-by-tour his figures were:

Year	Overs	Maidens	Runs	Wkts	Av'ge
1948	573.1	139	1349	86	15.68
1953	639.1	178	1394	85	16.40
1956	413.3	119	924	47	19.65
	1625.5	436	3667	218	16.84

Test cricket

Lindwall stands 4th on the list of Australian Test wicket-takers. He had 228 (av. 23.03) and he is only exceeded by D. K. Lillee (355), R. Benaud (248) and G. D. McKenzie (246).

When Lindwall took his 100th Test wicket, against West Indies at Sydney in 1951–52, he was the first Australian fast bowler to perform the feat. He subsequently became the first Australian paceman with 200 Test wickets.

Sonny Ramadhin

Born: Esperance Village, Trinidad 1.5.1929

CAREER RECORDS

First-class cricket: 1949 to 1965

Batting:

Matches	Inns	n.o.	Runs	H.S.	Av'ge	100s
184	191	65	1092	44	8.66	–

Bowling:

Runs Conceded	Wickets	Av'ge	Best	5 in inns	Ct/st
15345	758	20.24	8–15	51	38

Test cricket: 1950 to 1961

Batting:

Matches	Inns	n.o.	Runs	H.S.	Av'ge
43	58	14	361	44	8.20

Bowling:

Runs Conceded	Wickets	Av'ge	Best	5 in inns	Ct/st
4579	158	28.98	7–49	10	9

Highest Score: First-class cricket

44 West Indies *v.* New Zealand, Dunedin 1955–56

Highest Score: Test cricket

as above

Best Bowling Analysis: First-class cricket

8–15 West Indians *v.* Gloucestershire, Cheltenham 1950

Best Bowling Analysis: Test cricket

7–49 West Indies *v.* England, Edgbaston 1957.

Some Bowling Feats:

First-class cricket

Took 135 wickets for 2009 on his first tour of England in 1950; had played only two first-class matches before this tour. Exceeded 100 wickets on his second and last tour to England in 1957. Three best seasons in England were:

Year	Runs Conceded	Wickets	Av'ge
1950	2009	135	14.88
1957	1664	119	13.98
1964	2046	92	22.23

In 1950 and 1957 Ramadhin was a West Indian tourist; in 1964 he played for Lancashire.

Ramadhin's best bowling figures, 8–15 *v.* Gloucs at Cheltenham in 1950 were statistically the best figures for an innings for a tourist in England since A. J. Y. Hopkins' 7–10 for the 1902 Australians *v.* Cambridge University. Both his innings and match analyses (13–51) are the best by any West Indian tourist.

Ramadhin's only hat-trick came for West Indians *v.* Hyderabad at Hyderabad, 1958–59. His victims were M. L. Jaisimha, Sriram and Venkat Rao.

Test cricket

In 1955–56 Ramadhin became the second West Indian bowler (after A. L. Valentine) to take 100 Test wickets. His analysis of 9–81 during the match in which he took his 100th wicket – *v.* New Zealand at Dunedin – is still the best for a West Indian in New Zealand.

Ramadhin's return of 26 wickets in his first Test series – *v.* England in 1950 – was second only to A. L. Valentine, who took 33 wickets in the same series, among West Indian bowlers in their first Test series.

Ramadhin's match figures of 11–152 against England at Lord's in 1950 (his second Test match) were at the time the best by a West Indian in all Test cricket, beating the previous record set by A. L. Valentine in the previous Test. Ramadhin's figures remained the best in England until K. D. Boyce's 11–147 at The Oval in 1973.

In achieving match figures of 9 wickets for 228 runs against England at Edgbaston in 1957, Ramadhin set Test records by bowling 588 balls in the second innings and 774 in the match. 588 balls in an innings is in fact a record for all first-class cricket.

Alfred Lewis Valentine

Born: Kingston, Jamaica 29.4.1930

CAREER RECORDS

First-class cricket: 1949–50 to 1964–65

Batting:

Matches	Inns	n.o.	Runs	H.S.	Av'ge
125	142	48	470	24*	5.00

Bowling:

Runs Conceded	Wickets	Av'ge	Best	5 in inns	Ct/st
12452	475	26.22	8–26	32	45

Test cricket: 1950 to 1961–62

Batting:

Matches	Inns	n.o.	Runs	H.S.	Av'ge
36	51	21	141	14	4.70

Bowling:

Runs Conceded	Wickets	Av'ge	Best	5 in inns	Ct/st
4215	139	30.32	8–104	8	13

Highest Score: First-class cricket
24* Jamaica *v.* Cavaliers, Kingston 1963–64

Highest score: Test cricket
14 West Indies *v.* Australia, Melbourne 1951–52

Best Bowling Analysis: First-class cricket
8–26 West Indians *v.* Lancashire, Old Trafford 1950

Best Bowling Analysis: Test cricket
8–104 West Indies *v.* England, Old Trafford 1950

Some Bowling Feats:

Valentine made his Test debut with an innings analysis of 8–104 and match figures of 11–204 for West Indies *v.* England, Old Trafford 1950. This remains the best Test debut by any bowler for West Indies, both for an innings and a match.

Valentine took 33 wickets in his first Test series, *v.* England in 1950. This was equalled by C. E. H. Croft *v.* Pakistan in the West Indies in 1976–77 but has never been beaten by a West Indian bowler.

Valentine, who had taken only 2 first-class wickets for 190 runs in 2 matches before the 1950 West Indies tour of England took 28 wickets before the first Test.

Against Lancashire at Old Trafford in 1950, Valentine, a few weeks past his 20th birthday, took 8–26 in 22 overs in the Lancashire first innings of 103 and had match figures of 13–67 from 42.2 overs, the best match figures for a West Indian tourist until Ramadhin took 13–51 later in the same tour.

Against England at Georgetown in 1953–54 Valentine became the youngest bowler to take 100 Test wickets, aged 23 years and 302 days; this was later beaten by G. D. McKenzie.

Valentine's bowling figures in England in 1950 were outstanding:

Overs	Maidens	Runs	Wickets	Av'ge
1185.2	475	2207	123	17.94

Valentine obtained more first-class wickets than he scored runs. Other international players to achieve this unusual feat were W. E. Bowes, W. E. Hollies and B. S. Chandrasekhar.

Frederick Sewards Trueman

Born: Scotch Springs, Stainton, Yorkshire 6.2.1931

CAREER RECORDS

First-class cricket: 1949 to 1969

Batting:

Matches	Inns	n.o.	Runs	H.S.	Av'ge	100s
603	713	120	9231	104	15.56	3

Bowling:

Runs Conceded	Wickets	Av'ge	Best	5 in inns	Ct/st
42154	2304	18.29	8–28	126	439

Test cricket: 1952 to 1965

Batting:

Matches	Inns	n.o.	Runs	H.S.	Av'ge	100s
67	85	14	981	39*	13.81	–

Bowling:

Runs Conceded	Wickets	Av'ge	Best	5 in inns	Ct/st
6625	307	21.57	8–31	17	64

Highest Score: First-class cricket
104 Yorkshire *v.* Northants., Northampton 1963

Highest Score: Test cricket
39* England *v.* New Zealand, The Oval 1958

Best Bowling Analysis: First-class cricket
8–28 Yorkshire *v.* Kent, Dover 1954

Best Bowling Analysis: Test cricket
8–31 England *v.* India, Old Trafford 1952

Some Batting Feats:

When scoring his maiden century and highest score *v.* Northants at Northampton in 1963, Trueman added 166 for the 6th wicket in less than two hours with D. B. Close. Close scored 161, Trueman 104, and the next highest scorer was D. E. V. Padgett with 18.

Some Bowling Feats

First-class cricket

When achieving his best innings bowling figures, 8–28 *v.* Kent in 1954, Kent were all out for 76 before lunch on the first day, so Trueman obtained his 8 wickets during this period, a most unusual feat.

Trueman achieved the hat-trick on four occasions during his career. All were obtained for Yorkshire and he shares the county record with G. G. Macaulay, who also achieved four such feats. Trueman's hat-tricks were:

v. Notts at Trent Bridge 1951
v. Notts at Scarborough 1955
v. MCC at Lord's 1958
v. Notts at Bradford 1963

Only R. O. Jenkins *v.* Surrey in 1948 and 1949 equalled Fred Trueman's record of three hat-tricks against one county (Notts).

150 wickets in a season

Year	Runs Conceded	Wickets	Av'ge
1955	2454	153	16.03
1960	2447	175	13.98
1961	3000	155	19.35
1962	2717	153	17.75

Test cricket

Trueman became the first player to take 300 Test wickets, against Australia at The Oval in 1964. His total of 307 Test wickets was the best for England for many years, but subsequently overtaken by R. G. D. Willis and I. T. Botham.

Trueman has taken 86 Test wickets against the West Indies, a record for all countries.

Trueman took 29 wickets in his first Test series, against India in 1952, a record for a debut series for England at home. Trueman took 34 wickets against the West Indies in 1963, a record for one series against the West Indies for any country.

John Brian Statham

Born: Manchester 17.6.1930

CAREER RECORDS

First-class cricket: 1950 to 1968

Batting:

Matches	Inns	n.o.	Runs	H.S.	Av'ge	100s
559	647	145	5424	62	10.80	–

Bowling:

Runs Conceded	Wickets	Av'ge	Best	5 in inns	Ct/st
36995	2260	16.37	8–34	123	230

Test cricket: 1951 to 1965

Batting:

Matches	Inns	n.o.	Runs	H.S.	Av'ge	100s
70	87	28	675	38	11.44	–

Bowling:

Runs Conceded	Wickets	Av'ge	Best	5 in inns	Ct/st
6261	252	24.84	7–39	9	28

Highest Score: First-class cricket
62 Lancs *v.* Leics., Old Trafford 1955

Highest Score: Test cricket
38 England *v.* India, Lord's 1959

Best Bowling: First-class cricket
8–34 Lancashire *v.* Warwicks., Coventry 1957

Best Bowling: Test cricket
7–39 England *v.* South Africa, Lord's 1955

Some Bowling Feats:

Statham took 1816 wickets (av. 15.01) for Lancashire, a record for the county.

Statham's best innings bowling analysis, 8–34, is the best for Lancashire against Warwickshire, while his match analysis of 15–89 is the best for Lancashire against Warwickshire in Warwickshire. Statham also took 15 wickets in the match, for 108 runs, for Lancashire *v.* Leicestershire at Leicester in 1964.

Statham achieved three hat-tricks in his career. They were:

For Lancashire *v.* Sussex, Old Trafford 1956
For MCC *v.* Transvaal, Johannesburg 1956–57
For Lancashire *v.* Leicestershire, Old Trafford 1958

Test cricket

In 1965 he became the second player after F. S. Trueman to reach 250 Test wickets. Currently he stands fifth among English Test wicket takers. Statham's total of 69 Test wickets against South Africa is exceeded only by S. F. Barnes among English bowlers.

When Statham achieved match figures of 10–97 against South Africa in the Lord's Test of 1960 this was the first time a fast bowler had taken 10 wickets in a home Test for England since the Second World War.

Frank Holmes Tyson

Born: Farnsworth, Lancashire 6.6.1930

CAREER RECORDS

First-class cricket: 1952 to 1960

Batting:

Matches	Inns	n.o.	Runs	H.S.	Av'ge
244	316	76	4103	82	17.09

Bowling:

Runs Conceded	Wickets	Av'ge	Best	5 in inns	Ct/st
16030	767	20.89	8–60	34	85

Test cricket: 1954 to 1959

Batting:

Matches	Inns	n.o.	Runs	H.S.	Av'ge
17	24	3	230	37*	10.95

Bowling:

Runs Conceded	Wickets	Av'ge	Best	5 in inns	Ct/st
1411	76	18.56	7–27	4	4

Highest Score: First-class cricket
82 Northants *v.* Sussex, Hove 1960

Highest Score: Test cricket
37* England *v.* Australia, Brisbane 1954–55

Best Bowling Analysis: First-class cricket
8–60 Northants *v.* Surrey, The Oval 1957

Best Bowling Analysis: Test cricket
7–27 England *v.* Australia, Melbourne 1954–55

Some Bowling Feats:

First-class cricket

Tyson's best innings analysis, 8–60 for Northants *v.* Surrey at The Oval in 1957, was followed by second innings figures of 5–52, bringing a match analysis of 13–112. It was reported by Wisden that ' . . . nearly half the runs scored off him came from the edge'.

Tyson took 100 wickets once, 101 wickets (av. 21.47) in 1957. In 1958 he achieved 99 wickets (av. 18.04).

Test cricket

In his first series against Australia in 1954–55 Tyson's total of 28 wickets was the best in a first series against Australia by an English bowler since F. R. Foster's 32 wickets in 1911–12.

Tyson's match analysis of 10–130 against Australia at Sydney in 1954–55 was statistically the best for England on that ground since H. Larwood's 10–124 in 1932–33.

Peter Barker Howard May

Born: Reading, Berkshire 31.12.1929

CAREER RECORDS

First-class cricket: 1948 to 1963

Batting:

Matches	Inns	n.o.	Runs	H.S.	Av'ge	100s
388	618	77	27592	285*	51.00	85

Bowling:

Runs Conceded	Wickets	Av'ge	Best	5 in inns	Ct/st
49	0	–	–	–	282

Test cricket: 1951 to 1961

Batting:

Matches	Inns	n.o.	Runs	H.S.	Av'ge	100s	Ct/st
66	106	9	4537	285*	46.77	13	42

Highest Score: First-class cricket
285* England *v.* West Indies, Edgbaston 1957

Highest Score: Test cricket
As above.

Some Batting Feats:

First-class cricket

May scored more than 1000 runs in an English season on 11 occasions, plus three times overseas. He scored 2000 runs in a season on 5 occasions. These were as listed:

2000 runs in a season

Year	Inns	n.o.	Runs	H.S.	Av'ge	100s
1951	43	9	2339	178*	68.79	9
1952	47	7	2498	197	62.45	10
1953	59	9	2554	159	51.08	8
1957	41	3	2347	285*	61.76	7
1958	41	6	2231	174	63.74	8

May's 1270 runs (av. 55.21) in South Africa in 1956–57 were the most runs by a touring captain in South Africa until J. R. Reid's 1915 runs in 1961–62.

May scored centuries in his first four innings in South Africa – for MCC in 1956–57. Details of the innings were:

162 *v.* Western Province (Cape Town); 118 *v.* Eastern Province (Port Elizabeth); 124* *v.* Rhodesia, Bulawayo; 206 *v.* Rhodesia, Salisbury.

This was the first instance of a batsman scoring centuries in his first four innings in a particular country.

May scored three hundreds in consecutive innings on two occasions. The details are as follows:

197 Surrey *v.* Leics, Leicester; 174 & 100* MCC *v.* Yorks, Scarborough, in 1952
155 Surrey *v.* Yorks, The Oval; 101 England *v.* New Zealand, Old Trafford; 112* Surrey *v.* New Zealanders, The Oval; all in 1958.

Test Cricket

May became the 10th English batsman to score a century on Test debut when obtaining 138 *v.* South Africa at Headingley in 1951. It was the first instance in a South African Test in England and only the second time in England that a century had been scored in the *first* innings of a Test debut for the home country.

The stand of 411 between May and M. C. Cowdrey for England *v.* West Indies at Edgbaston in 1957 is the best for the 4th wicket in all Test cricket, the best for any wicket against West Indies and the best for the 4th wicket at Edgbaston.

Michael Colin Cowdrey

Born: Ootacamund, Malabar, India 24.12.1932

CAREER RECORDS

First-class cricket: 1950 to 1976

Batting:

Matches	Inns	n.o.	Runs	H.S.	Av'ge	100s
692	1130	134	42719	307	42.89	107

Bowling:

Runs Conceded	Wickets	Av'ge	Best	5 in inns	Ct/st
3329	65	51.21	4–22	–	638

Test cricket: 1954 to 1975

Batting:

Matches	Inns	n.o.	Runs	H.S.	Av'ge	100s
114	188	15	7624	182	44.06	22

Bowling:

Runs Conceded	Wickets	Av'ge	Best	5 in inns	Ct/st
104	0	–	–	–	120

Highest Score: First-class cricket
307 MCC *v.* South Australia, Adelaide 1962–63

Highest Score: Test cricket
182 England *v.* Pakistan, The Oval 1962

Best Bowling Analysis: First-class cricket
4–22 Kent *v.* Surrey, Blackheath 1951

Some Batting Feats:

First-class matches

Cowdrey's best score – 307 – was at the time the highest score by any member of an English touring team made outside Test matches, and remains the highest by any tourist in Australia.

Cowdrey achieved a century in each innings of a match three times. His 115* and 103* for Kent *v.* Essex at Gillingham in 1955 was the first instance of two not out hundreds in one match by a Kent batsman; A. P. E. Knott subsequently equalled this record.

Cowdrey twice scored more than 2000 runs in an English season. The details are as follows:

2000 runs in a season

Year	Inns	n.o.	Runs	H.S.	Av'ge	100s
1959	44	4	2008	250	50.20	6
1965	43	10	2093	196*	63.42	5

Cowdrey obtained 1000 runs in a season in Australia, South Africa and West Indies. Details are as follows:

Australia 1962–63 1028 runs (av. 48.95)
South Africa 1956–57 1035 runs (39.80)
West Indies 1959–60 1014 runs (63.37)

Counting tours spent in more than one country Cowdrey scored 1000 runs in six overseas seasons – a record for an Englishman.

Test cricket

The 411 he added for the 4th wicket with P. B. H. May for England *v.* West Indies at Edgbaston, 1957, remains the Test 4th wicket record and is the best 4th wicket partnership in any match at Edgbaston.

Cowdrey's 7624 runs in Test cricket constituted a record until beaten by G. S. Sobers, and was the English record until passed by G. Boycott in 1981. Cowdrey's 114 Test appearances were a record until passed by S. M. Gavaskar in 1986, while his 120 catches were a record until overtaken by G. S. Chappell in 1984. Cowdrey's 22 Test centuries place him equal with G. Boycott and W. R. Hammond for England.

Cowdrey was the first batsman to score Test centuries against every other country. The record has since been equalled for England by K. F. Barrington and G. Boycott.

Cowdrey's 1133 Test runs *v.* New Zealand are a record, while his 1751 runs *v.* West Indies place him second to G. Boycott.

The 163* added for the 9th wicket by Cowdrey and A. C. Smith *v.* New Zealand at Wellington, 1962–63, remains a record for England.

Garfield St Aubrun Sobers

Born: Bridgetown, Barbados 28.7.1936

CAREER RECORDS

First-class cricket: 1952–53 to 1974

Batting:

Matches	Inns	n.o.	Runs	H.S.	Av'ge	100s
383	609	93	28315	365*	54.87	86

Bowling:

Runs Conceded	Wickets	Av'ge	Best	5 in inns	Ct/st
28941	1043	27.74	9–49	36	407

Test cricket: 1953 to 1974

Batting:

Matches	Inns	n.o.	Runs	H.S.	Av'ge	100s
93	160	21	8032	365*	57.78	26

Bowling:

Runs Conceded	Wickets	Av'ge	Best	5 in inns	Ct/st
7999	235	34.03	6–73	6	109

Highest Score: First-class cricket
365* West Indies *v.* Pakistan, Kingston 1957–58

Highest Score: Test cricket
As above.

Best Bowling Analysis: First-class cricket
9–49 West Indians *v.* Kent, Canterbury 1966

Best Bowling Analysis: Test cricket
6–73 West Indies *v.* Australia, Brisbane 1968–69

Some Batting Feats:

Sobers' career best score is the highest in Test cricket; it beat the 364 by L. Hutton at The Oval in 1938. It is also the best score by a West Indian in first-class cricket, beating the 344* by G. A. Headley for Jamaica against Tennyson's XI in 1931–32.

During Sobers' innings of 72 for Notts *v.* Glamorgan at Swansea in 1968 he hit every ball of an over from M. A. Nash for six, the first time this had ever been done in first-class cricket. The record has since been equalled by R. J.

Shastri, who hit every ball of an over from Tilak Raj for six, Bombay *v.* Baroda, Bombay 1984–85.

While playing for South Australia in 1962–63 and 1963–64 Sobers twice performed the 'double' of 1000 runs and 50 wickets during the season, a unique achievement.

Test cricket

Sobers' 365* against Pakistan at Kingston, 1957–58, is the highest ever Test score.

Sobers was the first batsman to exceed 8000 runs in Test cricket; his record of 8032 runs remains the best for West Indies.

During his 365* Sobers added 446 for 2nd wicket with C. C. Hunte; when scoring 226 *v.* England at Bridgetown in 1959–60 Sobers added 399 for 4th wicket with F. M. M. Worrell; in 1966 Sobers added 274 with D. A. J. Holford for an unbeaten 6th wicket stand and at Headingley in the same series Sobers added 265 for the 5th wicket with S. M. Nurse. The first stand is a West Indian first-class record, all are West Indian Test records.

All-round Cricket:

First-class cricket

Sobers achieved the 'match double' for Notts *v.* Kent at Dover 1968, scoring 17 & 105* and recording bowling figures of 7–69 and 4–87. His century came in 77 minutes and was the fastest of that season.

Test cricket

Sobers was the first player to complete 4000 runs and 200 wickets in Test cricket; this has subsequently been equalled by I. T. Botham, of England.

Some Bowling Feats:

First-class cricket

When Sobers achieved his best bowling figures – 9–49 for West Indians at Canterbury in 1966 – he was the first West Indian to take 9 wickets in England. Eight of the wickets were taken before lunch on the third day of the match.

Geoffrey Boycott

Born: Fitzwilliam, Yorkshire 21.10.1940

CAREER RECORDS

First-class cricket: 1962 to date

Batting:

Matches	Inns	n.o.	Runs	H.S.	Av'ge	100s
596	994	161	47434	261*	56.94	149

Bowling:

Runs Conceded	Wickets	Av'ge	Best	5 in inns	Ct/st
1459	45	32.42	4–14	–	260

Test cricket: 1964 to 1981–82

Batting:

Matches	Inns	n.o.	Runs	H.S.	Av'ge	100s
108	193	23	8114	246*	47.72	22

Bowling:

Runs Conceded	Wickets	Av'ge	Best	5 in inns	Ct/st
382	7	54.57	3–47	–	33

Highest Score: First-class cricket
261* MCC *v.* West Indian Cricket Board President's XI, Bridgetown 1973–74

Highest Score: Test cricket
246* England *v.* India, Headingley 1967.

Best Bowling Analysis: First-class cricket
4–14 Yorkshire *v.* Lancashire, Headingley 1979

Best Bowling Analysis: Test cricket
3–47 England *v.* South Africa, Cape Town 1964–65

Some Batting Feats:

First-class cricket

Boycott is the only English batsman to have averaged 100 in a season, and the only batsman to have done it twice. Those who have averaged 100 are; D. G. Bradman (115.66) in 1938; G. Boycott (102.53 and 100.12) in 1971 and 1979; W. A. Johnston (102.00) in 1953.

Boycott is the only Yorkshire batsman to have scored a century and 1000 runs against every other county, and shares with H. Sutcliffe the record of over 100 centuries for the county.

Boycott has carried his bat through an innings on nine occasions, eight of them for Yorkshire. L. Hall holds the Yorkshire record with 14, but Boycott lies second.

At the start of the 1986 season, Boycott's 149 centuries placed him equal fifth with Sutcliffe among century scorers.

Boycott has exceeded 2000 runs in a season on three occasions:

Years	Inns	n.o.	Runs	H.S.	Av'ge	100s
1964	44	4	2110	177	52.75	6
1970	42	5	2051	260*	55.43	4
1971	30	5	2503	233	100.12	13

Boycott's 1535 runs (av. 95.93) in Australia in 1970–71 is the record aggregate by a tourist in Australia.

Test cricket

Boycott's 8114 Test runs is the record for an English batsman and he held the record for all countries until overtaken by S. M. Gavaskar. Boycott's total of 22 Test centuries equals the English record with W. R. Hammond and M. C. Cowdrey.

Boycott's 193 Test innings, 64 Test fifties, and 2205 runs against West Indies are all records for an English batsman.

When Boycott scored 107 and 80* against Australia at Trent Bridge in 1977 he became the first English batsman to bat on all five days of a Test. When he scored 99 and 112 *v.* West Indies at Port-of-Spain in 1973–74 he became the first batsman to score 99 and a hundred in the same Test.

Boycott's highest Test score – 246* *v.* India at Headingley in 1967 remains the best score in an England/India Test. Boycott was left out of the England side for the next Test because of his slow scoring.

Anthony William Greig

Born: Queenstown, South Africa 6.10.1946

CAREER RECORDS

First-class cricket: 1965 to 1978
Batting:

Matches	Inns	n.o.	Runs	H.S.	Av'ge	100s
350	579	45	16660	226	31.29	26

Bowling:

Runs Conceded	Wickets	Av'ge	Best	5 in inns	Ct/st
24702	856	28.85	8–25	33	345

Test cricket: 1972 to 1977
Batting:

Matches	Inns	n.o.	Runs	H.S.	Av'ge	100s
58	93	4	3599	148	40.43	8

Bowling:

Runs Conceded	Wickets	Av'ge	Best	5 in inns	Ct/st
4541	141	32.20	8–86	6	87

Highest Score: First-class cricket
226 Sussex *v.* Warwickshire, Hastings 1975

Highest Score: Test cricket
148 England *v.* India, Bombay 1972–73

Best Bowling Analysis: First-class cricket
8–25 Sussex *v.* Gloucs, Hove 1967

Best Bowling Analysis: Test cricket
8–86 England *v.* West Indies, Port-of-Spain 1973–74

Some Feats:
First-class cricket

During Greig's highest score – 226 *v.* Warwickshire in 1975 – he hit the first four balls of an over from P. J. Lewington for six and was caught out trying to repeat the stroke from the fifth ball. During the innings Greig added 191 for the 4th wicket with A. E. W. Parsons and 147 for the 5th wicket with J. A. Snow. Greig scored 71 in the second innings, declared, setting Warwickshire a target of 355 in 4¼ hours, and lost the match.

Playing for Eastern Province *v.* Natal at Port Elizabeth in 1971–72, Greig achieved the 'hat-trick', dismissing P. P. Henwood, A. R. Lilley and V. A. P. van der Bijl.

Test cricket

When Greig scored 103 *v.* India at Calcutta in 1976–77 he reached his century in 414 minutes; this was the slowest century in England/India Test matches.

Greig was the first England player to score 3000 runs and take 100 wickets in Test cricket; his figures have subsequently been exceeded by I. T. Botham.

During Greig's best Test score, *v.* India at Bombay 1972–73, he added 254 for the 5th wicket with K. W. R. Fletcher. This is still the best stand for that wicket for England in Tests. Greig added 163 for the 6th wicket with A. P. E. Knott *v.* West Indies at Bridgetown, 1973–74, the English record *v.* West Indies for this wicket.

Greig's best innings bowling analysis, 8–86 against West Indies at Port-of-Spain in 1973–74 is the best for England in any West Indian Test, while his match figures of 13–156 are the best for any Test team against West Indies.

Basil Lewis D'Oliveira

Born: Signal Hill, Cape Town, South Africa 4.10.1931

CAREER RECORDS

First-class cricket: 1961–62 to 1980

Batting:

Matches	Inns	n.o.	Runs	H.S.	Av'ge	100s
362	566	88	18919	227	39.57	43

Bowling:

Runs Conceded	Wickets	Av'ge	Best	5 in inns	Ct/st
15021	548	27.41	6–29	17	211

Test cricket: 1966 to 1972

Batting:

Matches	Inns	n.o.	Runs	H.S.	Av'ge	100s
44	70	8	2484	158	40.06	5

Bowling:

Runs Conceded	Wickets	Av'ge	Best	5 in inns	Ct/st
1859	47	39.55	3–56	–	29

Highest Score: First-class cricket
227 Worcs *v.* Yorkshire, Hull 1974

Highest Score: Test cricket
158 England *v.* Australia, The Oval 1968

Best Bowling Analysis: First-class cricket
6–29 Worcs *v.* Hants, Portsmouth 1968

Best Bowling Analysis: Test cricket
3–46 England *v.* Pakistan, Headingley 1971

Some Batting Feats:

First-class cricket

D'Oliveira's best first-class score – 227 *v.* Yorkshire in 1974 – took just over 6 hours and came out of a Worcestershire total of 373. Yorkshire were dismissed for 101 and 189 so their total scores for each innings were exceeded by D'Oliveira. D'Oliveira shared an 8th wicket stand of 125 with N. Gifford – the best for Worcs *v.* Yorkshire.

D'Oliveira achieved innings figures of 5–39 and 6–29 (his best) for Worcs *v.* Hants at Portsmouth in 1968. The match figures of 11–68 are easily D'Oliveira's best ever.

Test cricket

Of D'Oliveira's five Test centuries, his 109 *v.* India at Headingley in 1967 was his first, and came on his Test debut *v.* India.

D'Oliveira's Test Centuries

109 *v.* India, Headingley 1967
158 *v.* Australia, The Oval 1968
114* *v.* Pakistan, Dacca 1968–69
117 *v.* Australia, Melbourne 1970–71
100 *v.* New Zealand, Christchurch 1970–71

D'Oliveira added 252 for the 4th wicket with G. Boycott, *v.* India at Headingley 1967. This is the best stand for any wicket at Headingley and second only to the partnership of 266 between W. R. Hammond and T. S. Worthington at The Oval in 1936 for a home Test *v.* India.

Dennis Keith Lillee

Born: Subiaco, Perth, Western Australia 18.7.1949

CAREER RECORDS

First-class cricket: 1969–70 to 1983–84

Batting:

Matches	Inns	n.o.	Runs	H.S.	Av'ge	100s
184	223	65	2220	73*	14.05	–

Bowling:

Runs Conceded	Wickets	Av'ge	Best	5 in inns	Ct/st
19317	845	22.86	8–29	49	62

Test cricket: 1970–71 to 1983–84

Batting:

Matches	Inns	n.o.	Runs	H.S.	Av'ge	100s
70	90	24	905	73*	13.71	–

Bowling:

Runs Conceded	Wickets	Av'ge	Best	5 in inns	Ct/st
8493	355	23.92	7–83	23	23

Highest Score: First-class cricket
73* Australia v. England, Lord's 1975

Highest Score: Test cricket
As above.

Best Bowling Analysis: First-class cricket
8–29 Australians XI v. World XI, Perth 1971–72

Best Bowling Analysis: Test cricket
7–83 Australia v. West Indies, Melbourne 1981–82

Some Batting feats:

Test cricket

When obtaining his best score, above, Lillee went in at the fall of the 8th wicket, with the score 133–8. He added 66 with R. Edwards for the 9th wicket, and 69 for the 10th wicket with A. A. Mallett. Thus the score was more than doubled by the last two wickets.

Some Bowling Feats:

First-class cricket

When Lillee achieved his best innings bowling analysis – 8–29 in 57 balls for an Australian XI v. a World XI at Perth in 1971–72 – he followed with 4–63 in the second innings. His match figures were 12–92, statistically his best, and every victim was caught out.

On his retirement Lillee had taken 323 Sheffield Shield wickets. This is a record for Western Australia, beating the 302 of G. A. R. Lock. The only Sheffield Shield bowlers to exceed Lillee's total were C. V. Grimmett (Victoria & South Australia) and A. A. Mallett (South Australia). The leaders are:

G. V. Grimmett	513 wickets	(av. 25.29)
A. A. Mallett	344 wickets	(av. 23.75)
D. K. Lillee	323 wickets	(av. 23.35)

Lillee's total of wickets for Western Australia in all first-class cricket was 351 (av. 23.02), a record for the state.

Test cricket

Lillee holds the record for total of Test wickets at the time of writing. He took 355 (av. 23.92). He is followed by I. T. Botham (354), R. G. D. Willis 325 (25.20), R. J. Hadlee 315 (22.63), L. R. Gibbs 309 (29.09), F. S. Trueman 307 (21.57).

Lillee shares the Test record of having taken 10 wickets in a match on 7 occasions with C. V. Grimmett and S. F. Barnes.

Lillee holds the record for the most Test wickets in a calendar year; in 1981 he took 85 wickets (av. 20.95). In Anglo-Australian Test matches he took a record total of 167 wickets, 26 better than H. Trumble, who lies second.

Isaac Vivian Alexander Richards

Born: St John's, Antigua, 7.3.1952

CAREER RECORDS

First-class cricket: 1971–72 to date

Batting:

Matches	Inns	n.o.	Runs	H.S.	Av'ge	100s
368	583	39	27359	322	50.29	88

Bowling:

Runs Conceded	Wickets	Av'ge	Best	5 in inns	Ct/st
7184	168	42.76	5–88	1	335/1

Test cricket: 1974–75 to date

Batting:

Matches	Inns	n.o.	Runs	H.S.	Av'ge	100s
82	122	8	6220	291	54.56	20

Bowling:

Runs Conceded	Wickets	Av'ge	Best	5 in inns	Ct/st
1052	19	55.36	2–20	–	79

Highest Score: First-class cricket
322 Somerset *v.* Warwickshire, Taunton 1985

Highest Score: Test cricket
291 West Indies *v.* England, The Oval 1976

Best Bowling Analysis: First-class cricket
5–88 West Indians *v.* Queensland, Brisbane 1981–82

Best Bowling Analysis: Test cricket
2–20 West Indies *v.* Pakistan, Lahore 1980–81

Some Batting Feats:
First-class cricket

When Richards scored 322 *v.* Warwicks in 1985 this established a new record for a Somerset batsman; the previous record was H. Gimblett's 310 against Sussex at Eastbourne in 1948. The former record for a Somerset batsman at Taunton had also been held by Gimblett – 231 *v.* Middlesex in 1946; the Taunton record for any batsman is still 424 by A. C. MacLaren for Lancashire *v.* Somerset in 1895.

Richards has scored three centuries in consecutive innings on two occasions:

1980 for West Indies; 145 *v.* England, Lord's; 100 *v.* Glamorgan, Swansea; 103 *v.* Somerset, Taunton.

1985 for Somerset; 120 *v.* Lancs., Old Trafford; 123 *v.* Derbyshire, Derby; 112 *v.* Sussex, Taunton.

Richards has scored centuries against every first-class county, including Somerset (in 1980 above). This is a record he shares with G. M. Turner (Worcs & New Zealand).

Richards shares with I. T. Botham the Somerset 8th wicket record – 172 *v.* Leics at Leicester in 1983.

During his innings of 186 for Somerset *v.* Hants at Taunton in 1985, Richards hit ten sixes, equalling the Somerset record held by I. T. Botham. A few weeks later Botham set a new record of twelve sixes. Richards hit 9 sixes in an innings of 100 for West Indians *v.* Glamorgan at Swansea in 1980; this remains the best for a West Indian touring team.

Richards' 49 sixes in the 1985 season is the sixth best on record.

During his 322 mentioned above, Richards obtained 216 runs in boundaries. This is a Somerset record, beating I. T. Botham's 168 in boundaries during his 228 *v.* Gloucs at Taunton in 1980.

Test cricket

During 1976 Richards scored 1710 runs in 11 Test matches (av. 95.00); this remains the record for a batsman in Tests during a calendar year. His 7 centuries during the year are also a record.

Richards' aggregate of 829 runs (av. 118.42) in the series *v.* England in 1976 is the fourth highest ever, the best for a West Indian and for a batsman playing fewer than five Tests.

Richards' 291 *v.* England at The Oval in 1976 is the best for West Indies in England, and the best against England at The Oval. The previous records were held by F. M. M. Worrell, 261 at Trent Bridge in 1950, and W. H. Ponsford, 266 for Australia in 1934.

Richards' 110* *v.* England at St John's, 1985/86, included the fastest century in terms of balls received in all Test cricket. Richards reached his hundred from 56 balls, beating the previous record of 67 balls by J. M. Gregory, Australia *v.* South Africa, Johannesburg 1920–21. Richards reached his century in 81 minutes, the West Indian record previously held by C. H. Lloyd, who scored a hundred in 102 minutes *v.* India at Bangalore in 1974–75.

Ian Terrence Botham

Born: Heswall, Cheshire 24.11.1955

CAREER RECORDS

First-class cricket: 1974 to date

Batting:

Matches	Inns	n.o.	Runs	H.S.	Av'ge	100s
269	414	31	13437	228	35.08	29

Bowling:

Runs Conceded	Wickets	Av'ge	Best	5 in inns	Ct/st
22957	896	25.62	8–34	50	246

Test cricket: 1977 to date

Batting:

Matches	Inns	n.o.	Runs	H.S.	Av'ge	100s
84	135	3	4577	208	34.67	13

Bowling:

Runs Conceded	Wickets	Av'ge	Best	5 in inns	Ct/st
9581	354	27.06	8–34	26	96

Highest Score: First-class cricket
228 Somerset *v.* Gloucs, Taunton 1980

Highest Score: Test cricket
208 England *v.* India, The Oval 1982

Best Bowling Analysis: First-class cricket
8–34 England *v.* Pakistan, Lord's 1978

Best Bowling Analysis: Test cricket
As above.

Some Feats:

First-class cricket

During his 228 for Somerset *v.* Gloucs at Taunton in 1980, he achieved a Somerset record of 10 sixes in the innings. He equalled his own record in 1985, as did I. V. A. Richards, and against Warwickshire at Edgbaston in 1985 Botham's 138* included twelve sixes. This remains the Somerset record.

During Botham's 138* for Somerset *v.* Warwicks at Edgbaston in 1985 he reached his century in 49 minutes. This is the record for Somerset and his third century in less than one hour. They are:

49 minutes (138*) Som *v.* Warwicks., Edgbaston 1985
50 minutes (122) England XI *v.* Central Zone, Indore 1981–82
52 minutes (131*) Somerset *v.* Warwicks., Taunton 1982

During the 1985 season Botham hit 80 sixes in first-class cricket. This set a new record, beating A. W. Wellard's total of 66 set in 1935. Wellard also exceeded 50 sixes in 1933 (51), 1936 and 1938 (both 57). No other batsman has hit 50 sixes in a season.

Test cricket

Botham took his 100th Test wicket in 2 years, 9 days (then a record) and his 200th wicket in 4 years, 34 days (another record). Botham's Test 'double' of 1000 runs and 100 wickets came in 21 Tests (a record) and he achieved the 2000 runs/200 wickets 'double' in 42 Tests and 4 years 26 days. These are both records. In 1984 Botham became the first Test cricketer to score 4000 runs and take 300 wickets in Test matches.

In Australia/England Tests he achieved the 1000 runs/100 wickets 'double' in 22 Tests – another record.

Botham's Test wicket total stands at 354, one fewer than the record held by D. K. Lillee. Among English bowlers he leads second placed R. G. D. Willis by 29 wickets. F. S. Trueman stands third on 307.

Among current Test all-rounders, Botham is one of four with more than 2000 runs and 200 wickets. They are as follows:

Player & Country	Tests	Runs	Av'ge	Wickets	Runs	Av'ge
I. T. Botham (England)	84	4577	34.77	354	9581	27.06
Kapil Dev (India)	74	3051	30.21	281	8054	28.66
R. J. Hadlee (N. Zealand)	63	2304	25.60	315	7130	22.63
Imran Khan (Pak)	54	2086	31.13	249	5587	22.43

David Ivon Gower

Born: Tunbridge Wells, Kent 1.4.1957

CAREER RECORDS

First-class cricket: 1975 to date
Batting:

Matches	Inns	n.o.	Runs	H.S.	Av'ge	100s
276	438	38	16037	215	40.09	34

Bowling:

Runs Conceded	Wickets	Av'ge	Best	5 in inns	Ct/st
209	4	52.25	3–47	–	173

Test cricket: 1978 to date
Batting:

Matches	Inns	n.o.	Runs	H.S.	Av'ge	100s
81	139	11	5755	215	44.96	12

Bowling:

Runs Conceded	Wickets	Av'ge	Best		Ct/st
15	1	–	1–1		58

Highest Score: First-class cricket
215 England *v.* Australia, Edgbaston 1985

Highest Score: Test cricket
As above.

Best Bowling Analysis: First-class cricket
3–47 Leics *v.* Essex, Leicester 1977

Best Bowling Analysis: Test cricket
1–1 England *v.* India, Kanpur 1980–81

Some Batting Feats:
First-class cricket

In 1981 Gower and J. C. Balderstone added 289 unbeaten for the Leicestershire second wicket against Essex at Leicester. This beat the previous 2nd wicket record for the county – 287 by W. Watson and A. Wharton against Lancashire at Leicester 1961.

Gower has exceeded 1000 runs in a season on six occasions, his best season being 1982 when he averaged 46.36 for 1530 runs.

Test cricket

Gower's 5755 runs in Test cricket place him seventh on the list of English run-getters in all Test history, and make him the most prolific scoring English left hander of all time.

Gower's two Test double centuries – 200* *v.* India in 1979 and 215 *v.* Australia in 1985 were both scored at Edgbaston; Gower is the only Test batsman to obtain two double centuries at this ground for any Test team.

Gower's 200* in 1979 was scored on his Test debut against India. Only G. Boycott (246* at Headingley in 1967), B. L. D'Oliveira (109 at Headingley in 1967), and M. J. K. Smith (100 at Old Trafford in 1959) have achieved this feat in a home Test in addition to Gower.

Gower and V. J. Marks share the partnership record for the 7th wicket for England *v.* Pakistan in all Tests between the two countries. They added 167 together at Faisalabad in 1983–84.

APPENDIX B

TEST CRICKET RECORDS

Series by series analysis of England in Test cricket

1. v. Australia

SEASON	VENUE	SERIES RESULT
1876–77	Australia	Drawn (1 win each)
1878–79	Australia	Australia won (1–0)
1880	England	England won (1–0)
1881–82	Australia	Australia won (2–0, 2 drawn)
1882	England	Australia won (1–0)
1882–83	Australia	Drawn (2–2)
1884	England	England won (1–0, 2 drawn)
1884–85	Australia	England won (3–2)
1886	England	England won (3–0)
1886–87	Australia	England won (2–0)
1887–88	Australia	England won (1–0)
1888	England	England won (2–1)
1890	England	England won (2–0)
1891–92	Australia	Australia won (2–1)
1893	England	England won (1–0, 2 drawn)
1894–95	Australia	England won (3–2)
1896	England	England won (2–1)
1897–98	Australia	Australia won (4–1)
1899	England	Australia won (1–0, 4 drawn)
1901–02	Australia	Australia won (4–1)
1902	England	Australia won (2–1, 2 drawn)
1903–04	Australia	England won (3–2)
1905	England	England won (2–0, 3 drawn)
1907–08	Australia	Australia won (4–1)
1909	England	Australia won (2–1, 2 drawn)
1911–12	Australia	England won (4–1)
1912	England	England won (1–0, 2 drawn)
1920–21	Australia	Australia won (5–0)
1921	England	Australia won (3–0, 2 drawn)
1924–25	Australia	Australia won (4–1)
1926	England	England won (1–0, 4 drawn)
1928–29	Australia	England won (4–1)
1930	England	Australia won (2–1, 2 drawn)
1932–33	Australia	England won (4–1)
1934	England	Australia won (2–1, 2 drawn)
1936–37	Australia	Australia won (3–2)
1938	England	Drawn (1 win each, 2 drawn)
1946–47	Australia	Australia won (3–0, 2 drawn)
1948	England	Australia won (4–0, 1 drawn)
1950–51	Australia	Australia won (4–1)
1953	England	England won (1–0, 4 drawn)
1954–55	Australia	England won (3–1, 1 drawn)
1956	England	England won (2–1, 2 drawn)
1958–59	Australia	Australia won (4–0, 1 drawn)
1961	England	Australia won (2–1, 2 drawn)
1962–63	Australia	Drawn (1 win each, 3 drawn)
1964	England	Australia won (1–0, 4 drawn)
1965–66	Australia	Drawn (1 win each, 3 drawn)
1968	England	Drawn (1 win each, 3 drawn)
1970–71	Australia	England won (2–0, 4 drawn)
1972	England	Drawn (2 wins each, 1 drawn)
1974–75	Australia	Australia won (4–1, 1 drawn)
1975	England	Australia won (1–0, 3 drawn)
1976–77	Australia	Australia won (1–0)
1977	England	England won (3–0, 2 drawn)
1978–79	Australia	England won (5–1)
1979–80	Australia	Australia won (3–0)
1980	England	Drawn (1 drawn)
1981	England	England won (3–1, 2 drawn)
1982–83	Australia	Australia won (2–1, 2 drawn)
1985	England	England won (3–1, 2 drawn)

TOTALS	In Australia	Australia won 66
		England won 49
		Drawn 19
	In England	England won 37
		Australia won 30
		Drawn 56
	Altogether	Australia won 96
		England won 86
		Drawn 75
	Series	Australia 27
		England 26
		Drawn 8

2. v. South Africa

SEASON	VENUE	SERIES RESULT
1888–89	South Africa	England won (2–0)
1891–92	South Africa	England won (1–0)
1895–96	South Africa	England won (3–0)
1898–99	South Africa	England won (2–0)
1905–06	South Africa	South Africa won (4–1)
1907	England	England won (1–0, 2 drawn)
1909–10	South Africa	South Africa won (3–2)
1912	England	England won (3–0)
1913–14	South Africa	England won (4–0, 1 drawn)
1922–23	South Africa	England won (2–1, 2 drawn)
1924	England	England won (3–0, 2 drawn)
1927–28	South Africa	Drawn (2 wins each, 1 drawn)
1929	England	England won (2–0, 3 drawn)
1920–31	South Africa	South Africa won (1–0, 4 drawn)
1935	England	South Africa won (1–0, 4 drawn)
1938–39	South Africa	England won (1–0, 4 drawn)
1947	England	England won (3–0, 2 drawn)
1948–49	South Africa	England won (2–0, 3 drawn)
1951	England	England won (3–1, 1 drawn)

1955	England	England won (3–2)
1956–57	South Africa	Drawn (2 wins each, 1 drawn)
1960	England	England won (3–0, 2 drawn)
1964–65	South Africa	England won (1–0, 4 drawn)
1965	England	South Africa won (1–0, 2 drawn)

TOTALS	In South Africa	England won 25 South Africa won 13 Drawn 20
	In England	England won 21 South Africa won 5 Drawn 18
	Altogether	England won 46 South Africa won 18 Drawn 38
	Series	England 17 South Africa 5 Drawn 2

3. *v. West Indies*

SEASON	VENUE	SERIES RESULT
1928	England	England won (3–0)
1929–30	West Indies	Drawn (1 win each, 2 drawn)
1933	England	England won (2–0, 1 drawn)
1934–35	West Indies	West Indies won (2–1, 1 drawn)
1939	England	England won (1–0, 2 drawn)
1947–48	West Indies	West Indies won (2–0, 2 drawn)
1950	England	West Indies won (3–1)
1953–54	West Indies	Drawn (2 wins each, 1 drawn)
1957	England	England won (3–0, 2 drawn)
1959–60	West Indies	England won (1–0, 4 drawn)
1963	England	West Indies won (3–1, 1 drawn)
1966	England	West Indies won (3–1, 1 drawn)
1967–68	West Indies	England won (1–0, 4 drawn)
1969	England	England won (2–0, 1 drawn)
1973	England	West Indies won (2–0, 1 drawn)
1973–74	West Indies	Drawn (1 win each, 3 drawn)
1976	England	West Indies won (3–0, 2 drawn)
1980	England	West Indies won (1–0, 4 drawn)
1980–81	West Indies	West Indies won (2–0, 2 drawn)
1984	England	West Indies won (5–0)
1985–86	West Indies	West Indies won (5–0)

TOTALS	In England	West Indies won 20 England won 14 Drawn 15
	In West Indies	West Indies won 15 England won 7 Drawn 19
	Altogether	West Indies won 35 England won 21 Drawn 34

| | Series | West Indies 11
England 7
Drawn 3 |

4. *v. New Zealand*

SEASON	VENUE	SERIES RESULT
1929–30	New Zealand	England won (1–0, 3 drawn)
1931	England	England won (1–0, 2 drawn)
1932–33	New Zealand	Drawn (2 drawn)
1937	England	England won (1–0, 2 drawn)
1946–47	New Zealand	Drawn (1 draw)
1949	England	Drawn (4 drawn)
1950–51	New Zealand	England won (1–0, 1 drawn)
1954–55	New Zealand	England won (2–0)
1958	England	England won (4–0, 1 drawn)
1958–59	New Zealand	England won (1–0, 1 drawn)
1962–63	New Zealand	England won (3–0)
1965	England	England won (3–0)
1965–66	New Zealand	Drawn (3 drawn)
1969	England	England won (2–0, 1 drawn)
1970–71	New Zealand	England won (1–0, 1 drawn)
1973	England	England won (2–0, 1 drawn)
1974–75	New Zealand	England won (1–0, 1 drawn)
1977–78	New Zealand	Drawn (1–1, 1 drawn)
1978	England	England won (3–0)
1983	England	England won (3–1)
1983–84	New Zealand	New Zealand won (1–0, 2 drawn)

TOTALS	In New Zealand	England won 11 New Zealand won 2 Drawn 16
	In England	England won 19 New Zealand won 1 Drawn 11
	Altogether	England won 30 New Zealand won 3 Drawn 27
	Series	England 15 New Zealand 1 Drawn 5

5. *v. India*

SEASON	VENUE	SERIES RESULT
1932	England	England won (1–0)
1933–34	India	England won (2–0, 1 drawn)
1936	England	England won (2–0, 1 drawn)
1946	England	England won (1–0, 2 drawn)
1951–52	India	Drawn (1–1, 3 drawn)
1952	England	England won (3–0, 1 drawn)
1959	England	England won (5–0)
1961–62	India	India won (2–0, 3 drawn)
1963–64	India	Drawn (5 drawn)
1967	England	England won (3–0)
1971	England	India won (1–0, 2 drawn)
1972–73	India	India won (2–1, 2 drawn)
1974	England	England won (3–0)
1976–77	India	England won (3–1, 1 drawn)
1979	England	England won (1–0, 3 drawn)

1979–80	India	England won (1–0)
1981–82	India	India won (1–0, 5 drawn)
1982	England	England won (1–0, 2 drawn)
1984–85	India	England won (2–1, 2 drawn)
1986	England	India won (2–0, 1 drawn)

TOTALS	In England	England won 20
		India won 3
		Drawn 12
	In India	England won 10
		India won 8
		Drawn 22
	Altogether	England won 30
		India won 11
		Drawn 34
	Series	England 13
		India 5
		Drawn 2

6. v. Pakistan

SEASON	VENUE	SERIES RESULT
1954	England	Drawn (1–1, 2 drawn)
1961–62	Pakistan	England won (1–0, 2 drawn)
1962	England	England won (4–0, 1 drawn)
1967	England	England won (2–0, 1 drawn)
1968–69	Pakistan	Drawn (3 drawn)
1971	England	England won (1–0, 2 drawn)
1972–73	Pakistan	Drawn (3 drawn)
1974	England	Drawn (3 drawn)
1977–78	Pakistan	Drawn (3 drawn)

1978	England	England won (2–0, 1 drawn)
1982	England	England won (2–1)
1983–84	Pakistan	Pakistan won (1–0, 2 drawn)

TOTALS	In England	England won 12
		Pakistan won 2
		Drawn 10
	In Pakistan	England won 1
		Pakistan won 1
		Drawn 13
	Altogether	England won 13
		Pakistan won 3
		Drawn 23
	Series	England 6
		Pakistan 1
		Drawn 5

7. v. Sri Lanka

SEASON	VENUE	SERIES RESULT
1981–82	Sri Lanka	England won (1–0)
1984	England	Drawn (1 draw)

TOTALS	In Sri Lanka	England won 1
	In England	Drawn 1
	Altogether	England won 1
		Drawn 1
	Series	England won 1
		Drawn 1

Analysis of other countries in Test cricket

1. Australia v. South Africa

First Test Series: 1902–03

No. of Series; 12; Australia won 8; South Africa won 2; Drawn 2
No. of Tests; 53; Australia won 29; South Africa won 11; Drawn 13

2. Australia v. West Indies

First Test Series: 1930–31

No. of Series; 13; Australia won 7; West Indies won 5; Drawn 1
No. of Tests; 62; Australia won 27; West Indies won 19; Drawn 15; Tied 1

3. Australia v. New Zealand

First Test Series: 1945–46

No. of Series; 8; Australia won 4; New Zealand won 2; Drawn 2
No. of Tests; 21; Australia won 9; New Zealand won 5; drawn 7

4. Australia v. India

First Test Series: 1947–48

No. of Series; 10; Australia won 6; India won 1; Drawn 3
No. of Tests; 42; Australia won 20; India won 8; Drawn 14

5. Australia v. Pakistan

First Test Series: 1956–57

No. of Series; 11; Australia won 4; Pakistan won 3; Drawn 4
No. of Tests; 28; Australia won 11; Pakistan won 8; Drawn 9

6. Australia v. Sri Lanka

First Test Series: 1982–83

No. of Series; 1; Australia won 1
No. of Tests; 1; Australia won 1

7. South Africa v. New Zealand

First Test Series: 1931–32

No. of Series; 5; South Africa won 3; Drawn 2
No. of Tests; 17; South Africa won 9; New Zealand won 2; Drawn 6

8. West Indies v. New Zealand

First Test Series: 1951–52

No. of Series; 6; West Indies won 3; New Zealand won 1; Drawn 2
No. of Tests; 21; West Indies won 7; New Zealand won 3; Drawn 11

9. *West Indies v. India*

First Test Series: 1948–49

No. of Series; 11; West Indies won 9; India won 2
No. of Tests; 54; West Indies won 22; India won 5; Drawn 27

10. *West Indies v. Pakistan*

First Test Series: 1957–58

No. of Series; 5; West Indies won 3; Pakistan won 1; Drawn 1
No. of Tests; 19; West Indies won 7; Pakistan won 4; Drawn 8

11. *New Zealand v. India*

First Test Series: 1955–56

No. of Series; 7; India won 4; New Zealand won 1; Drawn 2
No. of Tests; 25; India won 10; New Zealand won 4; Drawn 11

12. *New Zealand v. Pakistan*

First Test Series: 1955–56

No. of Series; 9; Pakistan won 6; New Zealand won 2; Drawn 1

No. of Tests; 27; Pakistan won 10; New Zealand won 3; Drawn 14

13. *New Zealand v. Sri Lanka*

First Test Series: 1982–83

No. of Series; 2; New Zealand won 2
No. of Tests; 5; New Zealand won 4; Drawn 1

14. *India v. Pakistan*

First Test Series: 1952–53

No. of Series; 8; India won 2; Pakistan won 2; Drawn 4
No. of Tests; 35; Pakistan won 6; India won 4; Drawn 25

15. *India v. Sri Lanka*

First Test Series: 1982–83

No. of Series; 2; Sri Lanka won 1; Drawn 1
No. of Tests; 4; Sri Lanka won 1; Drawn 3

16. *Pakistan v. Sri Lanka*

First Test Series: 1981–82

No. of Series; 2; Pakistan won 2
No. of Tests; 6; Pakistan won 4; Drawn 2

APPENDIX C

IAN BOTHAM'S FAST SCORING

The recent batting feats of Ian Botham have naturally provoked much debate as to where he lies in the hitters' hierarchy; how he compares with the renowned smiters of the past.

In fact there can be no comparison with most of the past hitters. Arthur Wellard, whose six hit record for a season Botham beat in 1985 is naturally often mentioned but although a hitter of sixes – over 500 in his career – he scored only two centuries and averaged less than 20. Jim Smith, another legend, comes out even worse with one century and a career average of less than 15, and other noted hitters who can be immediately dismissed due to exaggeration of their prowess are A. E. Watt, F. Barratt, G. F. Earle, C. I. Thornton and G. J. Bonnor. All had their days, and the last-named in particular was at times a fair run-getter, but really, to compare any of them with Botham would be ludicrous. A player who is often named in this class, but who was in fact a far better batsman was L. N. Constantine. He did score his runs, including five centuries, at a rattling pace but his overall record was disappointing.

Another group often mentioned in the same breath as Botham are the specialist, high-scoring batsmen who generally score quickly and hit a large number of sixes. Certainly in the present day Vivian Richards and Gordon Greenidge score a lot of their runs from hits over the ropes and in the fairly recent past one can name Harold Gimblett, John Jameson and, for a time, W. J. Stewart. All have included a fair number of sixes among their runs but again one feels comparison with Botham is invalid.

When all others have been swept away however, one name remains against which even Ian Botham tends to pale. Gilbert Jessop played in the 21 seasons prior to the first world war and incredibly made at least 14 of his 53 centuries in one hour or less. (A figure of 15 has been mentioned in another source but I have been able to trace only 14.)

It is terribly difficult to compare even Jessop's feats with Botham, though on the face of it Jessop's 14 fast hundreds outshine Botham's 3 in under one hour. When one considers that until 1910 a ball usually required to be hit out of the ground for six to be awarded, Jessop's feat looks even better, but against this it is accepted that the over-rate in Jessop's time was generally substantially faster than now. Just how much faster is not possible to say, but after a lot of delving into match reports of Jessop's day I feel the difference may have been exaggerated somewhat.

I would however estimate that for every six ball over faced by Jessop, Botham faces only five balls. On the other hand account must be taken of the pre-1910 custom that sixes should be hit out of the ground; I would say this would have added perhaps three minutes to each Jessop century.

This tampering with the timings of Jessop's centuries is admittedly artificial, but perhaps it enables us to make a slightly more acceptable comparison. Certainly one sees a quite dramatic change, with Jessop's 14 centuries of one hour or less reduced to two, compared with Botham's three. Only the first two survive, with revised timings of 45 and 47 minutes respectively, as against timings of 49 and 50 minutes for Botham's top two.

It has to be said that if Jessop's conditions are transferred to Botham, Botham gains no centuries while Jessop still has a far higher proportion of really quick (75 minutes or less) innings even after 'adjustment'. However as an interesting exercise, not to be taken seriously, we detract nothing from Jessop but at the same time show that Botham, since his maturing as a batsman, has become almost Jessopian in prowess. Certainly one would rank him as the second best hitter of all time.

Centuries by Jessop in one hour or less

40 minutes; (101) Glos v. Yorks., Harrogate 1897
42 minutes; (191) Gents of South v. Players of South, Hastings 1907
53 minutes; (139) Glos v. Surrey, Bristol 1911
55 minute; (123*) South v. North, Hastings 1900
55 minutes; (126) Glos v. Notts., Trent Bridge 1902
55 minutes; (119) Glos v. Sussex, Hastings.1907
55 minutes; (116) Lord Londesborough's XI v. Kent, Scarborough 1913
57 minutes; (124) Glos v. Middlesex, Lord's 1901
59 minutes; (139) Glos v. Yorkshire, Bradford 1900
60 minutes; (112*) Rest v. Stoddart's XI, Hasting 1898
60 minutes; (126) Glos v. Notts., Trent Bridge 1899
60 minutes; (109) Glos v. Middlesex, Lord's 1900
60 minutes; (169) MCC v. Leics., Lord's 1901
60 minutes; (165) Glos v. Worcs., Stourbridge 1910.

NB: Jessop's 59 minute hundred v. Yorks in 1900 came in the second innings of a match in which he had scored 104 in 70 minutes in the first innings, reaching his century in 68 minutes.

Centuries by Botham in one hour or less

49 minutes; (138*) Somerset v. Warwickshire, Edgbaston 1985
50 minutes; (122) England XI v. Central Zone, Indore 1981–82
52 minutes (131*) Somerset v. Warwickshire, Taunton 1982

APPENDIX D

COMPARISON OF LEADING ALL-ROUNDERS

All cricketing comparisons are fraught with riders and qualifications – even the ostensibly straightforward batting and bowling averages, since only the simple-minded or one to whom figures are the be-all and end-all would argue that a higher average confirms batting superiority. Judgement of all-round worth is even more difficult since it is so hard to devise an 'averages' system to give even an approximate idea of individual merit.

It was part of my brief however to produce an assessment of all-rounder effectiveness among Test cricketers, so a method, or methods had to be evolved.

One way which has been in use for more than forty years is the simple division of batting average by bowling average. It may be felt that any all-rounder worth his salt should have a higher batting than bowling average and certainly the method prevents differing conditions helping one facet or the other. The results are also objective; no way can one adjust the figures to get the 'correct' conclusions.

Weaknesses? The high scoring batsman who bowls just enough to qualify is undoubtedly favoured while the conclusions are all about career figures. No account is taken of all-round performances in matches. Hammond's high placing owes everything to his batting average, while suspicions that Sobers' assessment figure is too high also tend to be confirmed. On the other hand Rhodes' comparatively low position comes as no surprise; he was in fact never a true Test all-rounder.

Generally the results seem, to me, convincing and reasonably fair.

A note on qualification; I decided that only those with 1000 runs and 80 wickets in Tests should be considered, and the final list included only those with an 'assessment' figure which exceeds 1.

Ranking of test all rounder by 'assessment figure'

PLAYER	RUNS	AV'GE	WICKETS	AV'GE	ASSESSMENT FIGURE
G. S. Sobers	8032	57.78	235	34.03	1.69
K. R. Miller	2958	36.97	170	22.97	1.60
W. R. Hammond	7249	58.45	83	37.80	1.54
G. A. Faulkner	1754	40.79	82	26.58	1.53
Imran Khan	2086	31.13	249	22.43	1.38
T. L. Goddard	2516	34.46	123	26.22	1.31
I. T. Botham	4577	34.77	354	27.06	1.28
A. W. Greig	3599	40.43	141	32.20	1.25
M. A. Noble	1997	30.25	121	25.00	1.21
A. K. Davidson	1328	24.59	186	20.53	1.19
J. M. Gregory	1146	36.96	85	31.15	1.18
R. J. Hadlee	2304	25.60	315	22.63	1.13
W. W. Armstrong	2863	38.68	87	33.59	1.15
W. Rhodes	2325	30.19	127	26.96	1.11
F. E. Woolley	3283	36.07	83	33.91	1.06

PLAYER	RUNS	AV'GE	WICKETS	AV'GE	ASSESSMENT FIGURE
Kapil Dev	3051	30.21	281	28.66	1.05
T. E. Bailey	2290	29.74	132	29.21	1.01

Of those who fail to qualify through not playing enough, the following seems the most impressive:

W. Bates	656	27.33	50	16.42	1.66

Bates' career was curtailed by a horrendous eye injury received at net practice. There is no certainty he would have maintained his form but one cannot help wondering at his final figures had he enjoyed a normal span.

It was surprising that Mankad's assessment figure – 0.97 – compelled his omission. This would have been rectified by a further 60 runs or 5 wickets. Others accepted as 'top' all-rounders qualified on runs and wickets but were well short in assessment figures. M. W. Tate was however a near-inclusion which may have surprised many. Like Mankad he needed just a handful of runs or wickets.

The true all-rounder should be capable of at least one outstanding *all-round* match performance during his Test career and I felt it not unreasonable to expect a Test all-rounder to be able to obtain match figures of at least 100 runs and 8 wickets. These figures are slightly harder to achieve than the alternative 'Century and five wickets in an innings' since they would normally require a concentrated effort over a whole match, and are therefore, I feel, more relevant.

The figures tend to suggest that this is the age of the 'true' all-rounder – expected, and able, to produce the goods with both bat and ball in the same match. Other supposedly leading all-rounders of the past obviously just could not do it all in one match.

Instances of 100 runs and 8 wickets by one player in a test match

G. Giffen	161, 41;	4–75, 4–164;	Australia v. England, Sydney 1894–95
A. E. Trott	38*, 72*;	0–9, 8–43;	Australia v. England, Adelaide 1894–95
J. H. Sinclair	106, 4;	6–26, 3–63;	South Africa v. England, Cape Town 1898–99
G. A. Faulkner	78, 123;	5–120, 3–40;	South Africa v. England, Jo'burg 1909–10
J. M. Gregory	100;	7–67, 1–32;	Australia v. England, Melbourne 1920–21
H. Larwood	70, 37;	6–32, 2–30;	England v. Australia, Brisbane 1928–29
G. O. B. Allen	35, 68;	3–71, 5–36;	England v. Australia, Brisbane 1936–37
W. J. Edrich	191, 22*;	4–95, 4–77;	England v. South Africa, Manchester 1947

K. R. Miller	109;	6–107; 2–58;	Australia *v.* West Indies, Kingston 1954–55	I. T. Botham	108;		0–17, 8–34;	England *v.* Pakistan, Lord's 1978
R. Benaud	100;	4–70, 5–84;	Australia *v.* South Africa, Johannesburg 1957–58	I. T. Botham	114;		6–58, 7–48;	England *v.* India, Bombay 1979–80
O. G. Smith	100;	3–94, 5–90;	West Indies *v.* India, Delhi 1958–59	I. T. Botham	30, 81;		8–103, 0–117;	England *v.* West Indies, Lord's 1984
A. K. Davidson	44, 80;	5–135, 6–87;	Australia *v.* West Indies, Brisbane 1960–61	Kapil Dev	41, 89;		5–125, 3–43;	India *v.* England, Lord's 1982
G. S. Sobers	174;	5–41, 3–39;	West Indies *v.* England, Leeds 1966	Imran Khan	67*, 46;		5–49, 3–66;	Pakistan *v.* England, Leeds 1982
Mushtaq Mohammed	121, 56;	5–28, 3–69;	Pakistan *v.* West Indies, Port of Spain 1976–77	Imran Khan	117;		6–98, 5–82;	Pakistan *v.* India, Faisalabad 1982–83
I. T. Botham	103;	5–73, 3–38;	England *v.* New Zealand, Christchurch, 1977–78	I. T. Botham	30, 81;		8–103, 0–117;	England *v.* West Indies, Lord's 1984

Index